For Sigrun

Wissenschaftlicher Beirat:

    Prof. Dr. R. Arnold
    Prof. Dr. U. Boehm
    Prof. Dr. W. Georg
    Prof. Dr. W.-D. Greinert

Studien zur Vergleichenden Berufspädagogik

Herausgegeben von der Deutschen Gesellschaft für
Technische Zusammenarbeit (GTZ) GmbH

Band 13

Manfred Diehl

Potentials and Limits of Culture-specific Vocational Training

A presentation using the example of vocational training measures in rural and urban regions and in the informal sector of Pakistan and India

Translated by the GTZ Language Service Team

Nomos Verlagsgesellschaft
Baden-Baden

The responsibility for the concept of this series lies with the publisher, in the »Vocational Training« Activity Area of the »Economic Development and Employment Promotion« Division of the Deutsche Gesellschaft für Technische Zusammenarbeit (GTZ) GmbH, Eschborn.

Die Deutsche Bibliothek – CIP-Einheitsaufnahme

Diehl, Manfred:
Potentials and Limits of Culture-specific Vocational Training ; A presentation using the example of vocational training measures in rural and urban regions and in the informal sector of Pakistan and India / Manfred Diehl. Transl. by the GTZ Language Service Team. – 1. engl. ed. – Baden-Baden : Nomos Verl.-Ges., 1999
  (Studien zur Vergleichenden Berufspädagogik ; Bd. 13)
  Einheitssacht.: Möglichkeiten und Grenzen kulturspezifisch orientierter Berufsbildung <engl.>
  Kassel, Gesamthochsch., Diss., 1994
  ISBN 3-7890-5806-8

Original Title of the German edition: »Möglichkeiten und Grenzen kulturspezifisch orientierter Berufsbildung«
© Peter Lang GmbH, Europäischer Verlag der Wissenschaften, Frankfurt am Main, 1994

1st English edition 1999
© Nomos Verlagsgesellschaft, Baden-Baden 1999. Printed in Germany. Alle Rechte, auch die des Nachdrucks von Auszügen, der photomechanischen Wiedergabe und der Übersetzung, vorbehalten. Gedruckt auf alterungsbeständigem Papier.

This work is subject to copyright. All rights are reserved, whether the whole or part of the material is concerned, specifically those of translation, reprinting, re-use of illustrations, broadcasting, reproduction by photocopying machine or similar means, and storage in data banks. Under § 54 of the German Copyright Law where copies are made for other than private use a fee is payable to »Verwertungsgesellschaft Wort«, Munich.

Foreword

Since the beginning of the 60ies, considerable financial, technical and human resources have been used to promote small and medium sized industry, vocational training and craft trades in countries of the Third World in the scope of technical and financial cooperation activities. These were carried out both as bilateral and multilateral cooperation programmes. The projects, often implemented with large-scale inputs of planning, studies, scientific investigations, different project approaches and promotion concepts have not brought about the targeted sustainable social and economic changes in these countries. On the contrary, many regions have suffered economic and social inroads and their situation today is worse than that 10 or 20 years ago. In the affected regions of Asia, Africa and Latin America considerable disappointment and disillusionment is felt, particularly as the social peace in these countries is jeopardised by the growing impoverisation of the lower and middle sections of the population. It is becoming apparent the world over that the informal sector is undergoing rapid growth. International organisations such as the World Bank, UNDP, ILO, etc. estimate that more than 70% of the population in countries of Asia, Africa and Latin America belong to the socalled informal sector, and this applies to economic activity and life in both urban and rural regions.
Vocational training aid did not begin to perceive the changes in these countries and its own lack of impact as from the 80ies, and only a few individual novel approaches and project concepts began to respond to this new, critical situation in Third World countries. The extensive literature on the genesis and expansion of the informal sector had to date concentrated on the development of socalled nonproductive work, i.e. services such as domestic work, rag collectors, scavengers, bootblacks, or criminal activities, prostitution etc. In my opinion, quite insufficient attention has been paid to the relationship between traditional craft trades and microenterprises in the informal sector, i.e. newly forming economic and employment structures and what connection this has with vocational training and the need to develop appropriate curricula. On the basis of many years of work as development expert and educational planner in countries of the third world I have keenly experienced this lack of practice-based scientific analyses and become aware of the

relative ineffectiveness of the existing instruments. This work therefore aims to contribute to the integration of the informal sector into educational and employment policy and deliver arguments for a targeted promotion of the informal sector by national and international donors. Improving both the subjective and also the objective educational preconditions for these groups and social classes is considered to be a major key to allow people in the informal sector to be recognised by official economic, employment and development policies.

But these improvements are only feasible if the official policies in the field of vocational training, education and employment tackle the problems of vocational training in the informal sector with the same inputs and commitment they apply in the formal sector; in this way, the preconditions would be set for integrating the informal sector on a long-term basis.

My studies are therefore oriented less to the theory of this problem but rather to improving the actual working and living conditions of the target groups in the informal sector and integrating these people into vocational training aid. It was necessary, therefore, to process my own experiences made in the research area involved in close cooperation with the affected and responsible persons in the countries selected for the study, India and Pakistan. Sincere thanks are expressed to my partners in India and Pakistan; without their cooperation this work could not have achieved its practice relevance. Special thanks go to V.M. Raghavan, M.S.S. Varadan, Ms. Pratima, K.E. Balakrishnan, M.S. Rama-Krishna, L.S.N. Guptha and the Directorate of Employment and Training DGE & T of the Government of India in New Delhi. In Pakistan, particularly valuable information and support was provided by the staff of the SEES/TAP in Peshawar. The assistance of the Team Leaders G. Marienfeld, J. Lette and particularly Hamish Khan, and also Halem Shah and Nizan Kahn and the responsible offices of the Provincial Government and the Directorate of Manpower and Training was most appreciated as were the efforts of so many people in India and Pakistan who willingly spared their time for interviews and consultations. I would also like to thank the Deutsche Gesellschaft für Technische Zusammenarbeit (GTZ) Eschborn, Germany, who permitted me to study important reference documents, project documents etc. The open and cooperative attitude of the former Head of the Vocational Training Division, Mr Rychetsky, is mentioned in particular.

My special gratitude is addressed to the professors and appraisers of this work, Prof. Dr. Helmut Nölker and Prof. Dr. Günter Spreth, for the abundant advice, suggestions and encouragement they gave to me.

Contents

1 *Introduction: problems, methodology and objectives*   11

    1.1   The problems   11
    1.2   Goals and limitations of the work   16
    1.3   Methods and approaches in formulating tasks
          (thematic key points)   17

2 *Defining key terminology in vocational pedagogics, defining the informal sector and describing the interfaces with the modern (formal) sector*   23

    2.1   Identification, interfaces and definition of the informal sector as distinct from the modern formal sector   24
    2.2   Defining work and its significance for the informal sector in the Third World   41
    2.3   Importance of culture and tradition in developing culture-specific approaches to vocational training in Third World countries   57
    2.4   Target groups in the informal sector, their social and economic position and importance for the development of the informal sector   70

3 *Presentation, development and analysis of selected approaches of German and international vocational training aid to promote the informal and traditional sectors in Pakistan and India*   91

    3.1   German-Pakistan Technical Cooperation in vocational training in the refugee-impacted province NWFP   91
          3.1.1   The project area: geography and key data on Pakistan and the North-West Frontier Province (NWFP)   94

3.1.2 Facts and data on the context of the German-Pakistan projects in the provinces of NWFP and Peshawar, which were impacted by refugee flows   105
3.1.3 Pakistan-German Technical Training Programme (PGTTP) – a project for the informal sector, with model status for vocational training measures in this sector   107
3.1.4 Didactical and methodological concept, project target groups and organisational structure of the Pakistan-German and Afghan-German Technical Training Programme   111
3.1.5 Conceptual and didactic considerations for project design   114
3.1.6 Conceptual structure of Afghan/Pak-German TTP and SES Programme at TTC Peshawar   118
3.1.7 Levels and interaction of the elements/programme components of the TTP/SES-Programme   143
3.1.8 Integration of vocational training measures for the informal sector into the NWFP vocational training system   144
3.1.9 Design and structure of the PAK-German Technical Training Programm (TTP)   147
3.1.10 Elements of the Afghan-PAK-German Technical Training Programme   148
3.1.11 Geographical Overview   149
3.1.12 Analysis of the survey of former graduates and small (micro) businessmen from the TTP/SES programme   153
3.1.13 Evaluation of the TTP/SES programme for promoting employment-oriented vocational training in the informal and traditional sector   169

3.2 The need for vocational training measures for target groups in the informal and traditional sector in India (using the example of the Federal States of Karnataka and Tamil Nadu)   173

3.2.1 Geographical, economic and development policy framework for India   173

	3.2.2 Study to develop requirement profiles for small (micro) businessmen and employees in the informal sector in the southern Indian cities of Bangalore and Madras	198
	3.2.3 Evaluation of the studies carried out in Bangalore and Madras	217
	3.2.4 Photo-documentation on the informal sector in southern India	220

4 *Employment-creating training for target groups in the informal sector – Approaches to holistic, target-group centred vocational pedagogics*   227

    4.1 The context and need for vocational pedagogics oriented towards the informal sector   227

    4.2 Target group orientation and developing a didactic basic structure for vocational training in the informal sector   233

    4.3 The concept of training in the context of job-creating vocational training in the informal sector   238

    4.4 Approaches to employment-oriented learning in the informal sector   246

    4.5 Integration of employment-oriented vocational training in the informal sector into the formal vocational training system or systemic aspects of projects in this area   252

    4.6 Summary and review of approaches to holistic vocational pedagogics for the informal sector   255

5 *Summary and conclusions*   261

    5.1 Vocational training for the informal sector: context, definitions and interfaces with the formal sector   261

    5.2 The importance of culture, tradition and the need to develop a concept of work intrinsic to the cultures   265

    5.3 Importance of culture and tradition for technical cooperation in the informal sector   266

    5.4 Potential target groups for measures to promote the informal sector   269

5.5	Results of the study on TTP/SES Peshawar, Pakistan	272
5.6	Review of the studies carried out in Bangalore and Madras	274
5.7	Summary and presentation of approaches for a holistic vocational pedagogics for the informal sector	276

Reference Literature   283

Annexes   297

1 Introduction: problems, methodology and objectives

1.1 *The problems*

Vocational training aid in technical cooperation with Third World countries is typically perceived in the context of the desired socio-cultural, socio-economic and technological development opportunities of the modern production and service sectors. Project-specific and didactic studies are accordingly primarily those parameters which set the environment and the framework for addressing methodological, didactic and curriculum implications to create training measures and institutions and vocational training systems[1].

As a result the training institutions, vocational training systems and approaches to capacity building in Technical Cooperation's partner countries in the Third World promoted during the past 40 years, have primarily – despite all the efforts to do just the opposite – repeatedly been oriented towards the so-called formal (i.e. modern and organised) economy in these countries. This applies equally to bilateral and multilateral vocational training aid programmes. The present study aims to investigate the reasons for this orientation and its evolution, together with the failure to pursue other, alternative approaches, although only to the extent necessary to answer relevant questions in the context of developing curricula with culture-specific orientation.

Individual projects regarded as highly successful or technical full-time training facilities seen as appropriate and well-functioning (particularly in German vocational training aid) have not to date – with a few exotic exceptions (e.g. Pak-German Technical Training-Programme, Peshawar/Pakistan)[2] – had any decisive influence on reorientation and system building in terms of the integration of socially-disadvantaged target groups and the informal sector.

---

1 Cf. W. Schulz: Umriß einer didaktischen Theorie der Schule, in: Die deutsche Schule 2, 1969, p. 63.
2 Projects of German-Pakistan technical cooperation for vocational training of Afghan refugees and Pakistani rural target groups (socially disadvantaged), BMZ/GTZ Project, source GTZ, Eschborn.

It is accordingly appropriate to adopt a critical approach to current practice in project identification, sectoral studies and project planning, implementation and evaluation.

The hope that well-functioning individual projects (stand-alone solutions) will initiate a trickle-up effect and have a favourable effect on systems has proved largely illusory. While the so-called Wissing Model[3], with off-company technical training facilities, has successfully produced qualified industrial skilled labour for selected technical disciplines, the model has not on its own favourably impacted the evolution and orientation of indigenous vocational training systems. The hoped-for trickle-up effect has not appeared. The model has also failed to generate coherent formulation of or successful model approaches to developing modern indigenous vocational training policies. In every case where this model has been followed in developing systems, the result has been priority for highly academic forms of vocational training, encouraging educational systems with a tendency to develop school based approaches to training (technical secondary schools)[4]. As a result, analyses of the manpower requirements[5] of the modern sector of the economy have played a decisive role in the orientation of German and international vocational training aid (with the World Bank as a particularly important influence). The quantitative and qualitative development of measures for vocational educational and training institutions and the development policy orientation of vocational training systems focuses on the need for skills as derived from labour market requirements (which reflect the needs of the formal sector of the economy). This need for skills can be seen as the guiding principle and justification of approaches to date in vocational training aid. As a result, the promotional approaches, the vocational training measures and concepts are almost entirely oriented towards the needs of the formal, modern sector of the economy. This, in turn, generally leads to concepts, strategies, methodological and didactic approaches, curricula, human resources upgrading concepts and institutions, organisational and system-influencing project approaches and proposals which are formulated exclusively in terms of experience in western industrialised economies and transferred directly to Third World countries. Often this

---

3 See J. Wissing: Modell einer Facharbeiterschule für Entwicklungsländer, Weinheim.
4 See K. Frey, Berichte und Reprints aus dem Institut für berufliche Bildung und Weiterbildungsforschung (IBW-Berichte), TU-Berlin, No. 7, 1/91.
5 See Michael A. Buchmann, Berufsstrukturen in Entwicklungsländern Erdmann, Tübingen 1979 and Heinz Werner, Glossare zur Arbeitsmarkt- und Berufsforschung, Institut für Arbeitsmarkt und Berufsforschung der Bundesanstalt für Arbeit, Nürnberg, 1979, p. 134 Educational economic approach primarily oriented towards the need of the formal labour market and the modern industrialised sector.

leads to inappropriate solutions or stand-alone solutions which, although perfectly capable on their own of performing their role as institutions for training skilled workers for a segment of the needs of modern industry, have only limited suitability (if at all) for multiplier use.

To date, vocational training aid has lacked key requirements and instruments for scientific and professional long-term backstopping for the measures that have been assisted. Such accompanying support is an essential factor of successful project implementation for comparable measures or projects in the Federal Republic of Germany[6]. For Third World projects and programmes this is one of the key reasons for the lacking analysis and systematic collection of experience by the teams responsible for project implementation and the development aid organisations and consulting firms behind them. This also applies extensively to the NGOs[7] active in this sector. Often these NGOs lack organisational and management structures, so that the experts assigned by NGOs are left entirely to their own resources. The advice they provide to Third World partner organisations is often based on inadequate vocational expertise. Mostly they are not aware of the consequences of their own advisory services, because issues of system building are only exceptionally part of the teacher training curriculum at German universities or teacher training institutions. As a result the advisory approaches and solutions encountered are often home-made, narrow and mostly technically-oriented, lacking the necessary complexity and broad development perspective.

The informal sector of the economy was almost entirely neglected for a long time, at least as far as bilateral and multilateral donor organisations and their promotional concepts for vocational training aid were concerned. For much of this time it was the domain of the NGOs and church development aid organisations, which were assumed to be more appropriate and efficient in this sector by virtue of their very strong social commitment. How far this assumption is justified would have to be investigated in detail in a separate study comparing goals with achievements. One result of this, however, is that bilateral and multilateral donor organisations suffer from a significant lack of experience in dealing with the target groups and the specific socio-cultural and socio-economic features of the informal sector. For all its good intentions, the designation "informal sector" also has its dubious aspects,

---

6 See K. Frey, Berichte und Reprints aus dem Institut für berufliche Bildung und Weiterbildungsforschung (IBW-Berichte), TU-Berlin, No. 7. 1/91.
7 Nongovernmental organisations.

because of the danger that large groups of the world population who have already been classified as Third World inhabitants will now be relegated to the status of people in the informal sector, with a further plunge into discrimination. The cultural and social development of the target groups involved certainly does not justify any downgrading[8].

There is also the danger that the complex and complicated way in which measures to improve the situation of the target group and the promotive framework in this living and economic context work, reduces the approaches for vocational training aid to political statements, and fashionable waves in bilateral and multilateral development aid organisations: This must be prevented in the interests of the target group, this vast mass of people forced to spend their lives in miserable conditions, and in the interests of the evolution of a more humane world.

In this context the clear commitment to these target groups[9] by the German Federal Ministry for Economic Cooperation and Development (BMZ) in "Vocational training", its January 1992 publication on its new sectoral concept, must be welcomed. This sectoral concept includes the following statement:

> It is intended to meet the needs of target groups in the informal sector, and especially the needs of disadvantaged population groups to improve their earnings potential and living conditions, through special offers in vocational training. These must specifically address the learning capabilities of the participants, their environment and the resulting concrete need for skills. Offers are also intended to create additional or improved opportunities for employment, self-employment or effective work in the subsistence economy.[10]

The informal sector is expanding all over the world. Today it is believed that c. 70% of the employable adult world population lives and works in this sector[11]. For this reason alone it seems essential to improve our understanding of this economic and social environment and tailor vocational training aid for its needs, in order to improve the opportunities for these (underprivileged) people to integrate themselves into world society. Vocational training here is understood simply as a means for the target groups in the informal sector to achieve a better starting point. It is obvious that the methods and processes devel-

---

8 In view of the more or less internationally established understanding of the "informal sector" this terminology is retained, but the background will be more closely defined in a separate section.
9 Sektorkonzept: Berufliche Bildung, BMZ-Referat 310, Bonn, Jan. 1992.
10 Op. Cit.
11 Cf. C. Lohmar-Kuhnle, Konzepte zur beschäftigungsorientierten Aus- und Fortbildung von Zielgruppen aus dem informellen Sektor, Weltforum Verlag Cologne 1991.

oped so far for integrating the informal sector and its population will fail to produce the promising approaches and results, given the lack of research to date on existing and traditional structures and the needs of the people and their potential employment in the informal sector, and the lack of adequate awareness (let alone mobilisation) of the innovative capabilities of the individuals in this sector.

Project identification, planning, implementation and evaluation have too often been viewed through the eyes of the range of methods in the modern (formal) sector of the economy and the approaches and experience developed there: this is particularly true of vocational pedagogy. Any vocational pedagogy or employment policy which is oriented exclusively towards the modern sector can be assumed by the same token to be lacking. Similar problems can also be observed in developed industrialised nations such as the Federal Republic of Germany, particularly after Reunification. Here too, economic stagnation is resulting in expansion of the informal sector.

The present study is intended as a contribution towards a more balanced consideration of this sector, specifically in terms of the needs and employment of the people in the informal sector, including the social-psychological, socio-cultural, socio-economic and technological-pedagogical factors, and the – often neglected – orientation and restrictions based on religious and ethical-moral factors.

The aim here is to counter the attempt to define the target groups of the informal sector as marginal social groups, with accompanying status as a special case for vocational pedagogy. It is assumed that the massive growth in the informal sector is due to the failure of economic and development policies, the past colonial structures still existing in the affected countries and, finally, the collapse of the Soviet Union as a global power, which is continuing to have disastrous consequences for the socially weak in this world.

With its specific problems and enormous importance for the national economy of many countries as a living and working environment for much of the population, the informal sector is accordingly viewed as a challenge for vocational pedagogy. It is accordingly not a matter of developing sophisticated vocational policy development and research approaches which dismiss the target groups as exotic objects with marginal status: instead, it is a matter of looking for concrete solutions as vocational education and training concepts, measures for economic and trade promotion and a general exercise for awareness raising among politicians and experts with regard to this sector and its special features.

The author's experience suggests that it is important in tackling this problem to avoid abstract generalities and advance to solutions and proposals which are as concrete as possible, e.g. for the areas and phases of project identification, planning and implementation, for concepts for evaluating and monitoring the success of vocational training measures and for developing self-help approaches for target groups and promoting greater economic, social and individual autonomy.

The aim is to draw on concrete experience from government and non-governmental projects in vocational training aid and economic aid, using selected case studies from India and Pakistan to analyse the success of these measures for the target groups and review the transferability of sub-components and developed concepts.

An attempt is made to develop new interactive partnership-oriented approaches and methods for producing curricula for the informal sector which are suitable for the target groups and adapted for specific cultural features. It is important in this to take into account experience to date in this sector in these countries. Following an analysis of the actual state of approaches to vocational training, the decisive influences of the modern sector on the traditional sector in the individual countries are investigated, and their significance for creating conditions in the informal sector and analysing the interface problem and links between the formal and informal sectors is studied.

Identification of the interfaces will provide information on approaches and indications of the influence of the informal sector for the macroeconomic importance, development and status of the industrial-modern sector. The conditions (the didactic analysis i.e. in the wider sense a learning theory) for the curricula development decision making can be identified on this basis. An attempt is made here to develop models which can be used to document in generalised form the main constituent factors for the development of curricula and vocational training measures appropriate to the target groups and take these into account in concrete project work. The curricula should be oriented towards the relevant areas of action and problems of the target groups and their future prospects for integration into the macroeconomic and social development process of the regional and national social structures.

1.2 *Goals and limitations of the work*

The concepts to date of the bilateral and multilateral organisations, NGOs and national development aid institutions and consulting firms in the field of vocational training aid for target groups in the informal sector show serious shortcomings in their development in terms of taking into account the needs and economic, social and traditional environment of the target groups.

It is not usual for established concepts of economic aid, educational aid and particularly vocational training aid to be transferred and their success presumed without further consideration of the specific regional or local situation of these groups.

On this basis the following practical goals were formulated for the present work:

* Scientific review of experience to date, using selected examples of German and international vocational training aid in Pakistan and India.
* Analysis of the effectiveness of the vocational training solutions and projects proposed in the above case studies and investigation of the underlying concepts and anticipated objectives.
* Analysis of the results achieved and variance from target based on a critical review and assessment of the effects among the target groups.
* Formulation of models for developing culture-specific curricula and methodological and didactic approaches to creating indigenous frameworks for vocational pedagogy and practice.
* Review (secondary analysis) of available foundations and materials on the problem of promoting the informal sector and consideration of possible ways of integrating this sector into the Third World educational and economic structure, i.e. an attempt to apply general economic and vocational educational fundamentals and adapt these to the central issue.
* The overall goal is to make a contribution in the present work to improving the effectiveness of vocational educators in their practical and theoretical work for the informal sector and the people affected, i.e. to contribute towards a human-centred vocational training aid concept for developing independent capability for action in vocational, self-help promoting and job-seeking terms among the target groups.

1.3 *Methods and approaches in formulating tasks (thematic key points)*

The methodological approach is determined by a critically constructive approach to and view of vocational training aid and the author's years of experience in technical cooperation, with the resulting call for proposals for solutions which are as concrete as possible in certain areas for developing culture-specific curricula and approaches in vocational training.

Development and analysis of the theoretical concept and theoretical and methodological evaluation of current practices in the field of developing appropriate curricula, concepts and vocational training policy guidelines for the informal sector cannot all be handled by a single uniform methodological approach. What is needed is a combination of hermeneutic methods and empirical-statistical, critically constructive and structuralist[12] paradigms.

In this case, the hermeneutic approach is not limited to an interpretative study of texts: here, "the educational process always developed in practice with its institutions and procedures is to some extent the text requiring interpretation and explanation in pedagogy"[13]. In principle there should be no methodological difference whether texts in the narrower sense of the term or other "documents" regarded as educationally important, e.g. institutions, trainers, actions by educators or young people etc, are taken as the subject for hermeneutic consideration In principle, there should be no difference between whether texts in the narrower sense or the "documents" – in other words objectives considered to be of pedagogic importance such as institutions, images, action by educators or young people, etc. are the objects of hermeneutic consideration.[14] It is planned to review the available studies and documents of relevance for project planning and implementation and to identify the core statements on concepts and theoretical approaches in the relevant material for the selected expert studies and the corresponding primary and secondary literature and to analyse and evaluate these statements. However, this will only be done to the extent required to establish the necessary theoretical and practical foundation and concepts for developing approaches to culture-specific curricula. According to the hypothesis put forward here, investigation of the rationale in technical projects, particularly in the informal sector, is frequently not based on rational planning and on a well defined theoretical foundation, but often developed as spontaneous solutions, as reactions and intuitive actions developed in the project environment. Practitioners basically lack possibilities for orientation and also time for an exact

---

12   Cf. Manfred Frank, Was ist Neostrukturalismus, ed. Suhrkamp, Frankfurt/M. 1984.
13   O.F. Bollnow: Pädagogische Forschung und philosophisches Denken, in: Erziehungswissenschaft und Erziehungswirklichkeit, ed. H. Röhrs, inter alia p. 229 from: W. Klafki, Aspekte kritisch-konstruktiver Erziehungswissenschaft, Beltz, Weinheim, 1976.
14   W. Klafki, Aspekte kritisch-konstruktiver Erziehungswissenschaft, Beltz, Weinheim, 1976, p. 25.

analysis of the circumstances under which specific developments or successes have emerged. However, as already noted, development of basic models and paradigms for advancing approaches in vocational educational thinking, analysis and action requires to some extent hermeneutic consideration of the practice to date of vocational educators in the informal sector[15]; besides a concrete opportunity to improve practice, this study is intended to contribute towards creating a theory for the question of "development of culture-specific curricula".

It should be noted that the term culture-specific does not see the term culture as static or preach culture as being absolute; rather it is seen as a very dynamic relationship between the situation at the outset which is western oriented and often aggressive, and an initially passive recipient and the target group in the informal sector called upon to change its behaviour patterns. In other words, it is expected that both sides will open themselves to the process and make the necessary qualitative and quantitative changes.

> "Culture is presently researched in the descriptive sense from the standpoint of the history of ideas and cultural morphology. It is regarded essentially as an autonomous and dominant entity vis-à-vis the individual. Viewing it as a dynamic structure, i.e. as dependent and at the same time special within the social overall process, does not by contrast involve any contemplative attitude to history. . . .
> In the struggle to improve the human condition there are times when the fact that theory takes only very superficial account of all these relationships is not particularly important in practice. . . .
> However, these periods are rare and brief, the structure which has deteriorated is quickly patched up and apparently renovated, . . . the obsolete cultural apparatus [acquires] new force as a spiritual quality of the people and as a context for intermeshing institutions"[16].

As Horkheimer indicates in this quote from: "Authority and Family", the process is always painful, particularly for those affected, since the necessary changes cannot take place without giving up traditional and much-loved habits and socially established modes of behaviour for individuals and communication structures between groups, classes and the existing authority structures.

Pedagogy and the subsector of vocational education at issue here can only make a contribution to the potential for change mentioned above if it can free itself to a great extent from its own theoretical and culture-specific shackles and measure itself against the relationships in devel-

---

15 Cf. J. Speck (Hrsg.), Handbuch wissenschaftstheoretischer Begriffe, vol. 2, pp. 279-278, WTB-Vandenhoeck, Göttingen, 1980.
16 Max Horkheimer, Traditionelle und kritische Theorie. Fünf Aufsätze, in: Autorität und Familie, pp. 135-136, Fischer, Frankfurt, 1992.

oping countries in the context of reviewing its theoretical and practical approaches[17].

This applies equally also to recipes and concepts practised and set up to date to overcome development policy catastrophes and manage crises in the developing country's employment system.

The study of the needs of people in the informal sector then goes on to analyse the existing data on the state of education and the labour market (employment and unemployment and data on general education and vocational training). The selected projects for promoting the informal sector are investigated for their efficiency in terms of retaining graduates of vocational training measures, using existing data and the sample survey. In addition, structured interviews are held with potential applicants and candidates and with the customers for the graduates – i.e. the employers and those responsible in the promotional institutions and programmes, and suggestions are collected for developing appropriate concepts for vocational training of the target groups in the informal sector. The empirical studies are, however, limited to a minimum because of the likely complexity in the countries involved, the political sensitivity and the associated high costs: they accordingly serve primarily as a check on the plausibility of the assumptions made and as a source for obtaining, formulating and developing quantitative and qualitative indicators to measure the success of such measures concerned with vocational training, employment and income creation.

Subsequently, two selected case studies are presented in vocational training aid to the informal sector by bilateral and international donor organisations and NGOs. The analysis draws on the results of limited field research, specifically two studies of the informal sector in Pakistan (TTP-Peshawar)[18] and India (Madras, Bangalore)[19].

---

17 Bronislaw Malinowski; Eine wissenschaftliche Theorie der Kultur, Suhrkamp, Frankfurt 1975 "We based our functional analysis of culture on the idea of the vital process, i.e. the combination of drive, its physiological effect and the state of organic satisfaction. It is helpful to summarise our recent results in the following diagram." Diagram of the instrumental process:

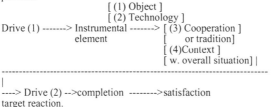

----> Drive (2) -->completion -------->satisfaction
target reaction.

18 Project to promote Afghan refugees and Pakistani rural population, promoted since 1981 by the BMZ and implemented by GTZ-Eschborn, source: GTZ-Eschborn, Dept. 4050 and author's research.
19 Author's research.

In addition, important information on the success and problems of such measures was collected through the author's personal contact with the ILO in Geneva, the World Bank in Washington D.C., the DMT of the NWFP Provincial Government in Pakistan, the DMT of the Baluchistan Provincial Government, the Government of India Directorate General Employment and Training, the DMT Tamilnadu-Madras, the DMT Kanataka-Bangalore and GTZ/BMZ[20] (and many others).

In this context, the present study will refer to the research and experience reports of the BMZ[21], the ILO[22], the World Bank[23], the Deutsche Gesellschaft für Technische Zusammenarbeit (GTZ), Eschborn[24] and other government and private sector organisations; this particularly applies to the empirical critical and descriptive part of the work referring to the historical and present situation in the informal sector and the people in this sector, i.e. the target groups of measures.

In ex post investigation of measures already implemented, it is also necessary to consider and analyse to a limited extent how far the organisations and experts commissioned to implement the measures are/were open to experimental approaches and which theoretical and educational concepts underlie the proposed solutions (concepts for implementation). For this reason the critical question must be posed how far these groups and the participants (in both the narrow and broad meanings of the term) in the developing countries were involved in the process, i.e. the seriousness of the projects studied must be questioned just as much as the goals achieved to date, which are generally regarded as very meagre by those familiar with this scene.

Again, attention is called to the lack of concepts, instruments and parallel measures, of targeted scientific backup to projects in the formal sector; because most of these are also projects that tread new ground in terms of the conceptual relevance to practice and acceptance of the target groups, and mostly have the character of sociological experiments. This is, however, only treated as a shortcoming if, as originally noted, the corresponding instruments for scientific back-up and structured collection of experience are absent[25]. Although the present work cannot make good shortcomings in project work to date, it can make a con-

---

20 See Annex IV, pp. 319 et seq.
21 Cornelia Lohmar-Kuhnle, Konzepte zur beschäftigungsorientierten Aus- und Fortbildung von Zielgruppen aus dem informellen Sektor, Weltforum Verlag, Cologne 1991, pub. Bundesministerium für wirtschaftliche Zusammenarbeit (BMZ) vol. 100.
22 Fred Fluitman, in Training for work in the informal Sector . . ., ILO, Geneva, 1989.
23 World Bank, W.D.C., Vocational and Technical Education and Training, 1991.
24 Orientation framework for the informal sector etc., GTZ, Eschborn.
25 Cf. R. Pàges, Das Experiment in der Soziologie, in: Handbuch der empirischen Sozialforschung, ed. René König, Stuttgart 1974.

tribution for future projects towards improving project identification, planning and implementation. It is accordingly necessary to supplement the analytical section of the work, which is extensively concerned with describing and analysing the situation in the selected case studies, by a critical and constructive section dealing with the future and potential for improving practice, with the focus on developing culture-specific curricula and hence an approach to developing and formulating culture-specific educational theories in the broader sense and vocational training theories in the narrower sense. The method used here is critical – constructive, i.e. the aim is to draft new approaches for curricula development in order to produce and identify differentiated interactions and draw up problem-solving recommendations that are adequate for the target groups in terms of culture-specificity of curricula and methods of didactics for training target groups in the informal sector. The situation of the organisations and experts commissioned with implementing projects in the informal sector is similar to the constructivist approach discussed by Paul Lorenzen[26] using the image (originating from Otto Neurath[27]) of a ship on the high seas: "All repair or conversion work ... must be done at sea"[28]. It is only possible to make a start if we take the given conditions and facts and accept them, i.e. acknowledge and analyse them accordingly, and know how to use the limited resources for the necessary conversion and rehabilitation of the ship. "Constructive thinking" seen in this way means:

1. We cannot make an absolute start – we are always in the middle of life and everyday language (= on the high seas).
2. Nevertheless, we can make an attempt to develop a language of science systematically from the start (= remodel the ship on the high seas).[29]

The critical-constructive (deductive) approach is particularly relevant in developing models for formulating culture-specific curricula and methodological educational approaches for developing vocational skills, self-help capability and job-seeking ability among the target groups in the informal sector.

---

26 Lorenzen, Denken, in: Einführung in die Wissenschaftstheorie 1, p. 128, by H. Seiffert, C.H. Beck, Munich 1975.
27 Lorenzen, Denken, op. cit. p. 128.
28 Helmut Seifert, Einführung in die Wissenschafts-Theorie 1, p. 129, C.H. Beck, Munich, 1975.
29 Helmut Seifert, Einführung in die Wissenschafts-Theorie 1, p. 129, C.H. Beck, Munich, 1975.

2 Defining key terminology in vocational pedagogics, defining the informal sector and describing the interfaces with the modern (formal) sector

The following sections look at key terms in vocational pedagogics and their significance, validity, transferability and relevance to the informal sector and the development of culture-specific approaches to vocational training aid in this sector. The emphasis is on developing appropriate concepts for training which are oriented towards employment and income, together with curricula for the target groups in the informal sector. Issues of culture, tradition and the assessment of the influence of existing economic, political and social systems are considered in the light of their importance for the problems and opportunities (goal conflicts) arising in the transfer, identification of development potential and integration of the informal sector into concepts for development promotion and strategies for vocational training aid in Third World countries and bilateral and multilateral development aid, and proposals for integration are formulated.

Particular attention is given to analysing the following problem areas:

- analysing the term *informal sector* in terms of its economic, political and social significance and implications for the people in this sector;[1]
- defining the informal sector and attempting to identify the interfaces with the formal sector;
- analysing the culture-specific conditions surrounding economic, political and social action and work in the informal sector, taking Pakistan and India as examples;
- considering the relationship between the modern and traditional sectors and its importance for defining the informal sector and relevance to designing appropriate vocational training, i.e. outlining guidelines for developing culture-specific vocational training concepts and curricula which are oriented towards the conditions in the informal and traditional sectors;

---

[1] The basis for this study includes the official development policy and sectoral policy papers and statements by the main bilateral and multilateral donor organisations and governments, and draws on the examples provided by the development policy approaches and strategies of India and Pakistan for promotion of the informal sector and the relevant primary and secondary literature.

- discussing potential for transferring vocational training approaches and experience and assessing the possibilities for transfers of technology and strategy for promoting self-employment from the formal to the informal sector;
- assessing the capability of the informal sector to absorb innovations and potential or need for developing separate and original human-centred and action-oriented approaches to developing curricula and concepts for vocational training in the informal sector;
- assessing the relevance of the informal sector on the basis of the examples of Pakistan and India; this is done through a review of the official planning documents and policy papers of these countries;
- assessing the significance of the informal sector for formulating national concepts and strategies for development, educational and economic policy, the interfaces with the formal sector and the recognition of the people in the informal sector (target groups) in terms of their economic, political and social significance for successful development and promotion of Third World countries by bilateral and multilateral donor organisations and their national governments.

2.1 Identification, interfaces and definition of the informal sector as distinct from the modern formal sector

The informal sector appeared as a term in international discussion of development policy at the beginning of the Seventies[2]. This sector now covers over 50 % of workers in these countries or persons capable of or available for work[3]. This applies not only to the African nations but also and equally to Latin America and Asia. The International Labour Office (ILO, Geneva) under a commission from the UN and the Deutsche Gesellschaft für Technische Zusammenarbeit (GTZ, Eschborn) has carried out a number of studies since the start of the Eighties to explore the informal sector for the purposes of international development aid (see note 1)[4]. However, there has been no significant improvement in the integration of the informal sector into economic and social policy strategies in development aid for these countries,

---

2 Cornelia Lohmar-Kuhnle, "Konzepte zur beschäftigungsorientierten Aus- und Fortbildung von Zielgruppen aus dem informellen Sektor", Cologne 1991.
3 Claudio de Moura Castro, "Training for Work in the Informal Sector", ILO, Geneva 1989.
4 Also deserving mention here are the conferences on the "informal sector" in the evangelic academy in Bad Boll (Rothermund, Karcher, Böhm) which made major contributions to reorientation in vocational training aid.

despite the misery and increasing poverty affecting these target groups for development aid which account for over 50% of the population in the countries of Asia, Latin America and Africa. In other words, these target groups continue to be largely neglected. Up to 1989 USD 52 billion of government funds was spent on development aid worldwide[5], but only a very small portion of this was oriented directly towards the needs of the target groups in the informal sector[6].

> "The "informal" sector of the developing economies has, in recent years, expanded so rapidly that it is now the source of livelihood for between one-third and three-quarters of the urban economically active population in the Third World. Current trends in urbanisation and population growth suggest that artisans and small commercial units may be expected to provide most of the employment to urban households by the year 2000, although the problem of employment may still remain. It is clear that while new horizons have opened for some activities, others are already showing obvious signs of saturation, and incomes will decline with new entrants looking for work. There might therefore be an involutionary trend with average income and capital accumulation rising very slowly or not at all"[7].

Given this, the question arises why international and German vocational training aid has so far responded so slowly to these developments in Third World countries.

> "Conventional approaches to development cooperation in the sector of vocational training is incompatible with the belated recognition of the informal sector in the Third World as a potential target group for forms of cooperation. As in addition the measures in vocational training aid in the modern sector frequently fail to produce the desired results (in the sense of comprehensive economic development), existing principles of development cooperation are being relativised and augmented[8]."

The main causes of the inadequate response of bilateral and multilateral donor organisations and official, government-controlled vocational training aid are the procedure for applications agreed with the Third World countries and the existence in these countries of elites mostly educated in the industrialised nations (and specifically their orientation towards the models of western industrial societies and the associated transfer of western value systems and concepts). It must also be said that the poorest groups do not have any strong lobby in the

---

5   Cf. R. Stockmann, "Die Nachhaltigkeit von Entwicklungsprojekten", Opladen, 1992.
6   Cf. C. Lohmar-Kuhnle, "Konzepte zur beschäftigungsorientierten Aus- und Fortbildung von Zielgruppen aus dem informellen Sektor", Cologne 1991.
7   Carlos Maldonada and S.V. Sethuraman, "Technological Capability in the Informal Sector", ILO publication p. 3, Geneva, 1992.
8   Manfred Wallenborn, "Legitimationsprobleme und Reflexionsbedarf praktischer Berufsbildungshilfe in: Berufliche Bildung und Entwicklung in den Ländern der Dritten Welt", ed. Rolf Arnold, Baden-Baden, 1989.

Third World countries and the rich industrialised nations to represent their interests effectively. This is why, as Wallenborn says, (see note 8) there has been a failure to shift paradigms or put a major effort into this.

> "The inaccuracy of the equation »vocational training – skilled jobs – economic development« led in the face of the debt and economic crisis in the developing countries to a relativisation of the manpower requirement approach and its implications for educational policy, and these effects have gradually spilled over to vocational training aid[9]."

Since 1986 there has accordingly been growing criticism of the "Sectoral concept for development cooperation in vocational training"[10] published by the German Federal Ministry of Economic Cooperation and Development. The CDU/CSU also reviewed the effect and concept of German Federal vocational training aid and criticised the following aspects to the Federal Government of the day[11]:
- the concentration on promoting elites, i.e. financing primarily or exclusively projects in the modern industrial sector and qualifying skilled labour for this sector;
- the fixation on industrialisation and neglect of the rural and informal sector[12];
- the lack of flexibility in vocational training aid as a response to increasing unemployment among graduates and the expansion of the informal sector, i.e. failure to act on the implications for new concepts, strategies and projects in vocational training aid;
- growing poverty of urban and rural population groups, i.e. failure to target the relevant groups in the informal sector.

The university conference "Vocational Training" in Essen in autumn 1986 offered a platform to critics of the sectoral concept and prevailing orientation of German vocational training aid which they used to express massive objections to and disappointment with the results and lack of orientation towards the genuine needs of the growing impoverished population in Third World countries[13]. In the course of the subse-

---

9 Op. Cit.
10 Pinger, W.: "Berufsausbildung als Schlüssel zur Armutsbekämpfung", Bonn, 1986.
11 [Cf. The citation in note 23] Cf. Arnold Rolf: "Der Streit um die Berufsbildungshilfe – Berufsbildung für die Dritte Welt im Widerstreit von Konzeptionen", p. 179-193, Baden-Baden, 1989.
12 Axt, H.-J./Karcher, W./Schleich, B. (eds) "Ausbildungs- und Beschäftigungskrise in der Dritten Welt?" Frankfurt, 1987.
13 Cf. Arnold, Rolf: Der Streit um die Berufsbildungshilfe. Berufsbildung für die Dritte Welt im Widerstreit von Konzeptionen, Baden-Baden, 1989; Axt, H.-J./Karcher, W./Schleich, B. (Hrsg.) see note 12; K. Frey, Bericht und Reprints aus dem Institut für berufliche Bildung und Weiterbildungsforschung (IBW-Berichte), TU-Berlin, Nr. 7 1/91.

quent debate the Federal Ministry of Economic Cooperation and Development (BMZ) presented a new "Sectoral concept for vocational training" in January 1992. In this the BMZ states the following goals and target groups for German Federal vocational training aid:

> "Vocational training is directed at acquiring specific skills and knowledge and inculcating social and political attitudes and modes of behaviour which have decisive importance for successful economic activity for people in employment or entrepreneurial or subsistence situations"[14].

The BMZ noted that the sectoral concept must be seen in context with the promotional concepts for other sectors, such as primary education, rural development, combating poverty through self-help aid, promoting the private sector and promoting women[15].
Vocational training should have great (if not central) importance in developing the opportunities for the individual and developing their competencies for economically successful action and improving their personal, family and social situation in life. The following areas should be noted in this context:

> "*Material security* for the individual and their family! The struggle to survive is replaced by shaping their life. Ideally, there is the possibility of prosperity, capital formation and improved security for old age. This becomes possible as a result of income, revenue, savings or more effective activity in the subsistence economy."[16]

It is striking that this only mentions the subsistence economy, avoiding the term "informal sector" altogether although this is given more attention (an entire chapter) under the heading "Promotion of target groups in the informal sector" in the sectoral concept[17].

> "*Establishing an identity*: the individual gains self-confidence and dignity and acquires new scope for action. This is promoted by occupational success, pleasure in work and creativity."[18]

> "*Social integration*: solidarity, social responsibility, help to self-help and social empowerment can develop. This is promoted through firm and structured membership of the company, production cooperative, vocational group, social group, commune and family."[19]

---

14 "Sektorkonzept, Berufliche Bildung", Division 310, German Federal Ministry for Economic Cooperation and Development (BMZ) p. 1 , Jan. 1992.
15 Op. cit.
16 Op. cit.
17 Op. cit., p. 21.
18 Loc. cit.
19 Op. cit., p. 3.

Taking the individual's view of themselves referred to here and the interpretation by the authors of the sectoral concept of the central terms they cite or identify "material security, establishing an identity and social integration"[20] it is doubtful whether this is sufficient for formulating development policy and vocational training policy measures in development aid. At least it lacks an important statement or orientation guidelines for groups or governments applying for vocational training measures showing the need to integrate target groups from the informal sector. This gap is not filled by the further statements about the risks in the socio-economic context which in the BMZ's view "give the individual the appearance of an investment with uncertain prospects of success"[21]. If it is assumed (as correctly described by the BMZ) that there are:

(1) "no suitable employment offer or lack of opportunity for self-employment despite qualified training,"
(2) "more difficult conditions for life, accommodation and economic activity, preventing utilisation of existing employment opportunities,"
(3) "discrimination against groups (e.g. women) blocking access to employment generally,"[22]

it is even harder to understand why the BMZ does not exert greater pressure on applicants (i.e. national agencies and governments submitting applications) or adopt a clearer development policy stance in reviewing applications in terms of the genuinely needy people living in total poverty in these countries and offer corresponding integrated aid measures. The recent frequent statements by Federal Minister Spranger about moving away from costly major projects with little broad impact in favour of future orientation (i.e. combating growing poverty in Third World countries) give grounds for hope that changes can be expected in the orientation of German Federal development aid. There is, however, every reason for scepticism, considering the efforts to date to give practical form to such orientation into practice. Any estimate of the potential for change must take into account in considering development policy, not only the interest groups active in the Federal Republic of Germany (development aid organisations, development banks, chambers, industry, political parties, foundations etc) but also those speaking for the Third World countries: governments, expert groups from these countries, national and multinational industries based there,

---

20   Loc. cit.
21   Loc. cit.
22   Loc. cit.

national political parties and the powerful lobby of these elites in Third World governments. The chances for rapid adaptation of development aid to meet the needs of the poor of the world and the informal sector described above are accordingly fraught with difficulty.

It is not intended to promote the illusion here that vocational training aimed at the informal sector and oriented towards combating poverty could play a key role. However, previous approaches – particularly in bilateral German development aid – have suffered from the defect that their analysis frequently treats vocational training in Third World countries as a crisis of training rather than employment[23]. Vocational training is not a "key to combating poverty"[24], as is made clear in a new "World Bank Policy Paper"[25] which cites five key areas for improving the efficiency and effectiveness of vocational training measures.

(1) "Analysis of the economic context of training, including labour market issues, should be improved and used in formulating national macroeconomic strategies and designing investment operations;

(2) Lending for prevocational courses should be replaced by programmes to strengthen quality and access in academic secondary education;

(3) Lending should address the policy changes needed to create a favourable economic climate for private training as well as direct measures to stimulate and improve training in the private sector;

(4) Lending should include measures to improve the responsiveness and efficiency of public training;

(5) World Bank lending should require the development of a longer term strategy for the evolution of the government's role in training and should encourage broadly based co-ordination of donor support."[26]

It should, however, be noted that these five key criteria for development policy cited by the World Bank ignore the informal sector, which is not even explicitly mentioned. This is a very important indication of the extent to which the formulation of these principles reflects specifically the official American view of the economic and social developments needed in Third World countries. In the chapter "Training as a

---

23 Cf. Arnold, Rolf, Der Streit um die Berufsbildungshilfe – Berufsausbildung für die Dritte Welt in Widerstreit von Konzestionen p. 182 – in Berufliche Bildung und Entwicklung in den Ländern der Dritten Welt, ed. Arnold, Baden-Baden 1989.
24 Cf. op. cit. and CDU/CSU, 1986, Berufsbildung als Schlüssel zur Armutsbekämpfung, Reihe Argumente, Neue Wege in der Entwicklungspolitik, Bonn 1986.
25 A World Bank Policy Paper, Vocational and Technical Education and Training, The World Bank, 1991, Washington D.C. USA.
26 Op. cit. p. 17-18.

Complement to Equity Strategies"[27] this is somewhat relativised in the following statements:

(1) "Most of the poor in developing countries are found in rural areas and in the urban informal sector. Their principal asset is their labour, and improving their productivity and earnings is the main road out of poverty. Reform of policies that discourage economic and employment growth -not training- is the first step along this road for the poor, as well as for women and minorities"[28]

(2) "The viability of rural self-employment depends fundamentally on the purchasing power of rural consumers and thus on the productivity and income of farmers;"

(3) "Farming, of course, is the predominant form of self-employment in developing countries;"

(4) "Basic education and agricultural extension help farmers to acquire and apply new information and skills";

(5) "Entrepreneurial economic activity provides a second source of income for many farm families, self employment and very small enterprises provide the main sources of income for others;"

(6) "Much urban informal sector employment is in low-skilled occupations in which entry is easy because of low capital requirements";

(7) "Again, access to markets, raw materials, credit and management advice are the keys to successful businesses."[29]

Despite the insights quoted here of the need to do something for the informal sector, the World Bank still puts the emphasis in its policy on lending and technical aid on improving and enhancing the efficiency of the modern industrialised sector, as shown in the projects supported by the bank. In the Eighties some USD 600 million was invested worldwide in vocational training by the World Bank (45 %), bilateral organisations (30 %) and other multilateral organisations (25 %).[30] In many countries this has led to rapid expansion of full-time academic training outside companies, with particularly striking examples evident in almost all countries in Asia, Africa and the Near East. No great importance was attached to concrete involvement of industry, the craft trades, service sector or agriculture as actors in providing and financing vocational training. This was in any event desirable for many countries in these regions, which were or still are adherents to social cen-

---

27 Op. cit. p. 58.
28 Op. cit. p. 58.
29 Op. cit. p. 59.
30 Op. cit. p. 65.

trally-planned economies with their dirigiste models and state structures[31]. In addition, most African and Asian countries are committed to the model of technical secondary schools as a result of their (frequently British) colonial past, resulting in vocational training which is heavily academic and focused on formal qualifications. This is why massive state facilities for formal vocational training have been and are still being established[32] and expanded. One consequence of this policy is that vocational training aid to date is mainly concentrated on developing modern and industrialised sectors of the economy and on its educational establishments and social powers, and the informal sector is often dismissed as a difficult and diffuse economic and social environment and ignored and underestimated in its development capability and potential for helping induce sustainable changes. However, this is obviously incorrect, since the economic and human catastrophe afflicting the populations of many countries in Asia, Latin America and Africa would be much greater in the absence of what has established itself generally as the informal sector in Third World countries. The situation found in many countries ruined by civil wars, tribal conflicts and repressed conflicts between national minorities is becoming the norm worldwide for these countries. In a study on the role of the informal sector and the economic development of Bangladesh, for example, A.T.M. Amin[33] explains some of the chief arguments clarifying the role of the informal sector for the development of the Bangladeshi national economy.

> "While rapidly growing numbers of rural migrants, formally educated and trained persons and female entrants are swelling the urban labour force, the establishment of new enterprises and the existing economic activities have significantly increased the urban economy's capacity to absorb Labour. Significantly but altogether insufficiently, owing above all to the failure of the modern manufacturing sector to provide the necessary lead[34]. In these circumstances the swiftly developing informal sector has acted as a shock absorber, particularly by providing

---

31 Cf. Karl-Hans Hartwig, H. Jörg Thieme (ed.) Transformationsprozesse in sozialistischen Wirtschaftssystemen, Springer, Berlin, 1991.
32 See also World Bank Report No. 7530-IN, Staff appraisal report, INDIA, Vocational training project, 04/1989, Washington, D. C. and India.
33 Assistant Professor, Division of Human Settlements Development, Asian Institute of Technology, Bangkok, The author is a member of the Department of Economics, Jahangirnagar University, Bangladesh. His analyses are mainly based on findings of an analysis of labour force and industrial organisations of the informal sector in Dhaka. He works also in close cooperation with ILO-ARTEP, New Delhi. (cf. note 35).
34 Even so no exact data are available here because the local labour market statistics and the population censuses are not collected sufficiently regularly in most Third World countries because of cost, technical facilities and frequently also the political delicacy of the likely results the author has acquired the impression in the course of many years of travel in these countries that the estimates have a realistic basis.

employment opportunities to many rural migrants pushed out of the agricultural sector by landlessness and other economic pressures."[35]

This is also true of most Asian countries, e.g. India, Pakistan, Indonesia and Thailand, despite their advanced industrialisation. The following comments in particular can be transferred wholesale:

> "The size of the informal sector in the cities of Bangladesh can by judged from the fact that about 65 percent of the total urban employment in Dhaka, the country's capital, is in this sector (see World Bank: Bangladesh urban sector memorandum, Report No. 3422-BD, Washington, DC, 1981)"...[36] The attention of planners and policy-makers needs to be drawn to this vast sector which does not enjoy any of the benefits and incentives that the Government provides to the formal sector and operates under constant threats and harassment both from a variety of law enforcement agencies and from local touts and musclemen."[37]

As the views and observations cited here show, the informal sector is left to its own devices in most countries and is not significantly supported or supplied with the corresponding knowhow in terms of concepts, planning or project implementation by the competent government agencies, financial community, formal sector, local economy or international and bilateral aid programmes. In view of this situation the informal sector could be regarded as the totality of the silent majority of men, women, young persons and children struggling for daily survival, outside the groups and lobbies described above and regarded by local, regional and international politicians, the main social decision-makers, the financial and commercial community and international aid as unofficial and voiceless.

With this group there is a need to address highly discriminated groups such as the unemployed masses or underemployed women and also children who have been degradingly exploited and robbed of their childhood and at the early age of 6 and 7 have to make a major contribution to the family income[38]. In this connection it is to be welcomed that the German Federal Ministry for Economic Cooperation and Development (BMZ) makes clear reference to the informal sector and

---

35   A.T.M. Nurul Amin, The role of the informal sector in economic development, some evidence from Dhaka, Bangladesh, in International Labour Review, Vol. 126 No. 5, Sept. 87, Geneva.
36   A.T.M. Nurul Amin, The role of the informal sector in economic development, some evidence from Dhaka, Bangladesh, in International Labour Review, Vol. 126 No. 5, Sept. 87, Geneva.
37   Op. cit.
38   Cf. Report of the national commission on self employed women and women in the informal sector, Shramshakti: commissioned by the Indian central government, New Delhi, 1988 p. 57.

disadvantaged population groups in its new "Sectoral concept for vocational training"[39] and cites the informal sector as a key principle for promotion:

> "The need of target groups in the informal sector (and particularly of disadvantaged population groups) to improve their earning opportunities and quality of life should be addressed through special offers in the field of vocational training. These must take explicit account of the learning ability of the participants and their living environment and the concrete needs for qualification arising out of this. The offers should lead to additional or improved opportunities for employment, self-employment or effective independent work in the subsistence economy."[40]
> It further says about the selection of the target groups:
> "Particularly in promoting target groups in the informal sector (and specifically disadvantaged population groups) . . . and intersectoral concepts for . . . "combating poverty through help to self-help movements as partners in development cooperation" and "promotion of women in developing countries".[41]

The concept of the informal sector also logically extends to all those economic activities of the target groups which are not covered by the formal economic sector as yet, i.e. "the large number of diverse small businesses, micro-businesses and one-person businesses on the edge or in the shadow of the modern economy, which are obviously economically relevant but virtually impossible to assign to the standard macroeconomic categories"[42].

On closer consideration this covers economic activity ranging from the traditional craft trades, through services to agriculture and modern industry to the countless nonspecific services supplied by the informal sector. The activities and necessary qualifications to provide the services of the informal sector accordingly cover a very wide range of technological, commercial and organisational levels. Generally, all areas of the formal sector and the modern economy are touched by the informal sector, although this often happens only at a very low economic, technological and (corporate) organisational level[43]. In the past, the economic and added-value importance of this sector to the national economy has been severely underestimated, and as a result the firms in the informal sector basically lack access to credit, marketing, information and decision-making systems; equally, they lack influence on the local and national economic and political environment. An exception here in the Asian cultures (e.g. India, Pakistan, Iran etc) are the baz-

---

39 Cf. BMZ, Sektorkonzept: Berufliche Bildung, Bonn 1992.
40 Op. cit. p. 13.
41 Op. cit. p. 14.
42 C. Lohmar-Kuhnle, Konzepte zur beschäftigungsorientierten Aus- und Fortbildung von Zielgruppen aus dem inform. Sektor, Cologne, 91, pp. 10-11.
43 Op. cit. p. 11.

aries[44] which are frequently highly impressive in their organisation and influence on social policy and the politicised lower strata of society, which in Iran inter alia played a major role in the overthrow of the shah and are also an important political and economic pillar of the integrative Shiite[45] Islamic-Iranian revolutionary movement. The influence of these political and religious movements and ideologies on Pakistan, India and Afghanistan is only indirectly apparent as a fundamentally anti-western political attitude, due to the predominantly Suni[46] orientation of the majority of the population. The influences of the Iranian revolutionary movement on social policy are accordingly only directly apparent where there are Shiite minorities (Karachi, Lahore, Bombay, New Delhi, etc) trying to intervene in the political life of these countries through their mullahs and political splinter groups[47]. The cultural, political and religious influence on thinking and acting, particularly in the Islamic culture of India and Islamic Pakistan, on the traditionally-oriented bazaries, the rural population and the landless poor groups in the population who essentially comprise the target groups of the informal sector, accordingly constitute a major influence and yardstick for the "social and economic action" of these groups[48]. However, for all the significance of Islam to the Indian subcontinent, it is important not to forget the vast influence of Hinduism[49], Buddhism and Christianity,

44 Cf. Religion und Politik im Iran, Gesellschaftspolitische Vorstellungen im shiitischen Islam: Differenzen in der "reinen Lehre", A. Shirazi, Syndikat, Frankfurt, 1981, pp. 172-174.
45 Anouar Abdel-Malek, La Pensée politique arabe contemporaine p. 43, "Shi`ah (Shiî`tes), tendance politico-religieuse musulmane dominant pricipalement en Iran, se rattachant à Alî, gendre et cousin du prophète (Mohammad), Seuil, Paris, 1970.
46 Op. cit. p. 43, "Sunnah (Sunnîtes), courant majoritaire au sein de l'islam; se considère comme seul détenteur de l'orthodoxie", which is why the Sunnite Islamic orientation is less interested in the current social policy debate and concentrated on the spiritual and religious life in the sense of Islam. With the exception of the Algerian FIS (Front islamique du Salut), which is inspired by the revolutionary Shiite influence of Iran and intervenes strongly in Algeria's political life despite the Sunnite Islamic majority in Algeria (the author).
47 Similar developments are increasingly apparent in Pakistan, India, Afghanistan and Egypt as well.
48 Cf.: Ende/Steinbach, Der Islam in der Gegenwart. C.H. Beck, Munich, 3rd edn. 1991, pp. 489 et seq.
In connection with the critical consideration of the term "popular Islam" F. De Jong presents interesting categories and levels which can be useful in understanding societies with an Islamic stamp, e.g. regional variants of Islam, the way that the broad mass of very largely illiterate people see themselves in Islam, forms of piety manifested in the cult of saints and mystical brotherhoods, ideas and practices which are identical with mysticism, superstition and heresy and, as already noted, the influence of political movements and parties in the regional and local context, which must not be underestimated (the author).
49 Cf. "The Tao of Physics", Fritjof Capra, New York 1984, p. 75:
Hinduism cannot be called a philosophy, nor is it a well defined religion. It is, rather, a large and complex socio-religious organism consisting of innumerable sects, cults and philosophical systems and involving various rituals, ceremonies, and spiritual disciplines, as well as worship of countless gods and goddesses. The many facets of this complex and yet persistent tradition mirror the geographical, racial, linguistic, and cultural complexities of India's vast subcontinent."

reflecting the colonial past and missionary efforts of the Christian church, which affected the process of civilisation, political culture and evolution of different social strata and traditions in these societies[50]. These problems of the relationship between culture and tradition will be explored in more detail in section 2.3. However, even the broad consideration here of the socio-cultural and socio-economic analysis of the informal sector are enough to indicate the complexity of focused development policy work in the educational and vocational training sector. Another important area for developing a better understanding of the problems of the informal sector are considerations and experience of the development policy and economic interfaces, or the fluid transitions to the formal sector.

"The interfaces between the economic structure of the informal sector and the modern sector are numerous and complex in most conurbations. The market economy of the informal sector is based on the supply of cheap goods and services for the bulk of the population with only minimal purchasing power, in both the modern and the informal sectors"[51]. Frequently there is accordingly no difference at all in the nature and form of the goods, products and services in the urban informal sector and the formal sector: the differences lie in the lack of complication, simplicity, low cost and direct availability to customers, naturally without any warranties. In many respects the services or products supplied are only as cheap as they are because they are not subject to any tax and do not comply with any official quality, production, performance or contractual requirements. From the customer's point of view, the performance is reasonable for the price. Here, the informal sector frequently fills in the gaps left by the formal sector as a result of frequently exaggerated overheads, profit expectations of entrepreneurs or suppliers and inadequate quality of products and services. It is not unusual for employees of nationalised facilities, corporations and service companies to have second or third jobs outside their normal working hours, selling their labour, skills and abilities in the informal sector. This is generally done without the knowledge of the employer or the tax authorities, so that buyers and sellers bypass the official agencies in their economic activities. It is accordingly true in part that the weaknesses of the formal sector in Third World countries are the strengths

---

50   This is also shown by the current conflict between the right-wing radical and fanatical Hindu political movements (destruction of the mosque at Ayodhia in Uttar Pradesh by the radical Shiv-Senamovement in India and construction of the RAM temple) in India and the Islamic so-called minorities in India (there are well over 100 million Muslims living in India). These conflicts emerge in India in particular where there are strong Islamic minorities or where Muslims even form the majority of the population.
51   C. Lohmar-Kuhnle, Konzepte zur . . ., see note 42, p. 33.

of the informal sector, contributing directly to the survival of buyers and sellers of products and services in the informal sector.

"Many economic activities in the urban informal sector in particular are only possible because of corresponding demand from the modern sector and a widespread (over)supply of cheap mass products and the "throw-away" mentality of middle-class consumers in the modern sector. Countless house employees live off this, the recycling economy of the informal sector in many cities is based on this, and the employment of many small production and service firms and day labourers depends on it"[52].

In addition there are many examples of the real economic links between the informal and formal sectors to the extent that the informal sector in some areas makes a key contribution towards ensuring the functioning of the production and service facilities in the formal sector[53, 54].

"In the rural area on the other hand the two sectors are often (still) largely separate from each other, i.e. there are relatively few mutual interactions. Paradoxically, however, it is even more difficult to define the boundary here than in urban centres between the modern and informal sectors, either theoretically or in real terms"[55]. There is also a number of countries in Africa, Asia and the south Pacific area, e.g. Papua New Guinea, where in regions remote from modern conurbations there is likely to be difficulty defining the formal sector properly at all alongside traditional social forms and relationships of production. Often the social groups in regional and local economic life are unfamiliar with monetary economies or the sale of goods or services. It becomes difficult here to talk in terms of an informal economy, since the social, economic and political action of these societies is frequently concerned solely with securing the group or the life of the clan as a whole. Goods are frequently exchanged directly through barter using socially defined barter commodities, and specialisation or division of labour within a group or clan often still falls short of the point where it could be assigned to vocational activities. It is even more difficult in these segmentary societies[56] to identify a traditional economic and employment

---

52 C. Lohmar-Kuhnle, Konzepte zur . . ., p. 32, see note 42, p. 33.
53 The author bases this on his own extensive experience where e.g. in Third World countries services for the home, e.g. installation and sanitary work, domestic services (ironing, washing, cooking etc), sealing wells for drinking water, security services, transport, removal services, refuse disposal etc. are exclusively provided by the informal sector.
54 This includes specifically the range of goods and services of small bazaar businesses such as transport, communication, energy etc.
55 C. Lohmar-Kuhnle, Konzepte zur . . ., p. 32, pp. 38 et seq. see note 42, p. 33.
56 Cf. C. Sigrist, Regulierte Anarchie, Texte und Dokumente zur Soziologie, Walter, Freiburg, 1967.

system based on the pattern of modern or Asian systems, and the related forms of informal economic sectors,[57] as these societies – if, as in Papua New Guinea, they are to be linked to the modern sector – must first create the key conditions for a social system oriented towards a modern state and community and economic system.[58] Educational and vocational training policy undoubtedly has an important function in this[59].

In contrast to the definition of the informal sector frequently cited in the literature based on contractual aspects of wage labour or the economy concerned[60], the informal sector here is *not* treated as the totality of illegal economic activities and unregistered establishments[61]. Equally, the informal sector cannot be equated with the traditional sector even if this is frequently identical to the traditional sector (as e.g. in many African countries)[62].

As already noted, in most countries the urban part of the informal sector frequently has more "modern" than traditional economic activities[63]. Turning to the many rural areas of the Third World countries, segmentation into modern, traditional and informal sectors is frequently not yet advanced, as the traditional rural and peasant establishments assume the necessary economic functions here and also provide employment for the labour market, with the exception of the administrative and service offices in rural areas of urban and government establishments.

The term *modern sector* is consequently preferred as the counterpart to the *informal sector*, as the term "formal sector" carries the implication

---

57 The author has faced these problems in the context of his work as expert and planner for GTZ/BMZ, and experience to date of the development aid organisations have not yet been systematically or scientifically analysed. Official ethnology has not yet approached these questions as a subject for research and the organisations and government agencies responsible have not yet invoked the help of experts from this sector.
58 Afghanistan is another example of how a modern system of government can collapse under the pressure of traditional tribal structures and the interests of the great clans and tribes, and how under the guise of politically and religiously justified conflicts the interests of individual groups/clans are the cause of the extensive military clashes. The weapons supplied are virtually unlimited and certainly sufficient to prevent the conflicts of interest from being resolved in a peaceful and democratic way.
59 Cf. Sektorstudie Berufliche Bildung Papua New Guinea, GTZ, Eschborn, 1991.
60 Dieter Borsutzky, p. 54, see note 64.
61 Cf. C. Lohmar-Kuhnle, Konzepte zur . . ., p. 10, see note 42, p. 33.
62 Loc. cit.
63 There are studies of the informal sector not only in the developing nations but also in modern industrial society, e.g. Berger et al. (1984). A review of the designations most frequently used in research for (sub)sectors of the informal sector is given in Huber (1983 :3);- shadow or underground economy, unofficial economy, alternative economy, counter, parallel or secondary econoblack economy, autonomous sector, self-help sector, vernacular sector, neighbourly help. On distinguishing shadow work from the informal sector cf. Evers (1987) in Dieter Borsutzky, p. 54, see note 64.

Definitions of the informal sector in terms of related concepts[64]

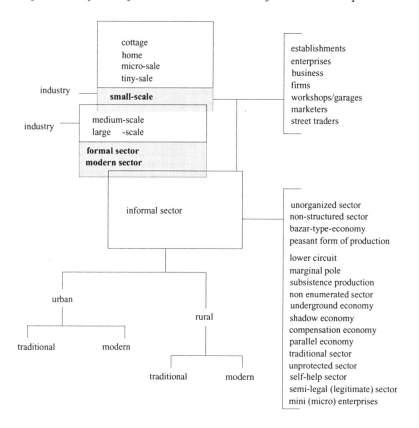

(unlike modern sector) that the informal sector covers criminal, illegal and noncontractual economic activity, which gives a completely inadequate picture of what happens in the informal sector.[65]

"The decisive priority is seen instead as the living and working relationships which show certain specific characteristics for economically and socially disadvantaged population groups which differ significantly from the structures, norms and functions of an urban industrial

---

64 Cf. Dieter Borsutzky, Die Industrialisierung im informellen Metallsektor: Das Maschinenkleingewerbe in Penang/Malaysia, Saarbrücken, 1992 p. 55.
65 Cf. C. Lohmar-Kuhnle, see note 42 on p. 33, pp. 11 et seq.

society with its culture and technology and style of living and working, all of which are described as "modern" in an age when standards are increasingly levelling worldwide[66]. Another link between the modern and informal sectors for development cooperation is the system of employment found in Third World countries and the problem for both sectors of inadequate employment opportunities. The employment system (or labour market) should not under any circumstances be limited to the modern sector, as it represents an important (and frequently highly fluid) interface between the modern and informal sectors[67].

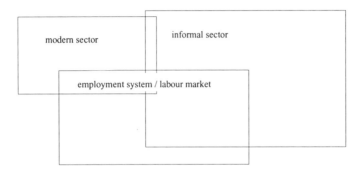

The interfaces between the modern and informal sectors in rural areas of the Third World are considerably easier to identify than in the urban areas, although they resemble the urban economy in their type and structure. However, the subsistence economy is largely decoupled from the modern sector[68]. According to C. Lohmar-Kuhnle[69] the interfaces in the rural area can be described as follows:
- procurement of raw materials, starter products and supplies such as cheap industrial products or waste products of modern industrial society which pass to the informal sector for further processing
- cheap products and services (repairs etc) supplied by the informal sector for consumers with low purchasing power in the rural area;

---

66   Cf. C. Lohmar-Kuhnle, source see note 42 on p. 33, pp. 11 et seq.
67   Job opportunities and labour markets in the informal sector are not covered by official statistics, labour offices and employment agencies. This area is generally little studied and there is hardly any reliable data. Multilateral and bilateral donors have not promoted this sector in the past as its importance deserves.
68   Cf. C. Lohmar-Kuhnle, Konzepte zur beschäftigungsorientierten Aus- und Fortbildung von Zielgruppen aus dem informellen Sektor, Weltforum Verlag, Cologne 1991, pp. 39 et seq.
69   Loc. cit.

these frequently replace more expensive equivalents from the modern sector;
- provision of community services by the informal sector (e.g. waste disposal etc);
- supply of cheap labour by the rural informal sector (landless peasants, seasonal workers and unemployed) to companies in industry and tourism in the urban modern sector such as construction, road construction, road cleaning, house employees, dock workers and cheap transport of goods (using e.g. ox carts, bicycles, handcarts, porters etc).

Conversely, the interfaces between the modern and informal sectors in conurbations are often extremely complex, as it is not possible to distinguish the sectors clearly. In many countries these sectors are interdependent, with a fluid boundary between the two. At the individual (employee) level, however, the interfaces are easier to identify clearly, and it is often the case that an employee in a company in the modern sector is forced by their poor pay to take a second or third job in the informal sector[70]. Studies in the informal sector accordingly need to look at concrete individual instances and also take a region specific and country specific approach if they are trying to identify more closely the processes in the interfaces between the modern and informal sectors in an urban environment. This is the only way of obtaining more exact data for analysing the labour market[71] and making possible vocational training which is oriented towards the informal sector and employment. From the standpoint of graduates of vocational training measures it is certainly irrelevant initially which sector offers them employment, since the important thing is a regular and secure income. Vocational pedagogics and development policy on the other hand should not be satisfied with this result, as the key issues here must be to create lasting employment with fair pay and to improve and secure income and create equal opportunity for all members of society. This is why the question here is not one of developing a *"special"* vocational pedagogics for the informal sector: instead, vocational pedagogics must first

---

70 The author has frequently observed that officials (teachers and trainers) in the education and employment ministries frequently run small repair businesses after working hours in the bazaars of India and Pakistan or are employed by a friend who is a small (micro) businessman, as a way of augmenting their poor salary.
71 The example of India and Pakistan shows the need to collect data on regionally or even locally oriented economic and employment structures, as the disparate economic and regional-specific development in the country and the size of these countries makes a central development strategy for the informal sector applying to the entire economy impossible. Measures and projects in the informal sector must accordingly be formulated in terms of regional characteristics and considered in terms of rural and urban structures of the informal sector.

acknowledge the existence of this sector and deal with it systematically. The corresponding techniques and didactics in vocational pedagogics will then have to be developed on the basis of information on this sector and the needs of the target group.

2.2 Defining work and its significance for the informal sector in the Third World

The meaning of work and its nature is understood in all cultures and all ages on the basis of its socio-cultural, socio-economic, historical, religious, political and ecological relationships and context. Work is directly linked with people and their existence: without people there would be no work and vice versa, so that people are both the subject and object of work.

> "People only take on historical reality and acquire their specific place in history through work. Whether they are machine minders, coal miners, shop assistants, public servants in a bureaucracy or academics teaching, they emerge from the immediate sphere of their personalities to take a specific place in an environment categorised, organised and structured by professions, occupations, classes etc, and their membership in these locates them within this environment."[72]

Work can accordingly reflect the socio-cultural, socio-economic and socio-political structure of societies through its significance and its assignment to the various strata of the societies under observation, including allocation of specific activities or entire vocational groups.

> "The concept of work is an ancient concept extensively explored and modified in religion, philosophy and education. The concern with this can even be described as a characteristic of western civilisation[73].

Work plays an important role as early as Greek mythology: Prometheus had to obtain compensation for humanity under his protection in the form of the divine gifts of fire and craft skills[74]. Prometheus later paid for his friendship with humanity with the gruesome fate imposed by Zeus. There are analogies with the creation story of the

---

72 Cf. Herbert Marcuse, Kultur und Gesellschaft 2. Suhrkamp 1967, Frankfurt, pp. 33/34.
73 Cf. Helmut Nölker, Arbeit und Polytechnische Bildung, Die zwiespältige Deutung der Arbeit, Ein historischer Exkurs, in E. Schoenfeldt (ed.) Polytechnik und Arbeit, S.B., Klinkhardt, 1979 Bad Heilbrunn. *Note on quote*: This applies particularly to the Christian view of work which has flowed into the western concept of occupation as an organisational form of work.
74 Loc. cit.

Christian religion: here, God expels the original human pair from Paradise because they violate his trust and eat of the forbidden fruit. As punishment, they are subjected to the curse of work, doomed to labour in the sweat of their brow in pain and suffering until the Last Judgement, which will restore the condition of Paradise for those who have lived and worked by God's law. Even the immortality proclaimed by Christianity and the eternal focus (reward for persecution and suffering) of human life is made conditional on the fruits of human work[75].
In his analysis of the economic concept of work, H. Marcuse emphasises inter alia the burden of work, i.e.

> "We could now try to capture the essential nature of work in its actual "negativity", which would at least suggest the fundamental significance of the burdensome nature of work: . . . This burdensome nature ultimately expresses nothing more than the negativity inherent in human existence: the fact that people can only achieve their own selves by passing through the other, that they can only gain themselves by passing through "Entäußerung" and "alienation"."[76]

It is clear that even attempts to reinterpret the concept of work on the basis of economic and materialist-dialectic ideas do not in principle lead to any other result or bring any significant relief to humanity compared to the Christian or ancient Greek interpretation of work, since work ultimately remains what it is. In Greek mythology and analogously in the Judaeo-Christian creation myth work came into the world as a result of human defiance of the divine law, although the creation myth subsequently transforms work into a blessing, provided that humanity follow God's law in this world and piously accept their lot, i.e. their daily burden of work[77].

> "For Christians, work is a divine commandment not only as a result of the work of creation and original sin but also of the example of God Himself as a great craftsman. The first thing that the Old Testament tells us is a statement about God's "labour": "In the Beginning, God created Heaven and Earth". An important motivation for Christian work is *imitatio dei*, the desire to emulate God. This also is the origin of the duty to work and the rejection of rest when there is no direct need to be satisfied."[78]

---

75 Loc. cit. and 1 Moses 1, 28; Matthew 6, 34, 2 Moses 20, 6.
76 Cf. H. Marcuse, Kultur und Gesellschaft 2. Suhrkamp, 1967, Frankfurt, S. 31/32.
77 Cf. H. Nölker, Arbeit und Polytechnische Bildung, Die zwiespältige Deutung der Arbeit, Ein historischer Exkurs, in E. Schoenfeldt (ed.), Polytechnik und Arbeit, p. 14, Klinkhardt, 1979, Bad Heilbrunn.
78 Op. cit., p. 15.

This contradiction in the concept of work in Christian thought and action also appears on further consideration of the results and effects of the Christian and western-oriented concept of humanity as an important cause of capitalism and the associated unrestrained exploitation of the earth and people by people in disregard of God's injunction[79]. The Protestant view of work and work ethic, particularly in Calivinism, is very important for the emergence of capitalism and its ideological orientation in the English-speaking world[80]. For Calvinism the theory of predestination is important, i.e. God determines what shall happen with individuals, whether they are destined for salvation or eternal death. As a result, the earthly acts (of people) are included in this predestination and human labour becomes a form of worship of God, in the words of Jesus "By their fruits shall ye know them." This encourages people with an eye on life after death to work harder and stops them consuming the fruits of their or their employees' labour, so that they only consume the minimum necessary and invest the surplus in new undertakings. "The reformed Christian accordingly lives in a state of great internal isolation. In an internal asceticism they drive themselves on to tireless industriousness on the principle that "God helps those who help themselves", to secure the mercy of God through the rich reward of their labour[81]. However, as Catholic social theory shows, this must not develop into "Mammonism and mammonist attitudes, i.e. in unrestrained acquisitiveness focusing entirely on this world and material things, as such a "capitalist mentality" is not Christian, it is un-Christian both for the haves ("capitalists") and for the have-nots ("proletariat")"[82]. These positions and interpretations of Christian social theory display key moments in the Christian-western idea of work and work ethic:

(a) the idea of the fruits of work and the resulting urge to profit and possessions
(b) the totality of work's claims on humanity, resulting from the idea that the fruits of work are an indicator of the blessing and mercy of God and that taking pleasure in ease is a sign of damnation

---

79 Cf. K. Marx, Lohnarbeit und Kapital, Dietz Verlag, Berlin, 1946, 10th edition.
80 Cf. Max Weber and R. H. Tawney, (a) Max Weber, Die Protestantische Ethik und der Geist des Kapitalismus, Gesammelte Aufsätze zur Religionssoziologie, vol. I Tübingen 1922, pp. 63 et seq. (b) R. H. Tawney, Religion and the Rise of Capitalism, London 1926.
81 Cf. H. Nölker, see note 77, p. 17 and Max Weber, Die Protestantische Ethik . . . see note 80.
82 Cf. Oswald von Nell-Breuning, Kapitalismus und gerechter Lohn, Herder, Freiburg, 1960, p. 97 et seq.

(c) the negation of the social nature of work through the integration of work in the issue of predestination with its isolating effect on individuals"[83].

Marx particularly criticised "the negation of the social nature of work" under the given capitalist economic relationships and in the national economy and introduced the term of the "alienation" of labour, i.e. the labourer or producer of products living from the results of their work is working for the capitalist who owns the means of production and receiving a wage in return. "The national economy conceals the alienation in the nature of work by ignoring the direct relationship between the worker (labour) and production[84]. For Marx, a further aspect of alienation is "the relationship of the workers to the product they create"[85], i.e. the worker must produce articles and products to survive which have no or only a very remote connection with their concrete needs. According to Marx these products benefit only the capitalists who also simultaneously determine the market and production, as they own the means of production (factories, machinery etc) and the associated capital. In this way, modern humanity and society have taken a major step towards work determined exclusively by society. This trend also separates this generation from previous generations who could only define their work on the basis of their own direct structure of needs. Today, however, we can only consider labour, product and the results of labour at the level of society as a whole. In analysing the significance and results of human labour, it is accordingly necessary to consider the overall social perspectives and different components, since in cultures other than western-oriented ones work also plays a major role in the life of people, depending on the degree of industrialisation and urbanisation of these societies.

Work can be understood, interpreted and experienced in terms of the Christian work ethic. However, in contrast to the concept of vocation, where these problems are even more evident as a result of the divine components of avocation, the concept of work has the advantage of being a universal category, as for all the global differences in the understanding of work, everybody still has to work in some way or other.

---

83 Cf. H. Nölker, Arbeit und Polytechnische Bildung, Die zwiespältige Deutung der Arbeit, Ein historischer Exkurs, in E. Schoenfeldt (ed.), Polytechnik und Arbeit, pp. 17/18, 1979, Klinkhardt, Bad Heilbrunn.
84 Cf. Karl Marx, Ökonomisch-philosophische Manuskripte. Reclam, Leipzig, 1970, pp. 154 et seq.
85 Op. cit., pp. 156 et seq.

As "work" plays an important role in vocational pedagogics in developing didactics, curricula and learning theories[86], care must be taken when transferring vocational training approaches to Third World countries to note which socio-cultural, socio-economic, religious, historical, political and social structures and post-colonial relationships are present. The situation becomes particularly complicated and complex where the informal sector is involved, as this operates at the margin as a subsector reaching deep into the modern sector and into rural areas, from indigenous cultural, economic and traditional social structures into surviving segments which are in part pure subsistence economies[87]. Ethnologists and anthropologists still classify these as "primitive forms of social life", forms of society and production still displaying their primeval nature. H. Marcuse offers a very interesting (and in the author's view highly illuminating) way of moving from the view of work in modern industrial society to an understanding of work purely aimed at the needs of "primitive humanity", which shows its primeval nature and moves us to mourn the loss of the paradise of these "primitive societies".

> "It has been repeatedly emphasised that among primitive peoples work seems to have an inherently different significance than among so-called civilised peoples[88]; – in fact, at a certain level of development it is actually not possible to talk about work in the strict meaning of the term. Here work is not a "regular activity", satisfying needs does not go beyond "momentary necessities" (even though these people are perfectly aware that they will suffer deprivation at some future time, e.g. in winter), there is a striking lack of proportion between the time spent working and the time spent playing, dancing, making jewellery etc. [making war, conflict etc. – the author]. Given this, there is a direct and striking connection between the relationship between existence and time (historicity) and work as a means of actualising this existence. Primitive peoples do not have the relationship with time which turns existence into history and which is also central to work as actualising existence.[89]"

---

86 "Work" is associated with the "world of work", which requires duly developed and standardised forms of behaviour to enable the "worker" to find their way around this "world of work" and do their "work". Effective vocational training is accordingly also concerned with meeting these forms and standards for the content of work and behaviour created by the social production and communication processes.
87 During a recent visit to a village in Papua (New Guinea) the author observed that the village neither had any clear division of labour (e.g. handicraft or the like) nor knew money as an economic means of transfer. The villagers, organised in extended families and clans, were only familiar with barter and otherwise performed all the work communally. This is certainly not to be understood as an empirically and scientifically established fact, but merely as an observation –indicating that there are still social forms of human coexistence which may have lost their original status but must still be accepted as surviving.
88 Op. cit., see sources, H. Marcuse p. 175.
89 Cf. Herbert Marcuse, Kultur und Gesellschaft 2. Suhrkamp, 1967, Frankfurt, pp. 35/36.

It is accordingly the temporal and historical dimension of human work which is important for documenting the historical and social development of our modern concept of work and its importance to the post-industrial society, since the historical and social development prompts a specific relationship of people to work.

> "The working individual is constantly maintaining the temporality of themselves and the objective world, and this behaviour is expressed in many different ways: in procurement, treatment and realisation of the working material, in the allocation and administration of the means of work and specifically in the general allocation of time which the working individual is more or less subject to.[90]"

In Hegel two further key aspects which have influenced our concept of work are emphasised:

(a) the individual aspect, its importance for the individual
(b) the social aspect, its importance for the state and society.[91]

The individual aspect of work is concerned with the anthropologically-determined nature of work, as according to Hegel humanity is distinguished from animals essentially by the fact that it is not directly adapted to the environment and cannot find the things needed for life at all times and on all occasions in nature. Humanity has to make a large number of arrangements and "create itself" to be able to "exist"[92]. The social aspect of labour is most apparent in the "social dimension" of labour, i.e. a human being (as an individual) depends for satisfying (their) needs on the help and specific skills of others, who in turn cannot do without the skills of the first individual[93].

> "In this way a "system of needs" develops in a society with division of labour which places individuals in a "system of mutual independence". These systems owe their emergence first to the self-discipline of human beings as individuals. But they also result in the realisation (to a certain extent "behind the individual's back") of the principle of a general morality which according to Hegel distinguishes life in a state. The totality of individual interests is "exalted" in a dialectical synthesis[94]. "Hegel sees middle-class society entirely as a modern society of work. This makes work the primary social legitimation of human beings"[95].

---

90 Op. cit. pp. 34/35.
91 Cf. Georg W. Friedrich Hegel, vol. II, Studienausgabe Fischer-Bücherei.
92 Loc. cit.
93 See note 82 on p. 43.
94 Loc. cit.
95 Op. cit., p. 26.

The importance of work to humans is again emphasised in an international context by the "Universal Declaration of Human Rights", adopted on 10.12.48 by the United Nations in Plenary Session[96]. Article 23 on the right to work states:

> "Article 23: [1] Everyone has the right to work, to free choice of employment, to just and favourable conditions of work and to protection against unemployment. [2] Everyone, without any discrimination, has the right to equal pay for equal work. [3] Everyone who works has the right to just and favourable remuneration ensuring for himself and his family an existence worthy of human dignity, and supplemented, if necessary, by other means of social protection. [4] Everyone has the right to form and to join trade unions for the protection of his interests.[97]"

Articles 24 and 25 include fundamental statements on working hours, leisure, quality of life, mothers and children and the availability of resources to satisfy fundamental human needs[98]. Another central article on human rights which is closely connected with the responsibilities of teachers and vocational training instructors is Article [26]:

> "Article 26. [1] Everyone has the right to education. Education shall be free, at least in the elementary and fundamental stages. Elementary education shall be compulsory. Technical and professional education shall be made generally available and higher education shall be equally accessible to all on the basis of merit. [2] Education shall be directed to the full development of the human personality and to the strengthening of respect for human rights and fundamental freedoms. . . . [3] Parents have a prior right to choose the kind of education that shall be given to their children.[99]"

The Federal Republic of Germany has accordingly acknowledged the principle of basic needs in the context of international development aid strategies and discussions[100]. The central points in the concept of basic needs include primarily securing the minimum needs of the individual and their family in terms of food, housing and clothing and ensuring the most important public services, specifically drinking water, sanitary facilities, transport, health and educational facilities[101]. In an

---

96 Cf. Willy Strzelewicz, Der Kampf um die Menschenrechte, Societäts-Verlag, Frankfurt, 1971, p. 247.
97 Op. cit. p. 248.
98 Op. cit. articles [24] and [25], p. 248.
99 Op. cit. pp. 248/249.
100 See "Grundlinien der Entwicklungspolitik der Bundesregierung", 19 March 1986.
101 Cf. Journalisten-Handbuch Entwicklungspolitik 87, pub. Bundesministerium für wirtschaftliche Zusammenarbeit (BMZ), Bonn, 1987; cf. the BMZ "basic needs concept", Bonn 1978; see also UNICEF Strategy for basic services (1976/1977); WHO programme for a basic medical service (1975) and ILO programme "Health for all by 2000" (1978); ILO action programme for promoting employment and meeting basic needs (1976); IDA programme to

extended sense it could be assumed that the "right to work" in satisfying human basic needs (particularly in the Third World) plays a central role in developing strategies to improve living conditions and develop the economic potential of these countries[102].

A further key aspect of documenting the multiple layers in the concept of work comprises the social, socio-cultural, traditional and religious values of the societies in which interventions are planned and implemented by the industrialised societies, e.g. in the form of development or technical assistance. India and Pakistan will serve as examples here for fundamental consideration of how the concept of labour developed to date has to be relativised through confrontation with the social, socio-cultural and traditional religious realities of these countries and how its significance shifts for vocational pedagogics in the development policy intervention fields in this sector. India and Pakistan (the former "Indian subcontinent") are characterised by their multiracial and multicultural populations. If we look at the historical development of these countries we see that these are highly-civilised peoples, in some cases with much older civilisations than their much-vaunted European counterparts. At the same time, both countries rank today as poor developing countries, despite the highly-industrialised sectors within their economies (the group of MSAC)[103]. In both countries the key problems for development are not primarily located in the structure of the domestic economies but rather the social structure of these countries. These social structures have developed on the basis of the evolved religious, social policy and cultural characteristics of the multi-ethnic nations India and Pakistan. The end of British colonial rule in 1947 and the associated tragic partition[104] of the subcontinent

---

increase productivity of people in rural areas (1973) and towns (1975) and the BMZ sectoral concepts (A) Berufliche Bildung (1992), (B) Sektorkonzepte: Förderung der Sektoren: Grundbildung, ländliche Entwicklung, Armutsbekämpfung und zur Förderung der Frauen.

102 The constantly expanding informal sector in Third World countries and the growing unemployment in the countries formerly in the Soviet Union are making it increasingly difficult to implement the principles formulated by the UN for securing basic needs and the "right to work". These are the causes for future social problems and conflicts in world society and the obstacles to peace in the world.

103 MSAC = Most Seriously Affected Countries: group of developing countries identified by the UN General Secretariat as being most seriously affected by the world economic crisis following the oil crisis. See Dieter Nohlen (ed.), Lexikon der Dritten Welt, rororo-Handbuch, Hamburg, 1989, p. 470.

104 Cf. Gunnar Myrdal, Asiatisches Drama, Suhrkamp, Frankfurt, 1980, p. 118 cf. Dieter Nohlen (ed.), Lexikon der Dritten Welt, rororo-Handbuch, Hamburg, 1989, pp. 318-319 "The partition was unexpected in this form (Muslim and Hindus) and resulted in three wars with Pakistan (1947/48, 1965 and 1975) and the persecution and ejection of the religious minorities in the two new states." Not only are these conflicts still unresolved, as the world media daily confirm, but there are new developments in both countries which suggest that new partitions could lie ahead. (The author).

into Pakistan and India gave rise to two countries which are still grappling with the consequences of colonisation and partition in the form of social, religious, economic and even geopolitical struggles. Besides the social problems in the two countries arising out of *realpolitik*, the evolved cultural and traditional structures of the Indian subcontinent, which have resulted in modern India in a caste system rooted in Hinduism and the diversity of other religions, are also very important for understanding the relationship to "work". Even if the Indian state in its progressive (1949) constitution did not formally abolish castes[105, 106], the formulations chosen in the constitution aim at the future disappearance of the caste system as a form of society[107]. However, India's historical development after independence (1947) has shown that issues of minorities and castes can have an incredible impact in the potential for influencing everyday policy, and this has for decades resulted in massive political and even violent confrontations between the various political groups and the disadvantaged segments of society, the religious minorities and the disadvantaged castes[108]. In the course of India's evolution into a "modern" state this has resulted in more and more special arrangements for these groups, the so-called "Reservation Policy"[109]. This "Reservation Policy" has had a decisive and adverse

---

105 At the time of the creation of the Indian state in the 40s Marc Glanter writes: "caste was in bad odour, viewed widely as an impediment to individualism and to broad national loyalties and inimical to progress and democracy. The hardships inflicted on the lowest castes inspired humanitarian revulsion. It was widely accepted that caste would have no place in independent India and the efforts to ameliorate past inequalities were in order", Marc Glanter, Competing Equalities: Law and Backward Classes in India, Delhi, Oxford Press 1984, p. 37.
106 Cf.: The Constitution of India, Nahabhi Publication, October 1992, New Delhi, India, p. 6 Article 15., "Prohibition of discrimination on grounds of religion, race, caste, sex or place of birth – (1) The State shall not discriminate against any citizen on grounds only of religion, race, caste, sex, place of birth or any of them." The following sections address other details of public and private life which are intended to ensure the equal treatment of all members of society with regard to their origin. The Indian constitution is dealing here with the problem that the members of society are not *de facto* equal by virtue of historical developments – this is a condition which has to be created.
107 Op. cit. p. 14, section *"Cultural and Educational Rights"*. paragraph 29. "Protection of interests of minorities – (1) Any section of the citizens residing in the territory of India or any part there of having a distinct language, script or culture of its own shall have the right to conserve the same. (2) No citizen shall be denied admission into any educational institution maintained by the State or receiving aid out of State funds on grounds only of religion, race, caste, language or any of them."
108 Op. cit. p. 24, paragraph 46. "Promotion of educational and economic interests of scheduled castes, scheduled Tribes and other weaker sections – The State shall promote with special care the educational and economic interests of the weaker sections of the people, and in particular, of the Scheduled Casteless and the Scheduled Tribes, and shall protect them from social injustice and all forms of exploitation."
109 Cf. Aniradh PRASAD, Reservation Policy and Practice in India, A Means to an End, Deep Publications, New Delhi, 1991, p. 33 "The issue of reservation is much sensitive. Even meritarian plea is charged to be based on the consideration of the perpetuation of dominant class

impact on Indian social coexistence by using quotas to exclude the former ruling castes (and specifically the Brahmins) from many state institutions, careers and educational opportunities (particularly universities). Here, policy has achieved the opposite of what was intended, resulting in the so-called Brain Drain to the western industrialised nations (and particularly the USA) by the stronger segments (Brahmins) of Indian society[110]. We cannot investigate the causes and implications of this specific problem of India (and partly of Pakistan) further in the present work. Nevertheless, we will consider the culture-specific features and traditional element in the evolved relationships of specific disadvantaged sections of Indian society and the important and dominant role of Islam in Pakistan in terms of their significance for transferring the western and industrial concept of work.

Besides the social problems described here of transcending castes (or to use the terminology preferred in India of "backward classes" instead of "scheduled castes and tribes")[111] it is also important to take into account the great nationalised and private industries which have arisen in India and have put India in tenth place in the world league table of industrial nations. However, as broad sections of Indian society and the Indian economy belong in the agricultural and informal (non-organised) sectors and this is dominated by the so-called "backward classes", it is important to consider the role of these social segments[112] and their values with respect to the concept of work. Indian society is (as noted above) still a multicultural and multiracial society, and any attempt to change this given the constellations that have evolved in the country inevitably results in chaotic situations. It is accordingly impor-

      interest. Both the Madras Communal G.O. involved in *State of Madras* v. Champkan, A.I.R. 1951 S.C. 226 and Mysore order in Balaji v. *State of Mysore* (1963), Supp. 1.S.C.439, are said to have been issued with specific purpose to oust the *Brahmins* from admission in Medical and Engineering colleges. In *Champkam*, it is said that had the quota not been fixed on the basis of marks alone *Brahmins* would have secured 249 admissions out of 395 seats in the Engineering Colleges, only 3 Muslims would have been admitted and no untouchable (lower castes and noncaste members) would have been admitted. But what the court did was to enforce the constitutional mandate. Objectives may be high but means may not be. The Court emphasized on means to achieve objectives and did not allow forbidden grounds of discrimination. The merit claim may have some interest but that should not be ineffectuated by evil means. Thorn by Thorn is not motto of our constitutional creed.

110 This policy is not the one and only reason for the brain drain, there is also the low level of incomes, conditions in work and research and the aggressive policy of the industrialised nations and other Asian countries of hiring away India's intellectuals and technical intelligentsia.

111 Cf. note 109, pp. 150-151.

112 These segments extend to the suburban and rural businesses and constitute a significant part of society at around 30% (defined as backward classes). In addition there are those who are (or will be) significantly increasing this segment as a result of urban impoverisation and unemployment.

tant to realise that this form of society exists and that the following aspects in particular must be taken into account:

> "Polytheism and tolerance of social pluralism (castes) are interrelated, while indifference to political unification of the heterogeneous society is endorsed by this plurality of paternal authority. The importance of solidarity pervades all the mutually interdependent groups. Responsibility is shared in common rather than exercised with personal authority. The tasks of all family and caste members are precisely determined; a child first begins to observe these by watching the highly stylised etiquette of family assemblies.[113]

Responsibilities and duties within the family and the extended social framework up to the overall social structure and division of labour are not reduced to the individual capabilities of the individual members of society, but rather applied to the group as a whole.

> "Duties are so arranged as to reduce the element of individual competition (as distinct from group competition); the ideal of the self-sufficient villages economy with its exchange of specialised services between the inhabitants (and a minimum exchange of cash) ensures that every man performs his allotted task, but does not excel above others."[114]

As a result, the performance of the individual is not particularly important, and is not or only rarely called for by the group.

> "The law of moral consequences, Karma[115], helps to co-ordinate those egoistic impulses with interests of society as a whole. Failure to do his duty, which before everything means caste duty, would spoil the individual's spiritual chances. Caste duty is by definition social duty and is recognised by all. In this way egoistic impulses are effectively harnessed to the interests of Society and kept in harmony with religion's goals."[116]
>
> "Personal ambition, on the other hand, tends to overreach prescribed rules ... Making action the means of expression of personal desires and ambitions merely enchains one in the fetters of Karma. Personal initiative cannot be beneficial to

---

113 Cf. Richard LANNOY, The Speaking Tree, A Study of Indian Culture and Society, Oxford University Press, London, 1975, p. 111.
114 Loc. cit.
  This also results in the development of a high level of division of labour in Indian society specialising in individual castes and casteless, e.g. trader, warrior, priest etc and the army of craftsmen and other service occupations not currently covered by the castes but organised in communal structures. Traditional Indian society accordingly has a very highly developed structure and is divided into many "*communal*" groups, each of which jealously insist on their identity. The individual plays a subordinate role in all this.
115 Karma = is part of the important Hindu texts, the UPANISHADS, dealing with the rules of Hinduism; the Upa-Veda, Karma-Veda and Sakha-Veda; the Karma-Veda deals with the moral aspects of a Hindu life, cf. Abbé J.A. Dubois Hindu Manners, Customs and Ceremonies, Asian Educational Services, New Delhi 1985 – reprint of the 1906 edn, Oxford, London.
116 Cf. note 113, text on p. 111.

moral progress because the essence of escape from Karma is to free oneself from one's desires"[117].

To identify the concept of labour it is accordingly necessary to include in the equation the Indian situation and the attitude towards egoism (i.e. the willingness to take individual initiative) in development policy measures. In the past it has seemed important for implementing successful industrialisation concepts and economic takeoff to assume not only the generally accepted economic indicators and factors but also a high degree of willingness to take individual initiative among the labour force. In India, as already shown, this can only be expected in the modern sector of the economy and in the field of formal education and the universities. The informal sector on the other hand (particularly in the suburban and rural areas) is still largely oriented towards traditional segments of society still permeated by caste and tribal structures and values[118]. Even so, it should not be forgotten that India with its many religions[119] is not focused only on Hinduism but also (with over 100 million Muslims[120] and some 20 million Christians[121] etc) experiences decisive contributions and impulses in the area of ethical, moral and other important social values from the Muslim and Christian minorities, with corresponding influences. Another major influence on changes in social values undoubtedly stems from Indian emigrants and Indian students living abroad, who still generally maintain very close links with their families in India and act as a channel for external influences on society. It can also be assumed that the many international economic links, the multinational companies and joint ventures in

117 Cf. note 113, text on p. 112.
118 Op. cit. p. 427.
"It is widely assumed that individualism is a precondition of industrialization and that without it there can be no "economic take-off". The irony is that in the West electronic technology and complexity of organisation no longer permit the survival of individualism, but encourage unified-field awareness and interdependence. Western youth has already rejected the extreme individualist position as a moral mistake and an intellectual error. The catalyst of individualism is claimed to be a necessity by those who have observed work-attitudes in countries like India where economic growth is proceeding too slowly. It is also based on the unfounded assumption that the pattern of technology in poorer nations will have to go through painful mechanistic phases of old-style industrial revolution, the tackling of all things and operations one bit at a time."
119 Buddhists 4.7 million; Christians 16.2 million; Hindus 549.8 million; Jains 3.2 million; Muslims 75.7 million; Sikhs 13.1 million etc. cf. Statistical Outline of India 1992-1993, TATA, New Delhi, 1992 these data can be grossed up proportionally using a corresponding figure for population growth of c. 25% since 1981.
120 India is one of the largest Islamic religious communities with a secular political system outside the Arab world, with c. 100 million Muslims today.
121 With c. 20 million Christians and many leading Christian primary and secondary schools, elite colleges and universities and the colonial history, Christianity in India is an influence to be taken very seriously in assessing social values and developments.

company formation are having substantial influence on the westernisation of the modern segments of Indian society and in some cases actually making possible the transfer of the concept of work familiar in industrialised societies. If we consider the situation in Pakistan, it is necessary to take into account the importance of Islam in Pakistan and look at the relationship of the Muslims to the range of concepts of labour presented here, extending and relativising this where necessary.

> "In view of the holistic view of Man, every human activity in Islam is an act of worship, provided it is performed with an honest intention. As a result, work in the narrower economic sense does not represent a religious issue for classical Islam.[122]"
>
> "The Koran, the Sunna and subsequently Islamic law all deal with the question which activities and vocations are allowed or prohibited for Muslims, but say virtually nothing about the anthropological question of the relationship of Man to his work generally"[123]

In the international discussion of solutions to the problems of development and industrialisation of the Islamic nations in the Third World, a frequent accusation (particularly by western critics) relates to the "fatalism" allegedly inherent in Islam[124]. This "fatalism" assumed in the Muslim faithful is then generally cited as the only explanation for the working behaviour, motivation and relationship to work generally of Muslims in Islamic societies[125]. There are accordingly efforts in many Islamic countries to redefine this concept and even develop a new and separate religious work ethic[126]. As already shown, the content and language of the concept of labour are rooted in the prevailing cultural, religious, traditional, economic and political conditions and relationships in the culture and society under review. Following the Partition, Pakistani society, Islam and the state have decided – in contrast to India – not to follow the path of a secular state or model of society. Today, Pakistan is an Islamic republic, and its constitution clearly reflects this, i.e. Islam is the state religion[127]. This gives religion far

---

122 Cf. M. TWORUSCHKA, Arbeit im Islam – Begriff und Ethik – in: CIBEDO-Texte, No. 33, Frankfurt 1985, p. 3.
123 Loc. cit.
124 Fatalism = the doctrine that events are dictated by fate = Lat. fatalis e.g. human acts are predetermined and are described as caused by natural law. Fatalism is always found in specific forms, e.g. in STOA and Islam, from: Alexander Ulfig, Lexikon der philosophischen Begriffe, Bechtermünz, Eltville, 1993, p. 131.
125 Cf. note 122.
126 Loc. cit.
127 Cf. S.N. AL-Attas (ed.), AIMS and Objectives of Islamic Education, paper by A.K. Brohi, Education in an Ideological State, p. 63 "Pakistan is an ideological state. And by that, at its irreducible minimum, is meant a state which is founded on a manner of thinking or an idea

greater and more extensive influence on the political, social and cultural processes in the country[128], and in addition there is naturally the question of the personal and individual attitude towards religion and the fundamental values and orientations anchored in this and passed on through it, which play a major role in the individual interpretation of the concept of work. In contrast, the Judaeo-Christian tradition (which as already shown essentially derives its concept of work from the biblical creation myth, i.e. God created the world and humanity in six days and on the seventh He rested) was a major incentive to the Christian to follow the example of God. Although Islam shares many features with the Judaeo-Christian creation myth, it reaches different conclusions for the people who are bound to follow God's example. According to the Koran, for example:

> God created the world in six days. However, He did not use the seventh day explicitly for rest: "In six days We created the heavens and the earth and all that lies between them; nor were We ever wearied " (50,38). The contrast between a resting God and a labouring God is alien to Islam: "Neither slumber nor sleep overtakes Him" (2,256).

In the Islamic view, a god who needs rest is a diminution of the concept of omnipotence. For "He has given you the night that you may rest in it" (28,73). "Prayer also counts as a time of rest before work" (62,10)[129]. As a result, Islam does not have any specific rest day[130]. "There is no Sabbath in Islam"[131]. The day most closely corresponding to the Christian Sunday or the Jewish Shabbat is Friday, the day of communal prayer. Formerly in Islamic countries work on Friday was

---

characteristic of people belonging to it. Our constitution declares that Islam shall be the State religion of Pakistan. It is also pledged to eradicate exploitation in all forms in order that the gradual fulfilment of fundamental principle "from each according to his ability to each according to his work" should be realized." Hodders and Stoughton, K.A. University, Jeddah, 1979.

128 E.g. in formulating laws in the fields of family, social and labour legislation, Islamic religious fundamental values play a decisive role, in the process decisively shaping the understanding of the law and the rulings of the courts. It must not be forgotten that Islam is also an instrument of decolonisation and the appeal to the fundamental values of Pakistan society. It is also a political instrument of a nation in search of its own identity, specifically with respect to the still incomplete partition from its large and influence neighbour, India (see the conflict over Kashmir, Punjab and Ayodhia).

129 The author has personally seen on hundreds of specific occasions in Pakistan and other Islamic countries how work is interrupted briefly "for the hour of prayer", e.g. at conferences, planning workshops or meetings, after which work is continued with undiminished motivation. This was always a great experience, given the naturalness and devotion shown, and partners generally made a great impression.

130 Cf. source note 122, p. 4.
131 Op. cit. M. Muhammad Ali, The Religion of Islam, Cairo, p. 432.

only interrupted for prayer: today, there is a trend in many Islamic countries to close businesses and schools "[132].

In Islam the goodness of God extends to the action and work of Man, i.e. men have no right to praise God according to their own lights. Instead, everything which men do is measured against this basic attitude and their relationship with God.

> "Through his acceptance of the oneness of God (*tauhid*), every action of a man – and not only his work – becomes an act of worship: "Just as (a man's) work cannot be regarded as an evil reduced to earning money, his leisure cannot be seen as a distraction from the true purpose of being. The *tauhid* view of the world, which sees existence as a unity, places him in a permanent process of perfection."[133]

A further important difference from the Judaeo-Christian tradition is the Islamic view that man cannot emulate God's "work" (the act of creation) at all, since this is reserved to God alone. Instead, the Muslim as God's representative places all his activities in the service of the All-Highest[134]. This interpretation shows how the western view of the "fatalism" of Islamic countries is based on a misunderstanding of the attitude of the Muslim to work and society. The opposite appears to be true: Islam is quite able to reproduce the modern definition of work because Muslims take a holistic view of the working day as one unit, i.e. working life, private life and religious life are a unit in a human's being; the whole of a person's life counts for the worship of God and to reach paradise. This is undoubtedly a crucial understanding for joint work if Technical Cooperation in education is to result in usable results and suggestions for the transfer of approaches shaped by western industrial society. In the specific case of Pakistan, however, it must be remembered that in addition to the factors described here the formerly strong Hindu and Indian cultural influence also play an important role in the existing and emerging social structures together with many pre-Islamic social structures (e.g. family, tribe and clan). This is particularly true of the North-West-Frontier province and Baluchistan, where even today society is essentially shaped not only by deep Islamic religious conviction but also by the great tribes and clans, i.e. individual interests are subordinated to the interests of the larger tribe, clan or family community[135] and the "Concept of Pukhtunwali, translated as

---

132 Op. cit. and H. Grotzfeld, Art. Freitag, in: K. Kreiser/W.Diem/H.-G.Majier, Lexikon der islamischen Welt, Stuttgart, 1974, p. 183.
133 Op. cit. pp. 5;6 and A. Mohibul Islam, Islam und Freizeit – ein Widerspruch, in: al-Fadir, No. 5, March 1984, p. 17 (Hamburg).
134 Op. cit. p. 6.
135 Cf. Sir Olaf Caroe, The Pathans, Oxford University Press, Karachi, pp. 9 et seq.

the Pukhtun Code or the way of the Pukhtuns"[136], plays the central role. In many areas of these two provinces, Pakistan law has limited application, "Pukhtunwali is the core of Pukhtun social behaviour"[137]. We can only conjecture how far these segments of Pakistani society may be removed from the development policy concepts and ideas of the central government or its foreign partners, the development aid organisations. This seems to be particularly important in conceiving measures for the informal sector in Pakistan, which in some cases reaches far into the areas of the Pukhtuns/Pathans and may conflict with the laws and values prevailing there.[138]

Summarising, the following points can serve as orientation in documenting and formulating culture and society specific concepts of work:

(•) The background of our own concept of work must first be clarified.
(•) The cultural and social context for partners in Third World countries must be investigated and the goals (including ethical, moral and religious etc) must be discussed and understood.
(•) The sectors and segments of society and the economy f the target groups to be addressed by measures to prepare them for "work" in society must be clarified, particularly where traditional and informal parts of the national economy are involved.
(•) The religious, traditional, social and ideological goals for education in Third World societies seeking Technical Cooperation in education must be clear to the partners involved.
(•) Education and vocational training must define its pedagogical methodology and didactics inter alia on the basis of the social and cultural relationships in the target societies. The concepts for Technical Cooperation consultancy projects in the field of vocational training can accordingly only be formulated and implemented in terms of the existing relationships in the target societies and their understanding of work.
(•) Vocational pedagogics, the instruments for formulating solutions, analyses and the groups of experts commissioned to do these must liberate themselves from their own approaches and aim at realistic

---

136 Cf. Akbar S. Ahmed, Pukhtun economy and society. Traditional structure and economic development of a tribal society, London, 1980, pp. 99 et seq.
137 Loc. cit.
138 From his own observations (many projects and visits to businesses) the author can state that the modern sector, i.e. modern industrial businesses, draw mainly on the traditionally much more industrialised Punjub and Sind, and specifically the Karachi conurbation, for skilled workers and labourers, as the cited provinces in Pakistan (NWFP and Baluchistan) are seen by the businesses as very backward in terms of their relationship with work.

solutions which are appropriate and acceptable to the systems, without at the same time abandoning the drive to innovation.

(•) Vocational training must arrive at new culture-specific, action-oriented approaches, geared to the definition of work and how the target group and the target society perceive work, and set up ways of assisting system building in vocational training that takes into account the employment situation and the prospects of the national economy.

(•) Changes in the understanding of work should basically be oriented towards the potential for change or development in the prevailing culture-determined division of labour. When following such an approach, care must be taken that the target groups and target societies have the opportunity to maintain their own identity or develop it further.

2.3 *Importance of culture and tradition in developing culture-specific approaches to vocational training in Third World countries*

The importance of culture and tradition is by no means an exclusively theoretical question in the context we are concerned with here, but rather a concrete and interactive relationship in development aid and Technical Cooperation between the countries offering assistance and countries receiving it. This relationship is generally dominated by the colonial past of these countries and their relationship with their former colonial rulers. The western industrialised nations (Europe, the USA and Japan etc) still have a very strong influence on the modern sector, the middle classes and the politicians of these countries. The way that the more economically developed "western" nations offer aid and the conditions and ideas associated with this aid for the weaker so-called "developing nation" together with the western-dominated ideas about the goals and so-called target "developed state" of the "recipient countries" are frequently permeated by the cultural and traditionally-evolved values of the western industrialised nations. This ethnocentricity[139] is accordingly often the cause of the arrogance of the aid workers or donor nations who prescribe what is or should be right for

---

139 Cf. Dieter Nohlen (ed.), Lexikon Dritte Welt, p. 231, "Ethnozentrismus: Unter Ethnozentrismus wird in der entwicklungstheoretischen Diskussion der Vorrang der Werte und Überzeugungen, beispielsweise der abendländischen, (Eurozentrismus) in der Beurteilung sozialer, wirtschaftlicher und politischer Verhältnisse und Prozesse in Ländern anderer Kulturbereiche verstanden."

the so-called "underdeveloped nations"[140]. This is particularly true of key programmes in development aid under Technical Cooperation (by bilateral and multilateral development aid organisations) which are heavily dependent on the donors' cultural, traditional, social policy and in part also ideological factors and the underlying paradigms. Elementary, vocational and general education[141] are some of the most important exports in the development aid of western industrialised nations, and particularly the Federal Republic of Germany. Vocational training is frequently regarded as playing a less problematical and less political role here than elementary and general education, but this is a major error, since vocational training is a direct product of the economic and social conditions and the cultural and traditional influences. The content, methodology, didactics and educational goals other than purely technical ones[142] are all subject to major social trends and influences[143]. This also extends to vocational training aid, as the debate about the old sectoral concept "Vocational training" of the German Federal Minister for Economic Cooperation and Development (BMZ) has shown[144]. There is also the general discussion stretching back years about the justification of expanding the formal educational and vocational training systems[145] and their institutions

---

140 Loc. cit.
 This is accompanied by the idea that merely an orientation towards the west in the actual or target state of social development of the culture perceived as having priority is sufficient to guarantee actual development.
141 Cf. E. Spranger, Kultur und Erziehung, Leipzig 1928, p. 189 Spranger's "three-stage law" of education makes a division into: "basic education, vocational training, general education", and according to his definition general education without vocational training is not possible: "The path to higher general education is through an occupation and only through an occupation" as in Kerschensteiner:
 "If there is such a thing as general education, then it belongs not at the start but at the end of life". G. Kerschensteiner, Das Grundaxiom des Bildungsprozesses, Munich 1953, p. 120.
142 Cf. Ludwig von Friedeburg, Bildungsreform in Deutschland, chapter Bildungsgesamtplan, pp. 404 et seq. Suhrkamp, Frankfurt, 1992.
143 Cf.: R. Arnold, Interkulturelle Berufspädagogik, BIS-OLDENBURG, 1991, p. 51 chapter 3, In der Dritten Welt lernt man anders. Here, Arnold tackles the problem of the transfer of methodologiy, didactics and training approaches and philosophies. "As we now know such a one-sided transfer of education can be counterproductive, also increasing underdevelopment if it undermines cultural identity and hence individual and social stability. What is important is accordingly to identify "culturally tolerable" pedagogical and didactic styles of action, to establish the receptiveness of training aid."
144 Cf.: R. Arnold (Pub.) Berufliche Bildung und Entwicklung in den Ländern der Dritten Welt, Nomos, Baden-Baden, 1989 and section 2.1.
145 Cf. T. Hauf, K. AMMAN et al.: Erziehung- ein Entwicklungshindernis ? In: Zeitschrift für Pädagogik No. 23 1977, pp. 9 et seq. U. Laaser, Bildung und Wissenschaft in der Entwicklungspolitik, In: Aus Politik und Zeitgeschichte, vol. 25/74, pp. 15 et seq U. Laaser, Bildungstransfer und Systemwandel Theorie und Praxis des industriestaatlichen Bildungstransfers in die Länder der Dritten Welt, Beltz, Weinheim 1981, pp. 92 et seq V., Lenhart: Bildung und Beschäftigung in der Dritten Welt. In: Haag, E. (ed.): Der Beitrag zur Berufsausbildung zur wirtschaftlichen Entwicklung in Partnerländern, DSE-Veröffentlichung Mannheim, 1982, pp. 73 et seq.

and facilities[146]. Here briefly are several of the issues and criticisms:
- the transfer of educational systems to Third World countries constitutes colonial or postcolonial exports by the industrialised nations;
- poor countries cannot fund schools and the dissemination of institutionalised forms of education in schools, which result in high follow-on costs primarily in vocational training:
- academic education is not very productive and produces dropouts, repeat students and potential unemployed with high expectations and an education which is irrelevant to the labour market;
- the educational infrastructure (teaching and learning materials, classrooms, laboratories, workshops and equipment) and available staff (teachers, administrators) do not meet the requirements of the educational system;
- the government bureaucracies in school administration and educational planning in most developing countries are unable to respond flexibly to the changing environment and needs of industry and society and orient themselves accordingly: they mostly produce rigid forms of didactically outdated teaching and learning systems, resulting in graduates destined for unemployment with qualifications irrelevant to the labour market;
- schools promote elitist thinking and graduates only learn to acquire much sought after diplomas and access to higher education institutions, continuing their education at universities etc[147].

Despite these criticisms, which are in part very realistic and true, the implication that promotion of state and formal educational and vocational training systems should be discontinued which played a central role in the controversy about the old BMZ sectoral concept is not feasible[148], as despite the functional and operational weaknesses so rightly criticised here the formal educational and vocational training systems in the developing countries also have very important social and social policy functions in the economic and social structure and modernisation of these countries. Laaser[149] cites the following aspects in this connection with the associated functions of modern educational institu-

---

146 I. Illich, Schulen helfen nicht. Über das mythenbildende Ritual der Industriegesellschaft, Rowohlt, Hamburg, 1982 G. Myrdal, Asiatisches Drama, Suhrkamp, Frankfurt, 1971, pp. 382 et seq. T. Hanf, Wenn die Schule zum Entwicklungshindernis wird. Bildungspolitik und Entwicklungspolitik in der Dritten Welt. In: Entwicklungspolitik, (ed.) Hauf/Oberndörfer, Stuttgart 1986 pp. 118 et seq.
147 Cf. U.H. Laaser, Bildungstransfer und Systemwandel, Theorie und Praxis, Beltz, Weinheim, 1981.
148 Cf. E. Schoenfeldt, Ziele, Motive und Erwartungen der bundesrepublikanischen Berufsbildungshilfe, in: Rolf Arnold (ed.) Berufliche Bildung und Entwicklung in der Dritten Welt, Nomos, Baden-Baden, 1989, pp. 21 et seq.
149 Cf. note 146, pp. 95 et seq.

tions in the efforts of Third World countries to modernise their societies:
- Education acts as a mechanism for recruiting, selecting and allocating political elites.
- Education is used as an instrument of political socialisation securing the authority of the institutional order and participation in this. It is used as an instrument of nation building.
- Education is seen as a medium of political integration linking economically and territorially disparate groups in a common system of political control.
- Education is also used as a field of action of political interest groups[150] with their educational agenda.[151]

The extrafunctional aspects, functions and objectives shown here which are represented by the state, the political system and the leading social groups and their importance for the management elites in these societies do not support the assumption that "the state" will withdraw from the educational and vocational training sector, as this is precisely how the groups which are politically, economically and socially strongest secure their influence over the masses and the formulated political, economic and social guidelines and ideas of the future managers and elites and the productive members of society in these countries. This should not, however, be taken as a given, as history has shown that the knowledge and education acquired can also be used to cause problems for or overthrow the ruling classes in these countries[152].
U. Laaser expresses his surprise at the former colonial nations in this respect and notes:

> "Given the obvious failure of political socialisation by the colonial powers, designed to be supportive but proving subversive in the event, it is in fact astonishing that most Third World governments still rely extensively on political socialisation through education to ensure authority and loyalty; ... It is, after all, beyond

---

150 Loc. cit.
151 It is helpful to recall here the former Soviet Union and German Democratic Republic, which assigned a very specific social and ideological role to educational institutions in addition to their usual functions.
152 Cf. the situation in Sri Lanka: President Premadasa commissioned UNESCO to carry out an educational study in 91/92 of the current orientation of official educational policy in Sri Lanka and its effect on the Sri Lankan social system. Premadasa's point was that despite the 96% literacy rate in Sri Lanka (Singalese and Tauitic population groups) Sri Lanka was experiencing previously unknown terrorist potential and resistance movements against the state, so that the national educational policy (source UNESCO/GTZ, 1991) had to be reoriented, i.e. "From the city to the land" Cf. also Nimal G. Gunatilleke, Human Resource Development in Sri Lanka-Inappropriate output or Failure to utilize resources, in: Human Resource Development and Utilisation: Issues and Policies (ed.) Dr.S.N.Hyder, Pakistan Manpower Institute and Friedrich Ebert Stiftung, Islamabad, Pakistan 1989, pp.188 et seq.

question that the political elites with their western education were at the forefront of the anti-colonial and anti-imperialist liberation movements – virtually independent of the nature and degree of political indoctrination at educational institutions"[153].

In a similar context Bassam Tibi raises the provocative question, "Are there any alternatives to the existing structures in these countries, if the western industrialised nations dominate the world in principle with the political, economic and social structures they have developed and increasing globalisation [means that] international economic and political ties are so strong that the Third World countries, which generally have serious structural and political weaknesses in their social systems, have no options, since whether they like it or not the changes will overtake them in one form or other?"[154] In addition, there is the fact that education for the economically better-off and the technocratic elites in these countries is still tied to the knowledge and approaches offered in the so-called "advanced" industrialised states. As a result, the question of identifying their "own way" and the search for possibilities and ways of integrating these countries and the masses not included in the above elites into development strategies and specifically into autonomous and progressive educational and vocational training policy remains unresolved. Traditional and regressive cultural attitudes of the target groups and the poor sections of the population in the developing countries are often blamed by development aid "experts" as the decisive reasons for the failure of concepts and strategies[155]. "Explicitly or otherwise there is the idea that traditional attitudes and anti-modernist behaviour are one of the reasons for poverty in the Third World[156]. However, all the indications from empirical experience in our own society and in Third World countries are that tradition is opposed to rationalism[157] and that traditionalism is a reaction of the poor and

---

153 Cf. note 146, p. 101.
154 Cf. Bassam Tibi, Der Islam und das Problem der kulturellen Bewältigung sozialen Wandels, chapter 10. Die persisch – schiitische Variante des religio- politischen Revivalismus, Suhrkamp, Frankfurt, 1985, pp. 187 et seq. The Islamic Iranians sought through revolution and the overthrow of the government to hold up the "westernisation" of Iran, but this only partly succeeded (the author), since as B. Tibi very rightly notes: "The social transformation was initiated from without. The gap between traditional forms of government and social structures changing in the course of the rapid transformation is not the only reason for traditional political systems to slip into crisis. The reception of new ideas through the modernisation of education and particularly study abroad (the governing classes) help shatter the legitimacy of existing forms of government".pp. 222 et seq.
155 Cf. G. Braun, Vom Mythos des Traditionalisierung, in: E + Z 8/9, 1986, p. 13-15.
156 Loc. cit.
157 Cf. Th. W. Adorno, Ohne Leitbild Parva Aesthetica, Suhrkamp, Frankfurt/M. 1968 pp. 29 et seq.
"Tradition comes from *tradere*, to pass on. The idea is the link between the generations,

oppressed to the threatened loss of their identity. This means that the traditionalist theory has to be stood on its head, so that instead of traditional behaviour being the cause of poverty, poverty could be the cause of so-called traditional behaviour[158]. This guarantees the survival in its traditional form of the members or groups of the segments of society displaying traditional behaviour and partly removes demand for modernisation[159] in these segments or (however cynical it may sound) ensures a certain delay in the process of impoverishment to the point of catastrophe. In many countries, however, these structures[160] have also been destroyed to the point where not even gaining time can help survival. Poverty is increasing rapidly worldwide. The post-colonial nations qualifying as Third World poor societies are accordingly developing traditional systems of values and norms which cannot generally be regarded as obstacles to innovation: instead, people are using available resources and skills to survive within the framework of their traditions. This implies that the "cultural system of poor societies can at best survive but not foster economic development, they guarantee efficient poverty"[161]. This can be extended to both the rural and urban

---

what is handed on from one member to the next, including craft skills. The image is one of physical proximity, immediacy, one hand receiving what another gives. This immediacy is the more or less naturally rooted relationship, for example a family. The category of tradition is essentially feudal, as Sombart described the feudal economy as traditionalist. Tradition is in contrast to rationality, although the former established itself in the latter. Its medium is not awareness but prescribed and unreflected obligation to social forms, the present of the past which has involuntarily transferred itself to the mental level. Tradition in the strict sense of the term is incompatible with a bourgeois society.

158 Cf. note 154, pp. 13 et seq.
159 Cf. Gunnar Myrdal, Asiatisches Drama, Suhrkamp, Frankfurt/M. 1973, pp. 51 et seq.
160 One of the leading examples of modern times is the situation in the Sahel-Zone (or other steppes and semidesert landscapes in Africa) where nomadic tribes live primarily from animal husbandry and the social status of the clans and tribes is often identical with the size of their herds (cattle, goats, camels etc). The traditional behaviour of these tribes led inter alia to the regional catastrophes and associated environmental damage presented and discussed in the international media. In this context this note should be seen only as an indication of the problems important (and requiring solution) for development aid, which cannot be covered in detail here. One thing is, however, certain, which is that the international and bilateral aid organisations have made a decisive contribution to this inappropriate behaviour and these economically defective developments, which in the southern Sahara have already led in some cases to armed conflict between the Touareg/Peul etc and the local governments of the Niger, Mali and Algeria. Future political developments are presently unforeseeable, but similar conditions to those in Somalia cannot be ruled out, given the desolate state of the governments in the region.
161 Third World societies should not be regarded generally as poor societies, since there are often approaches for prosperous middle classes (mostly bureaucrats, military, management in the modern sector) and wealthy minorities which hold political and economic power. This tradition is often only façade and is part of the pragmatic political power behaviour of these minorities. India and Pakistan can be regarded as examples of how interest groups operate as governments behind the mask of parliamentary democracy (India) and religion (Islam in Pakistan).

informal sector, since these (as many sectoral analyses by bilateral and multilateral aid organisations show) set limits to economic development and added value[162]. In addition, however, the statutory and tax provisions frequently designed exclusively for larger companies and craft establishments, the established ultracomplex system of approvals for banking, taxation and credit and the economic promotion programmes mainly tailored for the formal sector all form a decisive barrier to innovation and value added processes in the informal sector[163]. Finally, for individuals there are naturally also the traditional and cultural characteristics relating to different potentials for change and modes of behaviour. These particularly affect the agricultural small and microbusinesses in the Third World[164], but similar conditions apply to the urban and rural informal sectors when it comes to the use of modern processes and acceptance of innovations in production or manufacturing and launching new products. We can accordingly make the following statements in this context:

– Decisions on innovating or not are complex procedures for small farmers, independent craft workers and microbusiness owners. Cultural value systems play a selective and productive role in this. Such decisions are meant to produce established methods of ensuring income and survival[165].
– Avoiding untried innovations often appears sensible in poor societies, since bad decisions can put at risk the survival of whole groups or microbusiness owners. Conversely, innovative successes may disturb the "economic equilibrium" and consequently community solidarity. This is why traditional modes of behaviour should often be

---

[162] The informal sector, as described in section 2.1, must be regarded as an economic and social sector responding with great sensitivity to external intervention, as experience with many projects has already shown that major financial inputs or the associated powerful modernisation projects can lead to the collapse of this sector, so that the poor become welfare recipients. Africa is one example of the inappropriate development aid policy and strategy of the western nations.

[163] During his surveys of microbusiness owners in the informal sector in India (Madras, Bangalore) and Pakistan (Peshawar) the author frequently heard in response to the question "why small businessmen do not use bank loans" that banks (a) require security, (b) want evidence of income and sales. (c) demand tax records and (d) have set up a large number of forms and bureaucratic obstacles so that those involved, who are mostly also very insecure about their behaviour and their linguistic and social skills, prefer to do without such aid. They generally get their finance from other sources or give up on expansion. In addition it should be noted that traditional Muslims also reject the banks because of their interest rates, since Islam has what *in western eyes* is a distorted attitude to the whole issue of "moneylending". In the author's view this is a gross oversimplification and calumny of Islamic values and deserves greater consideration in technical cooperation projects.

[164] Cf. note 155, pp. 13 et seq.

[165] Loc. cit.

regarded as community measures protective against change and minimising risk. They produce "efficient poverty"[166].
- For vocational pedagogics and creating employment-oriented measures, this implies increased involvement of target groups in designing concrete projects and the development of special action-oriented approaches relating to the problems described here[167].

In this context the concept presented by G. Braun[168] is helpful for orienting, classifying and structuring the approaches to be formulated, with its perception of the behavioural modes and reactions in poor societies as classified in three key basic types appearing more or less consistently in all cultures and traditionally-oriented poor societies. Braun distinguishes three basic types or behavioural patterns for Third World people, namely type A: "The Modern Man"; type B: the limited rational or "Obstacle Man" and type C: the traditionalist or "Noble Savage". This classification is not encountered in reality in these countries in the pure types or social behavioural forms described here: instead, we always find mixed forms. For analysts and planners or measures or projects in Third World countries on the other hand, such classifications and orientation categories can be regarded as useful, as this can ensure that these measures take into account the key aspects of the target groups' behavioural modes.

---

166 Loc. cit.
167 Cf. C. Lohmar-Kuhnle, Konzepte zur beschäftigungsorientierten Aus- und Fortbildung von Zielgruppen aus dem informellen Sektor, pp. 165 et seq. Weltforum Verlag, Cologne 1991.
168 Cf. note 155, pp. 13 et seq. and p. 68.

2.3.1 Perception of behavioural modes in poor societies

1. *Observer categories in analysing behavioural modes*[169]

Categories/ type of observer	Type A "Modern Man"	Type B "Limited Rational"	Type C "Traditionalist"
Behaviour towards western economic values	Assumption of "rational" economic values	Limitation of needs	Extreme resistance
Wishes, ideas about target groups	Revolution of rising expectations	Idea of "limited" goods	Status quo oriented
Reaction to gaps between needs and level achieved	Attempt to satisfy growing needs	Attempt to limit or reduce needs	Gaps not perceived
Dominant form of economy	Individual competition, efficiency oriented	No dominant form of economy, unresolved variants	Communal subsistence production, defence of existing forms of economy

2. *Observer models in analysing behavioural modes*

	Type A	Type B	Type C
Models of individual	Maximiser	"Resistant" (obstacle man)	"Noble Savage"
Models of society	Modernising, industrialising, urban	Traditional, rural	Primitive
Specialisation (scientific method, instruments and background of experts and sector-specific specialisations)	Development economics	Sociology, social psychology	Social anthropology, ethnology

---

[169] Source: according to Hutton, Caroline; Cohen, Robin: African peasants and resistance to change: a reconsideration of sociological approaches. In: Oxaal Ivar; Barnett, Tony; Both, David (eds.): Beyond the sociology of development. Economy and society in Latin America and Africa. London and Boston 1975, p. 109 from: Gerald Braun, Mythos vom Traditionalismus, E + Z 8/9, 1986, pp. 13-15.

3. Development planner reaction to observer models

	Type A	Type B	Type C
Strategy of planner (without direct link to sectors, it is still necessary to develop sector-specific aspects, data, approaches etc. – i.e. the decisive factor is the composition of the planning group	Technical and financial development aid to enhance productivity among favoured groups	(1) Attempt to change values and cognitive orientation of "obstacle man" (2) Disseminating information and favourable "offers" for "corrigible" groups	(1) Maintain or isolate in "natural" conditions (2) Destroy means of community to survive

As shown here, tradition and traditional behaviour in Third World countries cannot be equated with culture, but rather a reaction to specific socio-economic, socio-cultural and historically rooted interrelationships and experience (colonialism etc) and religiously defined behavioural patterns and contexts. Culture, on the other hand, is (as Malinovski puts it):

> "The fundamental fact of culture as we know and experience it and as we observe it scientifically is the organisation of human beings into permanent groups. Such groups are related by means of some kind of agreement, specific traditional laws or customs, in short by something that corresponds to Rousseau's "contrat social"[170]. We always see them interacting within specific material circumstances: a part of the environment they act in, a number of tools and artefacts; a piece of riches to which they have a right. When working together they follow the technical rules of their class and their trade, the social rules of etiquette, customary subordination, or also religious, legal and moral mores which mould their behaviour. It is still always possible to determine and establish sociologically what impacts the action of a group of people organised in this way will have, what need they satisfy, what services they provide to themselves and to the community in its entirety."[171, 172]

---

170 Articles of incorporation (French).
171 Cf. Malinowski, B.: Eine wissenschaftliche Theorie der Kultur. Suhrkamp Verlag, Frankfurt 1975, pp. 80 et seq.
172 Cf. also the definition of the term *culture* in: Philosophisches Wörterbuch ed. G. Schischkoff, A. Kröner Verlag, Stuttgart, 1961, p. 322: "In the broad sense culture is the total collection of attitudes, acts and works of a people or group of peoples". It goes on to say that culture affects all areas of the societies under consideration, such as "morals and customs, language and script, clothing, settlement, work, education, economic and military systems, political institutions, law, science, technology, art, religion in all their manifestations for the people in question" etc.

If we now consider many projects in bilateral and multilateral Technical Cooperation we see that these projects were "correctly" planned with major technical and economic input and knowhow, but either failed to achieve their goals or had to be corrected subsequently with major inputs[173]. In this connection R. Stockmann[174] has made an important contribution with his study on the sustainability of development projects in the field of vocational training, casting extensive doubt on the elaborate technical planning, project implementation and evaluation of success and the associated concept of sustainability and its analysis using the GTZ/BMZ[175] review techniques and instruments. Essentially, he reaches a central conclusion of importance here, namely that elaborately-planned vocational training projects frequently fail to achieve the desired success and sustainability unless it is possible during the project implementation process in the partner country to achieve correspondingly close cooperation with local institutions and experts.

In other words, there is only a link between the quality of planning and the success (sustainability) of the project if the process of implementation and evaluation is professionally handled.[176] However, if we consider the study checklist and indicators Stockmann proposes for vocational training projects[177] we see that they ignore socio-cultural (cultural, traditional etc) issues in project planning, implementation and evaluation and concentrate almost entirely on economic, labour-market specific, technical and vocational pedagogical project results and data. The cultural and traditionally influenced contexts of vocational training projects already noted are neglected in this study. The recommendations for future project design and methodological suggestions for reviews of sustainability must accordingly be treated with caution, despite the essential correctness of the criticism of the BMZ and GTZ concepts for planning, implementation and evaluation[178]. In the view of the author, Stockmann does not go far enough: although he criticises the BMZ and GTZ for their inadequate approach (an evaluation concept oriented solely towards the level of project goals[179]) and proposes

---

173 Cf. Sozio-kulturelle Kriterien für Vorhaben der Entwicklungszusammenarbeit – Rahmenkonzept –, BMZ, Bonn, 1992.
174 Cf., R. Stockmann, Die Nachhaltigkeit von Entwicklungsprojekten, Westdeutscher Verlag, Opladen, 1992.
175 Op. cit. p. 15.
176 Op. cit. pp. 194 et seq.
177 Op. cit. pp. 42 et seq, cf. also diagrams on SECAP Quito impact profile p. 110 and passim. It is striking that no mention is made at all of any possibility that socio-cultural and traditional factors and indicators may have played a role in evaluating projects.
178 Op. cit. pp. 194 et seq.
179 Op. cit. pp. 37 et seq.

an approach which analyses and evaluates project success from the point of view of the target groups and the project environment (impact evaluation), he neglects the aspects of the socio-cultural and traditional area. The question to what extent a vocational training project is integrated and established sustainably as a socially accepted educational institution and the proposed or implemented didactic and pedagogical approaches are accepted by the target groups accordingly does not figure in his analysis. Particularly in the debate about the necessity for and development of culture-specific approaches to vocational pedagogics and the vocational training aid, this appears to be an important and previously neglected aspect, given its importance for implementing successful projects and constructive cooperation and creating sustainable changes in this sector. The decisive question in this context is "how can those involved, i.e. those supplying their knowledge and skill (consultancy firms, bilateral and multilateral organisations, NGOs etc) and the recipients, targets and initiators for the desired changes also jointly deploy their ability and intent to achieve change in such a way that the desired changes (objectives) ultimately occur?" It is accordingly necessary for a corresponding construction and intercultural cooperation between the industrialised nations with their economic superiority offering aid (donors) to create an atmosphere of maximum openness between the partners. G. Lachmann[180] makes the following recommendation in this context:

> "Taking into account socio-cultural factors in development cooperation means creating the greatest possible openness for independent social and cultural transformation, awareness of (un)intentional influence on this through technical, economic and administrative intervention, enablement of social acquisition of technology, i.e. overall increase in scope for action and freedom.[181]"

This cannot however lead to a neutral stance on the part of the "donor organisations", which need to act openly and with a clear intent to cooperate and open development policy concepts for assistance and change in the countries of the Third World.

> "This means abandoning the idea of neutral transfer of technical material, which would not involve any social intervention or creating "acceptance" or "social tolerance" through social engineering and also abandoning unilinear modernisation, conveying a solution which is technologically "more advanced". There is no

---

[180] Cf. G. Lachmann, Sozio-kulturelle Bedingungen und Wirkungen in der Entwicklungszusammenarbeit, Deutsches Institut für Entwicklungspolitik, Berlin, 1988.
[181] Loc. cit.

"administrative innovation" (Elwert); innovations arise through horizontal networking, communication, trial and error and direct experience. Development cooperation needs to reflect its involvement in "authoritarian control mechanisms" in the society (Achille Mbembe) and their reinforcement while conversely creating pluralism in opportunities and hence openness"[182].

The BMZ outline concept for socio-cultural criteria for development cooperation projects recommends taking into account three so-called "key factors":

"1. Legitimacy (acceptance)
2. Achieved state of development"
3. Socio-cultural heterogeneity[183]

These key factors are very generally formulated and need to be related in concrete instances and Technical Cooperation projects to the corresponding sectors and subsectors and duly expressed and taken into account in differentiated form. Particularly for the field of vocational training aid and job-creation measures the following additional factors need to be taken into account[184]:

1. To establish the society's *intent* the *legitimacy* is checked of individuals, groups, ideas and institutions involved in vocational training policy and its implementation in vocational training and the question is posed: what do the target groups and those involved in implementing projects in vocational training and job creation *want* to achieve and what role do they play in this.
2. An *analysis of the situation* is carried out with the objective of determining the state of development (current status) in terms of the *competencies* of the target groups and others involved. The situation (i.e. the status of the existing system) of the vocational training apparatus (in the formal, non-formal and informal sectors) is analysed to the extent necessary to formulate and elaborate approaches in terms of the potential identified under (1) above.
3. The *diversity* (i.e. the socio-cultural heterogeneity) of the target groups and others involved in such vocational training and job-creation systems is a complication in planning and implementing measures in these areas. This makes it necessary to achieve corresponding clarity in planning such projects regarding the diversity of the target groups and others involved and existing social roles and power relationships, with particular attention to the extent to which measures may contribute towards stabilising or shifting existing power relationships.
4. The different nature of the impacting cultures (the so-called "donor" and "recipient" countries) which is not expressed in the major categories of inter-

---

182 Loc. cit.
183 BMZ, 1992.
184 Cf. Sozio-kulturelle Kriterien für Vorhaben der Entwicklungszusammenarbeit – Rahmenkonzept –, BMZ, Bonn, 1992.

cultural communication "language" and "socialisation" can seriously impact (1)-(3) and cause joint projects to fail[185]. Care must accordingly be taken in vocational training aid to ensure that there is adequate competency in the expert team even in the analysis and planning phase, and that the team has an intercultural composition[186].

2.4 Target groups in the informal sector, their social and economic position and importance for the development of the informal sector

As already demonstrated in section 2.1, identification of the informal sector is an extremely complex issue, involving many different factors and aspects. In connection with the issue raised here of the economic and job-creating relevance of the informal sector to the national economy and its employment systems in Third World countries, these questions will necessarily be restricted in line with subsequent concrete project approaches for vocational training measures. This will yield key criteria for deriving the definition of the concept of target groups. In the context of the present book, target groups[187] are those groups whose situation is to be improved as an objective of concrete project measures[188]. In this context the economic and social position and the role of the genders have to be considered separately, which is important for identifying potential target groups in the informal sector. Using such a technique for identification it is also possible to exclude certain groups from the measures to be planned because of their dominant activities. An important criterion for this is the extent to which the tar-

---

185 Cf. M. Schürmann, Querschnittanalyse Sozio-kulturelle Faktoren, BMZ, Bonn, 1990. "Overview of socio-cultural factors in language"

Politics	Economics	Social structure	Personality
Learning difficulty	Educational opportunities		– acceptance – communicating interest – appropriate advice – communication barriers

186 Op. cit. M. Schürmann establishes in his cross-sectional analysis that the deficiencies in linguistic competence among the experts sent on mission from Germany frequently create obstacles in projects to achieving project goals and have an adverse impact on the development process and cooperation.
187 Cf. GTZ-Definition of target group(s) for project, from: Guidelines on formulating offers to the BMZ, internal memorandum on quality assurance, June 1992.
188 Cf. GTZ project definition: "A project is understood to be a package of activities limited in subject, region and time, carried out by an institution in a partner country supported by the GTZ and possibly by other organisations in order to achieve a number of results which will lead to achieving the project goal."

get group shows explicit or implicit development potential for successful economic activity and can be regarded as capable of development in the sense of sustainable economic changes[189]. To estimate this potential for change it is particularly important for planners and experts in implementing such projects to interact closely with the target groups. As far as possible, these groups need to be included in the process of planning and design as well as implementation. As already shown in sections 2.2 and 2.3, an important consideration here is that people in the informal sector react differently to innovations and changes in their lives and social environment by virtue of their social, religious and ethnic origins as well as their educational history. In any case, this also has direct effects on learning prequalifications, participation and the cultural and social value systems they represent. There are accordingly only a few joint or generally valid project strategies possible for groups with diverse origins and educational levels, so that fresh strategies have to be agreed and developed with the target groups for each project.

The following groups were identified and analysed in terms of their social status and dependencies within the economic system, based on examples from many projects in technical and development cooperation[190]:

2.4.1 (A) *Groups independently creating income and hence jobs for employees* (Table I):
– small (micro) entrepreneurs with few (up to 10) employees;
– individual entrepreneurs without employees or self-employed;
– small (micro) entrepreneurs in increasingly sophisticated technology and service areas.

2.4.2 (B) *Groups with income from employment in urban and rural economies* (Table II):
– wage earners and day labourers in the informal sector;
– wage earners and day labourers in establishments in the modern sector;
– wage earners and day labourers in the service sector;
– apprentices and child workers in establishments in the informal sector
– casual labourers, day labourers, street children;
– prostitutes and people earning a living by illegal methods;
– slave-like employment (bonded labour, c. 100 million people worldwide: source ILO statistics);

---

189 Cf. C. Lohmar-Kuhnle, note 42, text pp. 43 et seq.
190 The structure of the content of these synoptic views and tables is based on the author's years of experience in technical and development cooperation.

2.4.3 (C) *Groups in rural areas who have recently become employees performing their original activities and occupations as employees* (Table III):
- small (micro) entrepreneurs and employees from these establishments, generally traditional craft and service establishments unable to make an adequate income due to turnover problems;
- small (micro) farmers and family subsistence farms which (as above) are unable to make an adequate income;
- underemployed and unemployed young persons;
- landless rural labourers;
- underemployed and badly paid labourers in public services and other medium-sized companies.

2.4.4 (D) *Special groups in rural and urban areas who have lost their employment and traditional living area as a result of displacement and flight* (Table IV):
- refugees, victims of political persecution and asylum seekers.

In the following matrix developed from these criteria these additional criteria were regarded as important in identifying the target groups:

(1) dominant and significant economic activities of the group under consideration;
(2) nature of independent income-generating activities of the group of small (micro) entrepreneurs;
or
nature of income-generating employment of the groups;
(3) for the group of small (micro) entrepreneurs the extent to which they are involved or instrumental in creating new jobs is important;
(4) an important aspect of evaluating the relevance of the target group for development policy goals is the extent to which the groups under consideration are involved in "activities of social marginal groups or criminal activities" to secure their livelihood;
(5) the extent to which the economic activities and the living of potential target groups are located in the "urban environment and economic area";
(6) the extent to which the economic activities and living of potential target groups are located in the "rural environment and economic area";
(7) the "nature of the undertaking" and "the dominant activities" are other important criteria in identifying the target groups;
(8) the "formal education and vocational training requirements" are important for evaluating the target groups in terms of the con-

crete qualification measures to be planned and possible indicators for the success or failure of the groups under consideration with respect to their ability to adapt and develop.

The following tables I to IV can provide a structure and system of categories for more accurate planning, implementation and control of what has previously often been inadequate target group participation and definition. They also give a clear idea of how to classify the target groups and describe and characterise them in more detail on the basis of criteria (1) – (8). The content of these tables is based on the author's knowledge of the situation and his years of work in German "Technical Cooperation" and "development aid". The author is drawing here on concrete experience in countries in the Middle East (Turkey, Egypt, Jordan, Syria), the Maghreb states (Algeria, Morocco, Tunisia), Asia (India, Pakistan, Sri Lanka, Thailand, Indonesia, Burma (Myanmar)) southern Pacific islands (Papua New Guinea) and Central America (Mexico and Guatemala). Practical experience from years of concrete project work in Pakistan and India has been collected and analysed, and this experience will be used more obviously in the course of this work in the form of specific case studies.

The criteria (1) – (8) shown in tables I – IV for identifying target groups are not enough on their own to determine the potential of these groups and individuals. It is accordingly necessary to analyse the possibilities of these groups and individuals again and in greater detail for their potential for change, expansion and innovation in production for developing economic, social and employment-relevant opportunities in the informal sector. In this it is particularly important in vocational pedagogical terms and for designing concrete projects to study the learning prequalifications and the productive potential of the groups at issue and target groups in the informal sector in terms of the following[191]:

(a) analysis of the individual and group-specific learning prequalifications, motivations and socialisation of the target groups in the informal sector;

Continued on p. 81

---

191 Cf. The Dilemma of the Informal Sector, Report of the Director-General ILO, Geneva, 1991
In chapter 3, "Towards a Strategy" the following general goals were cited for the development of the informal sector:
– improvement of the productive potential, and therefore of the employment – and income-generating capacity, of the informal sector;
– improvement of the welfare of the poorest groups;
– establishment of an appropriate regulatory framework, including appropriate forms of social protection and regulation; and
– organisation of informal sector producers and workers.

Table I: *Summary table for identifying target groups in the urban and rural informal sector, broken down by non-employed income creating activities*

social position or group	(1) economic activities	(2) non-employed income-creating activities	(3) job creating activities	(4) activities of social marginal groups	(5) urban environment
1	small (micro) entrepreneur with few (< 10) employees	– owners of small establishments in craft production, services and repairs; – women rare; – seldom organised in associations, often working with family; – often subcontractors to larger companies with specified materials and products; – little depth of production, often same product for years; – little flexibility in production and little machinery; – often mobile work site (on building site, at customer's – near consumer).	– often employ up to 10 wage earners, often family members – often source of employment for children and family members	/	particularly evident in larger cities; in India and Pakistan located particularly close to the commercial centres, bazaars and traditional craft streets
2	one-person businesses	– owners of small mobile or fixed production, service or sales facilities; – often pay rent, business primarily for self-employment – often established as working at home (for women)	– no employees, often only second job to improve family income	/	particularly evident in urban areas, frequently established as mobile firms
3	small (micro) entrepreneurs in sophisticated technology and service sector	– entrepreneurs with relatively high level of education and financial background (family assistance) – in some cases entrepreneurs with university degree, e.g. in communications electronics, computer software, software applications, video technology etc. – illegal/grey cable TV, video services (copying etc.) and computer software copying services (India/Pakistan)	employers for: – camera operators – lighting technicians, etc. – technicians – skilled and semi-skilled workers – computer specialists	/	exclusively urban areas, partly also in rural areas (customers etc.)

(6) rural environment	(7) nature of business or activity	(8) formal education and vocational training	(9) comments
In semi-rural areas with high population growth and traditional crafts; also mobile service or repair business moving from place to place	e.g.: – cycle repairs; – installers; – cabinetmakers; – carpenters; – masons, i.e. builders; – roadbuilders; – mobile coffee shops and restaurants; – ironing and laundries; – transport companies (cycles, cycle rickshaw, ox cart, horse cart or human labour, i.e. porters); – smiths; – tailors; – locksmiths, welders – electricians – radio/TV technicians – refuse recycling	– often little academic education – however, often leaving certificate for 10th grade and more – often (as noted above) employed in public service or other companies and working as entrepreneur in the informal sector after normal working hours, i.e. untaxed second occupation	often no formal division visible between traditional establishments and establishments in the informal sector, in fact there is the impression that more and more establishments in the traditional sector are integrated into the informal sector
– less frequent in rural areas or seasonal and mobile work, i.e. market for services and products is in the city – women often work at home (knotting carpets etc)	e.g.: – tailors; – seamstresses – food stall owners – street vendors; – laundresses; – street vendors; – vegetable growers (cash crops); all activities under (1) possible; – domestic services e.g. sewer and well cleaning, gardening, party service etc	– often little academic education (6th grade) or even none – also employees in modern sector (second job) – women generally hardly any academic education or vocational training; – in India and Pakistan occupations also mostly reserved for specific castes	This kind of employment is often temporary: if demand or the market changes, self-employed individuals in the informal sector have to change their products or services. This is clearly a very special problem which vocational training concepts need to respond to.
– unusual in rural areas, but possible as contract work if there is a market	– production of wedding videos and similar celebrations; – repairing computers or modifying hardware; – using PC software, copying/selling software – tax advice, bookkeeping for small entrepreneurs in the modern sector; – second jobs to boost family income – brokering links to speed up services – cable TV, i.e. distribution of international TV networks received via satellite dishes through own cable network, including additional video programmes (India/Pakistan)	Often very high level of general education and vocational training, often completed advanced and even tertiary education. Almost exclusively unemployed or people with second job (moonlighting) to boost family income.	Thanks to its high level of education, this group has a relatively good chance of earning a living, provided individuals are not fixated on following their profession. It is important in this context to discover what corresponding entrepreneurial qualities are present in addition to subject qualifications.

Table II: *Summary table for identifying target groups in the urban and rural informal sector, broken down by employment*

(1) economic activities social position or group	(2) employment	(3) status of employee	(4) activities of social marginal groups	(5) urban environment	(6) rural environment
4 wage earner, day labourer etc. in establishments in the informal sector and lowest-paid labourers in modern sector (industry, construction or services)	production, repair and services	– no social security, .e.g. accident and health insurance, vacation, trade unions etc; – no contracts, guaranteed salaries, daily wages etc, often only piecework rates; – often lowest-paid day labourer, depressing wages; – no skilled work	/	– found particularly in cities; – women are often employed in households in such unclear circumstances – see (3) above – or in mass production factories (textiles, spinning mills, large cotton plantations etc) or carpet weaving shops;	– immigration or seasonal stay in urban areas where their earning opportunities are better; – employees often stay with family members already living in city; – they often have their second home in rural areas or are migrant workers with their families
5 apprentices and children in employment	production, repair and services and traditional establishments (craft) parental establishments and work at home	– no apprenticeship agreement or formal position; – often still very young (as early as 8-10) without any security; – in traditional craft establishments no formal security for apprenticeship, length of apprenticeship or diploma; – often related to master or contractual-type agreement between parents and master (Pakistan, India have established traditional apprenticeship arrangement, see section 3)	/	– particularly frequent in cities and particularly bazaars; – women and girls generally do not occur in this category, they are virtually never found in apprenticeships – women and girls frequently taught by mothers, grandmothers etc in cottage industry employment	less frequent; – if present, then immigration to city from country; – found in major rural settlements or villages
6 odd-job men, day labourers, casual labour, street children, prostitutes, unemployed and *others* stagnating on the edge of society or even those in slave-like dependency	production and service businesses, often in the *illegal* area, to acquire the material basis for survival	– prostitution is a very widespread phenomenon, arising out of the minimal opportunities for women to find employment – lowest social status, i.e. often without any identifiable allegiances; – in India and Pakistan often also equivalent to "*vassals and slaves*"; – or specific criminal status, e.g. illegal trade etc; – *street children*, difficult to classify, but mostly without parents or relatives, living on the street etc. – in Asia (India, Pakistan, etc) often living in slums	– the groups described here are marginal in bourgeois terms, but in view of the size of the groups it is difficult to define them as such; it is likely that every low-income stratum in the Third World has a substantial number of such people with this status	– primarily found in the urban environment of the informal sector; – generally relates to the lowest strata or castes in India and Pakistan, this is *also valid* for Africa, Latin America and Asia	– *vassals* or *slaves* are known as "*bonded labour*" in India and Pakistan (estimated at 5 – 10 million people) and mainly working in large-scale agriculture, brick production and growing and processing cotton

(7) nature of activities	(8) formal education and vocational training prequalifications	(9) comments
e.g.: – metalworking, blacksmithing – tailor's assistant, – construction labourer (mason, carpenter's assistant etc) – road construction etc – transportation – docker (port) – porter – cycle rickshaw – recycling sector, i.e. – collect and classify refuse etc – collect and sell old clothes etc – sellers or helpers in cafes, restaurants, households etc	– very low general education (often no more than 6th grade) or no schooling; – women generally have no formal education; – rarely formal vocational qualifications; – performance profile acquired through on-the-job training;	– women as cheap labour used in many Asian countries; – in countries with traditional Islamic conditions women can only be used in the economy to a limited extent, although they play an important role in agriculture and subsistence farming
– traditional craft work in bazaars, e.g.: – carpenter, cabinetmaker, smith, dyer – tanner, coppersmith, goldsmith – copper and sheet metal working – bicycle workshops – motorcycle and automotive workshops – women and girls are mostly active in the following traditional learned occupations: – embroidery, carpet weaving, weaving – domestic work, agriculture (small animal husbandry etc) – fruit drying – selling in markets, cash crops etc – India, also as helpers in road construction and house building	– no or very little general formal education; – seldom formal vocational qualifications, i.e. even after long period of apprenticeship there is no established diploma, the candidate qualifies by demonstrating their ability – outside the traditional sector in the informal sector there is no systematic approach or offer for acquiring specific knowledge and skills systematically – in the informal sector learning is almost exclusively on-the-job, with very much depending on the ability of the individual to make it	– child labour is a worldwide problem, particularly in developing countries; – apprentices often have very long training periods (up to 6-10 years) as a result of unregulated apprenticeships income of young people and children is important for the life or survival of the family
all activities needing non special qualifications and which are seriously hazardous to the environment and health, e.g. – tanning – sewer cleaning – crushing rock – road construction – street cleaning etc or activities crossing over into criminal or immoral activities e.g. – prostitution – theft, fraud – gangs etc	– no formal general educational or vocational training prequalifications	– the diversity and variation in incomes in the semi-legal and illegal area cannot be attributed to the informal sector: nevertheless, it is often people making their income in the informal sector who regard or need an illegal income as additional income

Table III: *Summary table for identifying target groups in the rural informal sector by employment*

	(1) social position or group / economic activities	(2) employment	(3) status of employee	(4) activities of social marginal groups	(5) urban environment
	small (micro) entrepreneurs and employees in their establishments	– these are frequently traditional craft establishments which are unable to survive in rural areas with their products and have to seek additional employed work	– originally qualified traditional craft workers, e.g.: – potter – smith – coppersmith – mason – carpenter – construction carpenter etc	/	– seeking new employment in the city to survive with their families
8	small (micro) farmers and family subsistence farms	– these are small farmers with their own or leased land and produce for their own consumption or surplus production for the local markets	– originally skilled independent farmers working their land in traditional style with animal husbandry on a very small scale – economic problems in rural areas and competition from products in the local market together with the increase in the price of seed and similar cost of living increases put an end to independence	/	– the subsistence farmers and their family members seek additional work in the city (in the informal sector) – women and "old" people continue to work the farm in the "best case"
9	– unemployed young persons, – underemployed young persons, – landless agricultural labourers	– the steady growth in population and deterioration in the age pyramid in Third World countries (and particularly in rural areas) worsens the chances for young persons; – landless agricultural labourers were often farmers who are impoverished and looking for work as farm labourers;	– no employment or only underemployed in family farms; – landless agricultural labourers generally have no further status in rural areas and can be hired or fired as needed;	/	– young persons migrate to the cities and increase the mass of unemployed, often drifting into illegal work or seeking any kind of employment (see above); – agricultural labourers seek work in cities as: – domestics, – odd-jobbers etc (see above)
10	*underemployed* and *poorly paid* salaried employees in government agencies and schools (middle class)	– this group has a steady income but cannot feed their family with this – the state as employer often has insufficient funds and is not able to improve the situation decisively	– salaried employees in the public service, e.g.: – teachers; – police officers; – medical staff; – extension workers; – administrative salaried employees etc	/	– public service employees generally do not give up their positions, so rarely migrate to cities

78

(6) rural environment	(7) nature of activity	(8) formal educational or vocational training prequalifications	(9) comments
– integrated into the rural and village and dependent on the rural market for products and services	– tailors, – cabinetmakers, – carpenters, – potters, – weavers, – smiths, – coppersmiths, – traders etc	– mostly well trained in traditional crafts and formal elementary education; – recognised craft knowledge and skills, correspondingly respected in village community	– traditionally very beautiful craft products, e.g. blacksmith work and pottery, are being forced out by industrial mass products and small (micro) businesses are facing difficulties
– the market no longer takes up the own products at the necessary prices; – structural changes in rural areas and urbanisation put an end to traditional production and lifestyles; – the result is flight from the land	– nonspecific activities, mostly in the informal sector, where very little is required in the way of prior knowledge or education, e.g. – transport worker – recycling industry, i.e. refusal disposal etc, – porter; – docker; – construction worker etc.	– mostly very little or no formal academic education; – no vocational qualifications apart from agricultural knowledge; – resulting restricted use in the informal sector, with resulting frequent unemployment or work as day or casual labourer	– families in such economic difficulties often survive at the existence level and with the help of relatives already settled in the cities;
– few opportunities for finding new or alternative employment; – generally too little economic or job-creating investment by government in rural areas; – lack of rural development programmes etc and informal sector often very poorly developed in rural areas	– young persons often have no or (over)specific knowledge and skills, and so have to accept any work offered; – experienced agricultural labourers (former) farmers, cannot sell their skills in the city and are mostly forced to survive as day labourers and *odd jobbers*	– general low level of education (if any); – vocational qualifications tied to agricultural knowledge (subsistence farming) with very little market value (if any) in the city; – little in the way of prequalifications for new (or any) occupational future to build on	– social tension due to high youth unemployment and rising criminality in rural areas; – migration to cities, further growth in urban misery and slums result from economic problems in rural areas
– salaried employees of government agencies in rural areas often offer their services as assistants against payment (corruption in this area is not unusual)	– all activities are conceivable which are related in any way with vocational qualification or government links, e.g. – teachers (private school) – police officers (night security) etc – often also helping (for compensation) with applications to government agencies etc	– often good formal education, in some cases with corresponding vocational qualification measures for the occupational groups listed, in some with tertiary education e.g. university (teacher, etc)	– this group is very flexible in terms of creating additional income, but generally is unwilling to abandon their high social status and seeks second/third jobs

Table IV: *Summary table for identifying target groups in rural and urban (see note) informal sector broken down by income-generating activities*

(1) social position or group	(2) income-generating activities	(3) status of worker	(4) activities of social marginal groups	(5) urban environment
refugees, victims of political persecution, asylum seekers	– no specific occupation sought, refugees, asylum-seekers and victims of political persecution are looking for temporary *refuge* with the opportunity to *survive:* often this only leaves the informal sector as an *economic* and *survival space*	– no recognised social status in the country providing refuge; – often accepted by local population under government and international pressure; – unresolved situation in terms of approval for developing economic activities and length of stay; – generally recognition as refugee by UNO, UNHCR required	– classed and treated as social marginal groups; – all kinds of criminal activities attributed to them; – often basis for political resistance movements aiming at change in their homeland	– live in special refugee camps, or specially equipped and isolated apartments, houses and sometimes entire city quarters, often in slums; – conflicts with local population – ethnic, religious and political potential for conflict etc.

(6) rural environment	(7) nature of activities	(8) formal educational and vocational training prequalifications	(9) comments
– generally live isolated in specially equipped refugee camps or on the edge of villages in slums or similar camps – conflicts with local population as often not enough land available for building – ethnic, political and religious potential for conflict etc	– mostly seek or create work in the informal sector e.g. work which also brings in money: – gather firewood; – sell off valuables; – transport (if automobiles available from flight); – or follow occupation already learned as craft worker, teacher, lawyer etc; – if there are no openings in their established occupation they try to settle in the informal sector	– often farmers and animal farmers from rural areas without formal education or vocational training; – or come from urban areas and are traders, entrepreneurs, craft workers, salaried employees, intellectuals and unemployed young persons and adults, with all conceivable educational qualifications from university degrees down to illiterates, i.e. highly heterogeneous in terms of education and social status	– the number of refugees and asylum seekers is growing worldwide: some of these with higher educational qualifications and corresponding social position in their countries of origin are trying to emigrate to western industrialised nations, the others stay in neighbouring countries and try to survive there – UN statistics show c. 100 million refugees worldwide

Note: Tables I – IV are based on the author's knowledge of the situation in the informal sector and refugee programmes in Jordan, Syria, Egypt, India, Sri Lanka, Pakistan, Thailand, Indonesia (Myamnar (=Burma)), Papua New Guinea and Afghanistan. In addition, internal information was used from the Deutsche Gesellschaft für Technische Zusammenarbeit (GTZ) and international organisations the author has worked with for years. In this context the study by Ms C. Lohmar-Kuhnle (see note 42, p. 32) deserves special mention as an outstanding suggestion for the organisation used here.

(b) analysis of the necessary individual and group-specific competencies in the target groups which are oriented towards the field of action;
(c) analysis of the potential for change and innovation of the target groups in question in the informal sector;
(d) analysis of approaches to improving the living and working conditions in the informal sector;
(e) analysis of approaches to improving the productive potential in terms of creating opportunities for employment and self-employment;
(f) analysis and description of local and geographical accessibility of the target groups' working and living area.

To show the complexity of the interrelationships, a matrix presentation was chosen for the learning potential and learning prequalifications[192] of the potential target groups in the informal sector analysed in tables I – IV with the target groups forming the columns and the individual content and relationships forming the rows:

2.4.5–I. *Objective requirements and features for target groups (1)-(10)* (Tables V, VI):

The objective requirements for analysing learning potential, learning behaviour and learning prequalifications include the following factors[193]:

(a) socio-cultural factors
(b) socio-economic factors
(c) socio-ecological factors
(d) factors creating ideological norms

---

192 Cf. Helmut Skowronek, Lernen und Lernfähigkeit, Grundfragen der Erziehungswissenschaft. 6th ed., 1975, Munich, pp. 102 et seq, and pp. 9 et seq.
193 Cf., Wilhelm H. Peterßen, Handbuch Unterrichtsplanung, Grundfragen, Modelle, Stufen und Dimensionen, 3rd. ed., Munich, 1988, pp. 409 et seq. The analysis of learning potential is broken down as follows:
  (a) *Socio-cultural* factors must be clarified in the context of the social, political and cultural requirements of the teaching and the target groups.
  (b) *Socio-economic* factors must be formulated in the context of the financial and economically-based requirements.
  (c) *Socio-ecological* factors must be identified in the context of the social and environmentally-caused problems.
  (d) *Ideological normative* factors are shaped by parents, groups, families and the social environment and by state considerations and concrete educational policy requirements. Cf. Herwig Blankertz, Theorien und Modelle der Didaktik, Grundfragen der Erziehungswissenschaft, 10th. ed., Munich, 1977, pp. 192 et seq.

2.4.6–II. *Subjective requirements and features for target groups (1)-(10)* (Tables V, VI):

The subjective requirements for analysing personal learning potential, learning behaviour and learning prequalifications include the following factors regarded as determinants[194]:

(a) *learning ability* – abilities/attitude
– knowledge
– skills
(b) *learning style* – physical
– intellectual
– social

2.4.7–III. *Special features and political dimensions of target groups (1)-(10)* (Tables V, VI):

The target groups identified in the informal sector should not be regarded as groups in isolation, but in the context of the objective and subjective requirements. Defining learning potential and learning prequalifications also requires investigation of the specific social, development policy and institutional policy behaviour of the target groups and the relationship to the society which this expresses[195]. The following individual areas are studied here:

---

194 Cf. W.H. Peterßen, see note 193, p. 410.
    Structural aid for teachers' planning

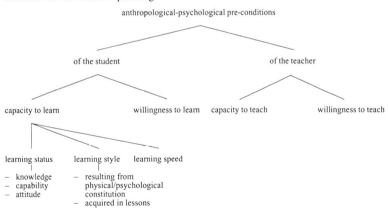

195 Cf. Handbuchreihe Ländliche Entwicklung, Landwirtschaftliche Beratung, vol. 2, eds. G. Payr, R. Sülzer. GTZ, Eschborn 1981, pp. 153 et seq.

(a) *social recognition* of these groups and individuals;
(b) *development policy strategies* and concept for solving the problems of these groups and individuals;
(c) *institutional frameworks* and lobbies for solving the problems of these groups and individuals.

2.4.8 – IV. *Other important factors for describing the learning situation in the informal sector*

Besides the problems and factors listed under I – III for analysing learning potential, learning behaviour and learning prequalifications, the specific external conditions of the target groups in the informal sector are particularly important, such as geographical factors, availability of the target group, time factors and the motivation of the target groups to participate in specific vocational training and upgrading measures[196]. Specifically, the following areas and issues are included in tables V and VI:
(a) *accessibility* of target groups and geographical factors;
(b) *availability* of target groups and time factors;
(c) *motivation* of target groups to participate in changes and specific vocational training and upgrading measures.

In this section we have seen that the informal sector comprises a large number of potential target groups for development aid measures. The target groups in this differentiated sector which is not subject to any obvious structure can, however, be organised in terms of the planning and implementation processes in technical cooperation etc. This shows that the learning potential, learning behaviour, learning prequalifications and needs of these groups and individuals from concrete aid and development measures (projects) can be very different and depend on a range of country-specific or region-specific factors. It will accordingly not be possible to formulate a uniform and general vocational pedagogic approach to solving training and upgrading problems in the informal sector, i.e. approaches need to be developed and formulated

---

196 Cf. C. Lohmar-Kuhnle, see note 42, pp. 32, et seq.
Learning opportunities:
The accessibility of the training facility in terms of the availability of transport, costs, knowledge of the location, permission to leave the place of residence (refugees) and the like (geographical factor);
The opportunity to free oneself to the necessary extent from other obligations in the home or in agriculture in order to participate in a training programme, or the ability to interrupt these without difficulty (time factor); etc., in the context of this section C. Lohmar-Kuhnle cites a number of other important influences affecting planning training and advanced training measures in the informal sector. The author has integrated those which he felt were important in tables V and VI.

Table V (see note on page 85):
Learning potential and prequalifications for small (micro) entrepreneurs and self-employed in the traditional and informal sector

	Target groups in Informal sector (from tables I – VI) learning potential and prequalifications of target groups	(1) small (micro) businesses (< 10 employees), establishments in traditional and informal sector (production, repairs and services)	(2) individual entrepreneurs and self-employed (production, repairs and services)
I. Objective preconditions and circumstances of target groups (1) – (6)	• *socio-cultural factors* • *socio-economic factors* • *socio-ecological factors* • *ideological and normative factors*	– position in social environment; – role of men and women; – traditional values and division of labour; – availability of funding and time; – readiness to spend on training and upgrading; – consciousness and knowledge of environmental problems and traditional values; – living situation in city/rural area; – role of parents, groups and social or occupational organisation; – government programmes	– acceptance by society as entrepreneur, i.e. social status – will and potential for change on the part of individuals; – role of men and women; – financial position and access to credits, funds or equipment etc; – legal authority for contracts etc; – problem consciousness and traditional values; – living situation in city and rural areas; – role of parents, groups and social status; – political programmes, promotion;

II. Subjective preconditions and circumstances of target groups (1) – (6)	• *ability to learn*
	  – abilities, attitude
	  – knowledge
	  – skills
	 • *learning style*:
	  – physical
	  – mental
	  – social
		– development, change in abilities and attitude;
		 – development, expansion of knowledge;
		 – development, expansion of existing knowledge *[sic: skills?]*;
		 – shaped by traditional schools;
		 – memories and principle of imitation;
		 – use of more than traditional methods of working and learning;
		 – introduce participative and problem-solving methods;
			– possibilities for developing entrepreneurial skills and competencies;
			 – developing, changing traditional behavioural norms and forms in terms of quality, market, price, product;
			 – developing existing and new skills;
			 – removing traditional barriers;
			 – accepting new roles and implementing them in social environment;

III. Specificities and political dimensions of target groups (1) – (6)	• *social recognition* of these groups, individuals • *development policy strategies* and concepts for solving problems • *institutional framework* and representation of the interests of these groups to solve problems	– development of acceptance and social potential for change; – past concepts have ended with classic SME promotional programmes or relatively successful individual projects without widespread effect; – except for occupational organisations already existing in many countries, there have been no successful concepts to date in the informal sector; – concepts have to be developed	– developing social acceptance and new role of candidates; – current concepts (see column 1) have not been developed for this target group and duly have only limited suitability; – as already noted in section 2.1 the informal sector is not a priority in developing countries; – concepts have to be developed
IV. Other major factors describing the learning situation in the informal sector	• *accessibility* of target groups, geographical factors • *availability* of target groups, time factors • *motivation* in target groups to participate in changes	– not a problem (relatively) in urban areas if travel money reimbursed; – problem in rural areas so that local measures required; – temporal availability for training and upgrading measures limited because of financial restrictions; – motivation relatively high if prospects for success in implementing what is learned	– relatively little problem in access in urban areas, if mobile services created; – major problem in rural areas; – temporal availability for training and upgrading measures very difficult if candidate is established because of loss of income and orders; – motivation very limited as above problems have not been well solved so far

(3) small (micro) farmers and subsistence farming establishments	(4) small (micro) entrepreneurs and self-employed outside traditional area, i.e. possible modern technologies
– position in social environment; – traditional attitudes; – role of men and women; – traditional techniques and products; – availability of finance from (a) products (cash crops) and (b) special credits; – problem consciousness and farming methods etc; – tradition and situation in life; – role of parents, groups, clans and social or occupational organisations; – government promotional programmes;	– relatively high social status (middle class and higher); – role of men and women dependent on financial background; – availability of finance and credits due to high social competencies; – problem consciousness not very strong; – mostly urban or semi-urban environment; – government promotional programmes;
– development of opportunities to expand products and production, i.e. cash crops etc; – development of entrepreneurial thinking and action; – expansion of existing knowledge and skills; – traditional barriers from family, clan and village etc – innovations where prospects for success very good	– development of entrepreneurial capability generally favourable as this group chose this area very much on own initiative; – high level of formal and technical or commercial knowledge; – shortcomings in management and relatively low flexibility in identifying new markets – open to modern learning and teaching concepts, self-teaching methods etc
– social acceptance outside traditional framework very difficult, so little dynamic potential; – development policy strategies to date in rural regional development involving high inputs and relatively low success; – rural development today paid lip service in many developing countries but not adequately taken into account in funding and policy; – concepts have to be developed	– social acceptance of this group relatively high; – development policy strategies unknown except for SME promotion mentioned under (1); – this group has not so far been recognised as an important target group; – no lobby, more individual fighters as no structures or traditional organisations available – major potential, and concepts need to be developed
– accessibility depends on geographical and infrastructural conditions in the developing countries, but generally difficult and disadvantageous; – farmers are not available for systematic training and upgrading, which has to be done locally and dependent on the prevailing situation; – motivation very low for such measures	– accessibility of this group is good, as they are generally economically active n urban or semi-urban areas and have their market there; – availability for training and upgrading, if implementation ensured (cost-benefit ratio); – motivation is high, but measures have to be brief

Note: Tables V and VI are based on the author's knowledge of the situation in the informal sector and the refugee programmes etc (see also note 4), review of the educational literature (see notes 6-10) and the view that vocational training measures in the informal sector require detailed studies of learning potential, learning behaviour and learning prequalifications for the target groups identified in (1) – (10). Tables V and VI accordingly have to be modified in concrete specific cases and are only intended as orientation.

Table VI (see note on page 85):
Learning potential and prequalifications of employees and specific target groups in the informal sector

	target groups in Informal sector (from tables I – VI) / learning potential and prequalifications of target groups (1) – (6)	(5) wage labourers, day labourers, odd jobbers etc. (employees)	(6) apprentices (in traditional and informal sector)
I. Objective preconditions and circumstances of target groups (1) – (6)	• *socio-cultural factors* • *socio-economic factors* • *socio-ecological factors* • *ideological and normative factors*	– employees, mostly without contracts; – low social position, mostly underclass; – no financial base (savings etc), very weak and underpaid; – does not relate to these ecological questions, not meaningful; – role of parents, group, social stratum has great influence;	– employees mostly without apprenticeship contract with very long terms (4-10 years); – weak social position, heavy dependence, mostly underclass; – no financial base, weak link in company and no rights or security; – does not relate to ecological questions, not meaningful; – parents, group, family, employer have great influence;
II. Subjective preconditions and circumstances of target groups (1) – (6)	• *ability to learn* – abilities, attitude – knowledge – skills • *learning style*: – physical – mental – social	– very limited due to typical lack of formal prior education; – no clear possibility of transfer for own development; – narrowly-defined skills; – on-the-job training; – traditional narrow concept; – plays virtually no role in society and has no representation;	– very limited due to general lack of prior education and poor training concepts; – skills, knowledge and ability only very narrowly developed; – traditional teaching concept, little autonomy; – plays no role in social life and has no representation;
III. Specificities and political dimensions of target groups (1) – (6)	• *social recognition* of these groups, individuals • *development policy strategies* and concepts for solving problems • *institutional framework* and representation of the interests of these groups to solve problems	– virtually no recognition; – virtually no chances for future due to social position; – no target group successfully promoted in development policy; – no concepts, strategies for promotion; – no lobby, no political representation in Third World countries	– status as apprentice not socially secured; – no position in society; – attempts but no successful concepts to date in promoting crafts; – only successes in individual projects; – no lobby, no social representation, virtually no priority to date in local development policy;
IV. Other major factors describing the learning situation in the informal sector	• *accessibility* of target groups, geographical factors • *availability* of target groups, time factors • *motivation* in target groups to participate in changes	– accessible in urban areas; – difficult access in rural areas; – access only possible through employer, i.e. special programmes; – motivation of this group is very low, requiring special programmes	– possible in urban areas; – accessible in rural areas only through special programmes; – accessible only with master's agreement, possible; – high motivation, great willingness to learn

(7) street children, child labour, working minors	(8) youth underemployment and unemployment	(9) prostitution and social marginal groups in urban environments	(10) refugees
– street children grow up without parents and are difficult to reach; – child labour as part of family work (carpet knotting, road building, farming etc) – influence only possible through change in situation of parents, families or clans;	– children of lower and middle class families, poor formal basic education; – behavioural problems as a result of long unemployment, e.g. aggression, antisocial acts, learning disturbances etc; – role of parents, family and social group without positive influence, specifically in urban environments; – tendency to criminality and prostitution as source of income	– mostly daughters of families in urban underclass or poor rural population; – on top of their wretched state they often make a monthly contribution to their families; – they generally have little or no education and hardly any future prospects;	This group unites all the target groups described in the previous categories and their problems. In addition, this group is often lodged in special camps and lives in a specific and mostly unresolved legal situation. This is why aid is only possible with the agreement and pressure of the international community. The case study of Pakistan (which will be described in the course of this work) will take a closer look at the problems
– ability to learn is only a problem here if the family social and economic situation is fundamentally changed; – mostly illiterates with no basis;	– learning ability very limited as a result of behavioural patterns; – special programmes required; – socially isolated and rejected;	– the social situation means that little can be expected in terms of ability and willingness to learn; – special programmes are required which can be successful; – socially isolated and mostly rejected applying a corresponding double standard;	
– no social recognition; – live and die in total exploitation, with no future; – development policy is incapable, helpless, no successful programmes and concepts so far;	– no recognition by society and family, seen as burden; – development policy and urban employment policy are starting to take this target group seriously, as it is becoming a security problem for society in rural and urban areas;	– no recognition as group requiring aid, family benefits while allegedly not knowing what the daughters are doing; – development policy and national social policy have discovered this group in only a few countries, e.g. Thailand (damage to tourism)	
– access to target groups is very difficult as they have to stay mobile in the struggle for survival and do not live in fixed social structures; – motivation to lead a better life is the struggle for survival	– target group easily accessible through families and with special programmes; – availability of target group possible if corresponding funds available; – motivation to change a problem: special programmes required	– target group difficult to access; – motivation to change own situation doubtful, as no alternatives available	

for specific target groups and their situations. Conversely, analytical approaches to identifying demand for (self) employment and for training and upgrading for potential target groups (see tables I – VI) which are based on a uniform concept are possible and feasible. While training and upgrading do not create any jobs for those involved in the informal sector, measures in this area lead to an overall improvement in the initial and development conditions for these target groups and the opportunities for the informal sector[197]. In principle, measures (projects) for improving the situation of the informal sector accordingly also include components for increasing general education and vocational training for target groups in the informal sector. Vocational training measures in this context essentially create the basis for initiating positive developments of this kind in the informal sector and should accordingly also be used in the context of other measures as major instruments to secure project success and achievement of goals[198]. Some of the important elements for identifying, planning and implementing successful measures in the informal sector are[199]:

- Careful and extensive analysis of target groups and the integration of general education and vocational training measures in projects and improving the income and living conditions of these groups in the informal sector.
- Definition and description of clear set targets, i.e. the measures conceived must embrace and cover the specific needs and problems of the target groups; care must be taken here to ensure that the specific needs of the target groups are taken into account in:
  (a) rural areas
  (b) urban areas
  (c) rural-urban areas of the informal sector.
- The context for measures for the informal sector must be investigated accurately and in terms of the positive impact of the projects politically, economically, socially and culturally and other elements important to the target group for securing long-term success.
- Involvement of beneficiaries (i.e. the target groups, responsible government agencies and other major institutions and groups associated with the project) must be ensured in all stages of identification, planning and implementation of measures.
- The role of women, men and children in the informal sector must be taken into account in designing projects, which must be planned and implemented in accordance with the principles of equal opportunity for men and women and

---

197 While vocational training measures alone do not create jobs for the target groups, jobs are created many administrators, teachers and trainers etc.
198 Cf. Fred Fluitman, in: Strategien Selbsthilfefördernder und Beschäftigungsinitiativer Berufsbildung in der Dritten Welt; Ausbildung für den informellen Sektor: Ein Tagungsordnungspunkt für die Neunziger Jahre pp. 32 et seq, Berlin, Expertentagung Juni 89, DSE-ZGB, Mannheim, 1989.
199 Op. cit. pp. 32 et seq.

- the international laws and regulations for the protection of children and young people.
- Planning and implementing measures in the informal sector must proceed on the basis that the informal sector already has its own micro-economic structures and generally follows the laws of the free market. This requires caution in conceiving promotional measures and ensuring that these structures are not destroyed from outside by the promotion. The goal must be to improve existing structures as far as acceptable and act towards integration.
- The measures must accordingly focus in principle on *the people* in the informal sector – the goal must be anthropocentric projects[200]. Projects provide complementary impetus to existing structures and represent a concentration of different measures such as:
  (a) general education and vocational training measures;
  (b) measures promoting craft trades;
  (c) health and hygiene measures;
  (d) measures to protect children and young persons;
  (e) job creation programmes etc.
- Training and upgrading projects in the informal sector need to develop flexible concepts which permit ongoing adjustment to employment and economic structures, i.e. the contents, methodology and didactics must be oriented towards need.
- Projects must show quick success and require competent and flexible management and committed personnel qualified for the needs of the informal sector.
- Measures must be planned and funded with a long enough horizon to ensure sustainability of the desired successes, with corresponding backstopping and follow-up services to ensure long-term prospects for development.
- Projects in this sector should be scientifically supported with specially adapted methodologies to collect and analyse project experience, errors and successes. This should ensure reproducibility and the multiplier effect in development cooperation.

These are just some important criteria for constructive integration of the target groups presented in this section (tables I – IV). In conclusion, however, it should be remembered that besides the elements listed here, successful project implementation in the informal sector also requires very specifically
(a) ongoing involvement of the target groups at every stage of project identification, planning and implementation, and
(b) development of willingness on the part of the responsible agencies in the local governments to promote commitment in the informal sector (an important point). In the long term, we must ensure that the informal sector is given the political, economic and development policy importance due to it on the basis of its size and relevance for employment policy.

---

200 Cf. C. Lohmar-Kuhnle, note 42, pp. 32 et seq.

3 Presentation, development and analysis of selected approaches of German and international vocational training aid to promote the informal and traditional sectors in Pakistan and India

3.1 German-Pakistan Technical Cooperation in vocational training in the refugee-impacted province NWFP

The ongoing Technical Cooperation lasting more than 30 years between the Islamic republic of Pakistan and the Federal Republic of Germany in the sector of vocational training indicates that both governments have identified this area as a special key point of development policy[1]. Pakistan has been a key country for years in German Federal development aid and Technical Cooperation, since together with India, China and Indonesia it represents c. 50% of the world population (China c. 1,100 million; India c. 850 million; Indonesia c. 180 million and Pakistan c. 110 million inhabitants)[2].
The official presentations and statements of the Federal Republic of Germany indicate that the following key areas have been identified for Technical and Financial Cooperation with Pakistan:
– family planning as part of health policy;
– direct and indirect combating of poverty through creation of productive job openings;
– vocational and technical/commercial training and upgrading and basic education;
– environmental protection, resource and nature conservation;
– advisory services on economic and social policy and upgrading in this sector[3].

In the years of the major Afghanistan conflict with the former Soviet Union, uncontrolled refugee flows from Afghanistan impacted particularly the Pakistan North-West Frontier Province (NWFP) and Baluchistan. Pakistan provided a new home to well over 3 million refugees.

---

[1] Cf. M. Diehl, Die Naturwissenschaften in Pakistan, eds. S. Laik Ali, W. Voelter, Z.H. Zaidi, Deutsch-Pakistan. Forum e.V. 1986, Mayen 1986, pp. 39 et seq.
[2] Cf. W. Preuss, Entwicklungspolitische Zusammenarbeit mit Asien, internal BMZ paper, Bonn 1990.
[3] Cf. bfai, Pakistan-Wirtschaftsentwicklung 1989, Bundesstelle für Außenhandelsinformationen, Cologne 1991.

Many of these Afghanistan refugees have still not returned to their homeland, where rival liberation fighters (mujahiddin) and political groups are still fighting savagely for final power positions in the capital of Kabul. This is the context in which German development aid (headed by BMZ and many other semi-governmental and NGOs) has for years provided substantial funds and personnel to support the provinces impacted by refugees (Baluchistan and NWFP)[4].

The long-term nature of the German commitment through Technical Cooperation in the sector of elementary education, vocational training and creating income-generating structures and craft promoting measures have led in the past 10 years to demonstrable if modest success. In particular, there are the many graduates of the vocational qualification measures in the TTP-TTC Peshawar and its promotion for small autonomous craft workers in the bazaars of the city of Peshawar and NWFP[5].

The measures promoted by the Federal Republic of Germany were agreed and implemented in consultation with the local central government, the NWFP government, the international organisations (World Bank, ILO, UNHCR etc) and many domestic and international NGOs[6].

---

4   Cf. section 3.1.2.
5   Cf. Project Progress Reports for TTC-TTP-Peshawar, internal GTZ reports on the cited projects and GTZ Study: U. Böhm and U. Ebeling, Berufsbildung und Kleingewerbeförderung in flüchtlingsbetroffenen Gebieten Pakistans sowie in Afghanistan Eschborn, 1992. Up to the start of 1993 c. 16,000 young Afghans and Pakistanis received training and advanced training at TTP/TTC-Peshawar, of these c. 65 % found employment or self-employment in the formal or informal sector.
6   The World Bank is running a programme together with the central government to improve the effectiveness and efficiency of the Pakistan vocational training system. This also partly affects the measures described here. The ILO is responsible for implementing the project in parts or was involved in a decisive capacity in its conception. The UNHCR is responsible for monitoring and implementing the UN contribution to refugee aid.

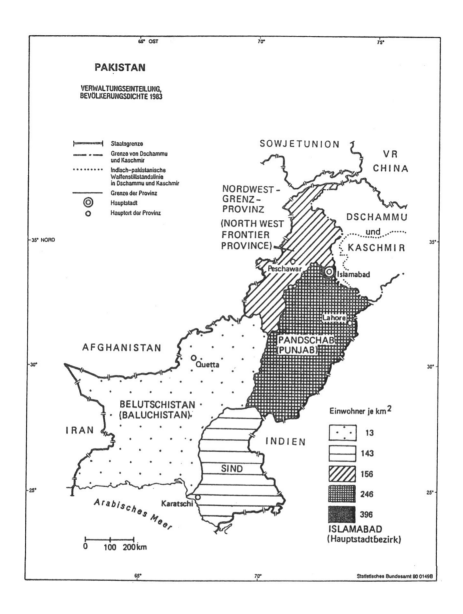

Official German language map of Pakistan (Political districts and population density). Source: Statistisches Bundesamt.

3.1.1 *The project area: geography and key data on Pakistan and the North-West Frontier Province (NWFP)*

Pakistan lies between the 23rd and 36th parallel. Its territory covers c. 804,000 km², more than twice the size of the Federal Republic of Germany. This does not include the disputed area of Jamnu and Kashmir, whose unresolved border and political status has fed the Pakistan-Indian conflict for decades and already resulted in two wars. Pakistan is the seventh-largest country in Asia, comprising part of south-east Asia (the Indian subcontinent) and part of the Near East (from Afghanistan to Bangladesh/ASSAM). The country is bordered to the west by the CIS (former Soviet Union), the Peoples Republic of China to the north, India to the east and the Arabian Sea to the south. Pakistan is notable for its striking variation in scenery, ranging from desert and steppe in the south and east to the Indus river plain in the middle and the mountains in the north and east (Himalayas etc)[7]. There is a desert covering c. 1,400 km² which is virtually undeveloped on the Arabian Sea with its only natural harbour, Karachi. Karachi is also Pakistan's largest city with over 8 million inhabitants: it is the country's industrial centre and most important transportation hub.

The climate in Pakistan ist subtropical and continental, but there are very substantial climatic variations in line with the topography[8]. The Indus plain, which covers about one third of the country is climatically too dry for cultivation. However, an extensive and highly developed irrigation system based on the largest rivers in the north of the country has made it a densely-populated agricultural area[9]. Monsoon rains and melting snow in the high mountain ranges in the north and east are another source for the steady volume of water. However, the high rate of evaporation due to the tropical climate in the plains (semi-arid) involves a high risk of soil salination, posing a continuous threat to the agricultural and cultivated areas. Pakistan has population growth of c. 3.1% a year, and as of mid-1991 it had c. 117 million inhabitants[10]. Pakistan's fertility rate (6.5) has remained consistently high compared to the falling rates in other Asian nations, e.g. India (4.5), Indonesia (3.6), Bangladesh (2.3) and China (2.3). The reasons for this include

---

7 Cf. Länderbericht Pakistan 1990, Statistisches Bundesamt, Wiesbaden October 1990, in J.B. Metzler-Poeschel, Stuttgart 1990 and bfai (Bundesstelle für Außenhandelsinformationen), Kurzmerkblatt, July 1992, Cologne and bfai, Wirtschaftslage, Pakistan am Jahreswechsel 1992/93, March 1993, Cologne.
8 Cf. Länderbericht Pakistan 1990, Statistisches Bundesamt Wiesbaden, October 1990, Metzler-Poeschel, Stuttgart, p. 17 and bfai, Wirtschaft aktuell/Pakistan, Stand 1992, Cologne.
9 Op. cit. p. 18.
10 Op. cit. p. 19.

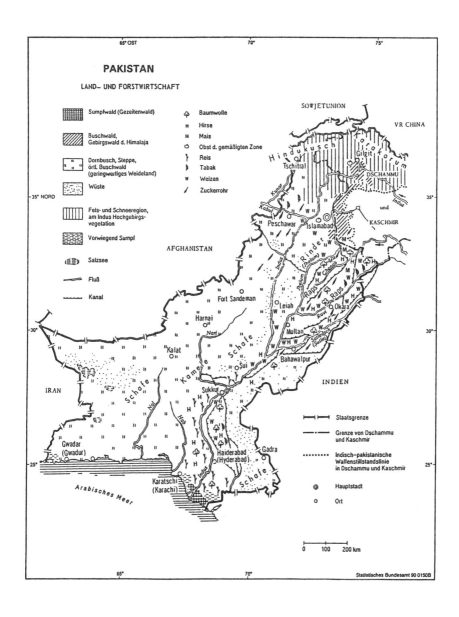

Official German langugage map of Pakistan (Agriculture and forestry). Source: Statistisches Bundesamt.

the lack of an effective and efficient social and family policy in Pakistan which might encourage a reduction in the number of children per family[11]. This unrestrained population growth is ultimately leading to the unfavourable population breakdown by age group, resulting in a difficult age structure for the population. Today, c. 54.4 % of the Pakistan population is under 20, c. 43 % are 20-60 and only c. 4.3 % reach an age of 60 and over[12]. The following table shows the breakdown of the population by the individual provinces:

Table I:
Population, by province (as at the beginning of 1986) (in thousands)[13]

Province	1965	1970	1975	1980	1986	1992[a]
Punjab	30,039	34,626	39,562	45,994	55,214	/
NWFP and tribal areas	8,636	9,955	11,014	12,804	15,804[b]	18,000
Baluchistan	1,928	2,223	3,598	4,183	5,020[c]	6,000
Sind	11,233	12,948	15,805	18,375	22,064	/

a. Figures are not available for 1992, but with an annual growth rate of 3.1 % it can be assumed that in 1993 there were some 18 million people in N.W.F.P. and some 6 million in Baluchistan.
b. The sharp rise in the population of these provinces is due to the flood of refugees from Afghanistan since the start of 1980.
c. The sharp rise in the population of these provinces is due to the flood of refugees from Afghanistan since the start of 1980.

Despite all the efforts of the Pakistan government, the health service has not been able to keep pace with the high population growth. The inadequate health education, poor sanitary conditions in urban and rural areas and poor nutrition (particularly among the lower classes) all have an adverse effect on the general state of health of the population. Here are just a few alarming figures: c. 12 % of infants die in their first year, 25% die before their fifth birthday. Four fifths of all children suffer from diarrhoea and chronic nasal discharge, 70% of all child deaths are due to parasites, malaria, diarrhoea or tuberculosis. Almost three quarters of Pakistan's population still is still without access to clean

11 Op. cit. p. 20
12 Op. cit. p. 22
13 Op. cit. p. 22

drinking water[14]. Besides the lack of funds to improve the infrastructure in health service, preventive health care, sanitation (sewerage etc) and the lack of medical services, another important reasons (particularly for the rural population and the urban lower classes) are the low level of education and poor educational opportunities. This is a major challenge for Pakistan's politicians and middle and upper classes.

Despite the substantial growth of Pakistan's educational system with international (and German) aid, illiteracy is still extremely high at c. 70%. This is particularly true for women in rural areas, where the 1981 census gave a rate of c. 92.7%[15], while men in urban and rural areas have an illiteracy rate of 40-50%. This rate is extremely high compared to the neighbouring Asian countries, where in comparable social classes only c. 47% are illiterate (although in the author's view this is still intolerably high). Pakistan also compares very poorly with its neighbours in terms of expenditure on education as a percentage of gnp (in 1985 Pakistan spent c. 2.1% of gnp on education, while its Asian neighbours spent 4-5% of gnp)[16].

Table II: *Literacy rates 1951-1987 (%)*

Years	Both Sexes			Male			Female		
	Total	Urban	Rural	Total	Urban	Rural	Total	Urban	Rural
1951	13.2	–	–	17.0	–	–	8.6	–	–
1961	18.4	–	–	26.9	–	–	8.2	–	–
1972	21.71	41.5	14.3	30.2	50.0	22.6	11.6	31.0	4.7
1981	26.17	47.1	17.3	35.0	55.3	26.3	16.0	37.3	7.3
1986/87	30.00	46.4	22.5	41.0	55.0	34.8	17.7	36.8	9.2

Source: Naushin (1978), Population Census Organization (1984) and Federal Bureau of Statistics (Labour Force Survey, 1986/87)

---

14 Cf. note 8, p. 27
15 Op. cit. p. 31
16 Loc. cit.

Population density in the North-West Frontier Province (N.W.F.P.), Pakistan, as at: 1981

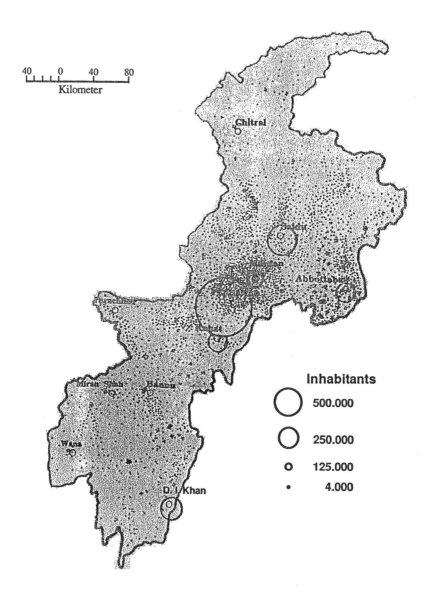

Source: Study Böhm/Ebeling, GTZ, Eschborn 1992

Table III:
Number of educational facilities by type, level and gender, 1947/48 and 1978/79 (T = total, F = female)[17]

	(1) Primary schools		(2) Middle schools		(3) High schools		(4) Secondary vocational schools		(5) Arts and Science colleges		(6) Professional colleges		(7) Universities	
Year	T	F	T	F	T	F	T	F	T	F	T	F	T	F
1947/48	8,413	1,549	1,549	153	408	64	46	18	45	5	19	2	n/a	
1978/79	54,549	16,551	5,062	1,364	3,302	896	245	83	477	130	99	8	19	
1988/89	87,545	26,250	6,560	2,028	5,183	1,469	235	108	698	190	included in (5)		22	

As table III shows, although there is an increase in the number of educational facilities for the various courses of education, these fall well short of what is needed to absorb the steady increase in the number of students and trainees. These problems are not solved by internal links between the individual courses (cf. table IV), i.e. creating transferability between general, vocational and tertiary education.

At an international conference[18] organised by the Pakistan Manpower Institute (PMI), Islamabad, and the Friedrich Ebert Foundation the following central recommendations were made for improving human resource development and education[19]:

3.1.1.1 – (A) *General and tertiary education:*

(1) Pakistan should raise its educational budget in line with UNESCO guidelines to 4% of gnp;
(2) elementary education should be made available for all Pakistan children of school age, the quality of education, the curricula and the teachers should be improved and adapted to needs;
(3) corresponding adult literacy measures must be implemented;

---

17 Cf. The integration of general and technical and vocational education, UNESCO-Publication, 1986, Paris paper by: Mohammad Aslam Popalzai and Khadim Ali Hashmi, Case study Pakistan, p. 197 and cf. note 18, p. 33 – Table 5.3 Schools and other educational facilities.
18 The Regional Workshop on Development and Utilisation of Human Resources: Issues and Policies, October 10-12, 1988, Islamabad, Pakistan.
19 Cf. Human Resource Development and Utilisation: Issues and Policies, pub. Pakistan Manpower Institute, Islamabad, 1989 Pakistan, pp. 9 et seq.

Table IV: The educational system in Pakistan (general, technical and vocational education)[a]

a) Cf. note 19 on page 99, p. 198.

(4) curricula in general schools must be reviewed and oriented towards the needs of graduates and the labour market;
(5) expansion and reform of secondary schooling must be made a top priority: for many young Pakistanis, the leaving certificate is their final educational qualification and route into the labour market, and the curricula in secondary education must be oriented accordingly;
(6) this involves the need for teacher training and upgrading, which in turn requires reorientation of training centres and colleges for this purpose, i.e. the equipment, teaching and learning materials, locations etc must meet the relevant needs;
(7) the situation is similar in the university/tertiary stage of education, which needs to be oriented more towards the needs and employment of graduates and the labour market;
(8) the socio-economic conditions of the rural and semi-rural areas of Pakistan should be given greater weight in developing appropriate curricula in secondary education: the dropout rate[20] for students in the courses offered must be reduced by greater adaptation and orientation to the needs of the graduates of these courses, i.e. an effort must be made to increase cooperation between the relevant social forces in education;
(9) the *private sector* must be more strongly interested and involved in education and its financial input must be increased;
(10) students from the poorer urban classes, rural and semi-rural areas of Pakistan must be given scholarships or adequate assistance and motivation measures; this is to improve the basis for more even development of Pakistan community structures, the chance to improve the lot of the socially disadvantaged and develop the local economy (eliminate location-based disadvantages);
(11) an approach should be developed and implemented at the national level (covering all provinces) to integrated development of general, vocational and tertiary education, development of educational planning and improving the employment prospects for graduates of the educational system: this requires cooperation between all social forces and the development of an educational policy oriented towards the future needs of the country.

---

20 Dropout-rate = students failing to gain the target qualification, frequently students failing to get even a minimum educational qualification.

3.1.1.2 – (B) *Vocational training and relationship to human resource development* [21, 22]

The high rate of growth of the Pakistan population (as described above) has led to a corresponding increase in the number of labour market entrants. Between 1970/71 and 1988/89 the active population[23] rose from c. 18.7 million to 30.9 million, equivalent to annual growth of c. 2.8%. As women are mainly employed in the subsistence economy, they are obviously not included in the active labour force.

Table V: *Labour market data (labour force and employment)*[24]

	87-88	88-89	89-90
Population(million)	103.82	107.04	110.36
Labour force (million)	29.93	30.87	31.82
Employed labour force (million)	28.99	29.90	30.82
Unemployment rate (%)	3.31	3.13	3.13[a)]
Labour force participation rate (%)	28.83	28.83	28.83

a. The unemployment rate shown here naturally does not realistically reflect the actual situation in Pakistan. It can be assumed the number of potentially underemployed and unregistered unemployed will substantially increase this figure. Any visitor or tourist in Pakistan is immediately struck by the fact that large numbers of young people are clearly without work and waiting or offering to perform any kind of job for tourists. The number must accordingly be regarded as an uninformative statistic with a political justification, and in the author's view does not in any way reflect reality.

If we now consider the result of the system of general and tertiary education and vocational training in terms of the quality and quantity of the labour prepared for the labour market, we find major discrepancies. These are partly quantitative (see the population figures below) and

21 Op. cit. pp. 10 et seq and Manpower Employment and Training services in Pakistan, pub. Employment Promotion Unit Technical Wing, Islamabad, 1990, Pakistan.
22 Cf. note 6, p. 16, and text p. 35.
23 Economically active population: gainfully employed individuals are all those engaged in an activity which is directly or indirectly gainful. This includes individuals in employment (including soldiers and family members acting as helpers), self-employed craft or agricultural workers or members of the liberal professions. Gainfully employed individuals and unemployed individuals together make up the economically active population. This definition makes it clear that the informal and traditional sector and family members acting as helpers are also included.
24 Cf. Manpower Employment and Training Services in Pakistan, pub. Employment Promotion Unit Technical Wing, Islamabad, 1990, Pakistan.

partly qualitative, if we look at the relevance of general and tertiary education and vocational training for employability and the very high dropout rate of students from these sectors. The Pakistan Manpower Institute has accordingly made the following recommendations for improving vocational and technical training in Pakistan[25]:

(1) The available supply of technical and vocational training in Pakistan must be substantially increased and diversified in order to achieve a quantitative and qualitative solution to the problems of the mismatch between the supply of labour and jobs;
(2) Training and advanced training institutions and the training and advanced training programmes offered and run there must be more closely oriented towards the needs of the employment system;
(3) The technological and job-related requirements must be met by the technical and vocational educational system;
(4) Technical and vocational education must be so broadly based in qualifying skilled workers that the graduates of educational facilities have adequate mobility in terms of their flexibility and eligibility for deployment;
(5) Private and state enterprises and other important employers must be involved in conceiving and implementing the qualification process in a way that ensures that trainees are given a suitable introduction to the "world of work" during training and that this is integrated into the training process;
(6) Employers (and associations) are urged to join with state and private entities implementing vocational and technical training measures in developing and implementing corresponding cooperative concepts for training and advanced training;
(7) The present Pakistan "Apprenticeship Training"[26] should be implemented in close cooperation between the public and private sector and the organisations responsible for the training and advanced training institutions. This applies particularly to the

---

25 Cf. Human Resource Development & Utilisation: Issues and Policies, pub. Pakistan Manpower Institute, Islamabad, 1989, pp. 11 et seq
26 Cf. Pakistan Apprenticeship Ordinance, 1962. This ordinance regulates the key features for implementing cooperative vocational training. The Pakistan central and provincial government is responsible for implementing this ordinance, which has accordingly not been very successful to date, as the responsible government offices at the Ministries of Labour and Employment operate exclusively through the channels of government control functions and attempt to activate this sector of vocational training through administrative measures. Industry, and specifically the private sector, is not cooperating in this, as it feels that its interests are not properly represented by the government. As a result, "Apprenticeship Training" has been unsuccessful to date.

selection and hiring of trainees by industry, to joint curriculum development, to monitoring the success of training measures and final examinations and to the quality and qualifications of trainers and teachers;

(8) The implementing organisations and partners cooperating in the sector of vocational training are called on to do more for the image in society of the skilled worker and to carry out corresponding PR measures to bring this training sector in Pakistan closer to the potential target groups and make it more attractive to them. This includes specifically paying regular minimum apprenticeship or trainee salaries on an appropriate scale, setting the duration of training and recognising final diplomas;

(9) The informal and traditional sector (artisans) should not be ignored in creating training and advanced training places.

(10) The existing training institutes, such as the Technical Training Center (TTC), Vocational Training Center (VTC) and Skill Development Center (SDC)[27] need to be equipped better for this task and the trainers, managers and other instructors at these centres must be prepared better for this task. These centres should also cooperate very closely with industry and craft trades and implement appropriate "dual" forms of vocational training[28].

(11) The curricula, the teaching and learning materials, the qualifications of the trainers and teachers at these centres must be adapted to the changing requirements of the labour market and updated or improved on an ongoing basis.

The Workshop also made special recommendations for the integration of disadvantaged groups, consideration of the needs of the informal sector and special consideration of women as a very heavily underprivileged group in Pakistan society. In addition a series of other important recommendations were made for creating better social conditions for successful implementation of training and upgrading measures and promoting job-creating measures. Many of these conceptual considerations and recommendations for improving the design of vocational

---

27 The TTCs, VTLs and SDCs are government off-the-job training and advanced training facilities which in Pakistan come under the Ministry of Labour. These training and advanced training facilities are classified under the non-formal training sector (ILO-World Bank definition), but in the author's view belong in the secondary education system.

28 Cf. Die berufsbildende Schule, March 93 M. Diehl, Probleme beim Transfer des dualen Systems in die Länder der Dritten Welt, pp. 93 et seq "-biliteral and multilateral development aid is generally too heavily focused on the state-dominated vocational training sector (due to the application procedure which has been standard in the past, which is dominated by planning procedures, planning and finance agencies in Third World countries with a mostly central government orientation).

and technical training can be better understood on the basis of the case study of TTC-TTP, Peshawar, as the German partner was directly monitoring and able to influence implementation and the results achieved.

3.1.2 Facts and data on the context of the German-Pakistan projects in the provinces of NWFP and Peshawar, which were impacted by refugee flows

Since its creation as an independent nation (1947)[29] Pakistan has been a place of refuge for countless exiles and persecuted minorities from the region. In the late Forties after the partition of India and Pakistan, Indian religious refugees (muhajjerin) found a new home in Pakistan, the new Islamic nation *(Dar al Islam = the house of Islam)*. Later, at the start of the Seventies, the partition of East and West Pakistan and the creation of the new nation of Bangladesh[30] resulted in new flows of refugees to Pakistan. The next political catastrophe in the region followed shortly, initiated by the Communist takeover (1978) in Afghanistan and associated massive resistance by the Afghan rural population (particularly in the provinces bordering Iran and Pakistan, with the activities of the Islamic fundamentalists) and the consequent destabilisation of internal political conditions in Afghanistan. This was followed in 1979 by military intervention by the former Soviet Union, which will probably go down in history as the Soviet version of Vietnam. This was another pointless war with many dead, injured and otherwise damaged on both sides. Soviet intervention in Afghanistan led to the largest movement of refugees in the region[31] since the partition of India (1947). Between 3-3.5 million Afghans left their country. They came particularly from the cities (Kabul, Khandahar, Khost etc) and the border provinces. The Afghan refugees settled mainly in the Pakistan provinces bordering Afghanistan – Baluchistan and North-

---

29 Pakistan became independent at the same time as India on 14.08.1947, and consists of the North-West Frontier Province, Baluchistan, Sind, Punjab and the Bengali part (East Pakistan) cf. Dieter Nohlen (ed.), Lexikon Dritte Welt; Länder, Organisationen, Theorien, Begriffe, Personen. Rowohlt, Reinbek bei Hamburg, 1989, p. 526.
30 Bangladesh (formerly East Pakistan) has been an independent state since 1971 and has been regarded since as the hopeless case in the history of international development aid and policy, cf. Dieter Nohlen (ed.), note 29.
31 Cf. David Busby Edwards; Frontier, Boundaries and Frames: The Marginal Identity of Afghan Refugees – in: Akbar S. Ahmed (ed.); Pakistan, The Social Sciences Perspective, Oxford Press Karachi, 1990 and cf. Dieter Nohlen (ed.) note (1) "The unsuccessful Afghanistan venture (Soviet Union) was probably one of the decisive factors in the transformation of the Soviet Union (1989) and "undoubtedly contributed to its collapse (the author)". The Soviet invasion of Afghanistan ended with the withdrawal of the last troops on 15.02.1989."

West Frontier Province (NWFP) – near the provincial capitals of Quetta and Peshawar. They were housed in refugee camps where they have mostly stayed since the beginning of the Eighties. Unlike the religious refugees from India and the refugees from Bangladesh, they are not seeking a new home in Pakistan but waiting in their temporary and poor accommodation for a chance to return to Afghanistan. Following the breakup of the Soviet Union and the change of government in Kabul, a form of coalition emerged between the subsequently opposed factions of the *mujahiddin* (freedom fighters)[32], although they are now locked in a bitter struggle and have again stopped the return flow of refugees from Pakistan to Afghanistan. Today, the civilian population is again fleeing the centres of the military confrontation (mainly the capital, Kabul), mostly heading for NWFP and Peshawar where they are refilling the refugee camps vacated by their many relatives who have returned. No end of the conflict is in sight, as the *mujahiddin* are still superbly equipped with weapons and ammunition, thanks to the western nations and the former Soviet Union. Afghanistan remains a security risk for peace in the region, and there seems no sign of a solution to these problems or a lasting compromise between the warring leaders and tribes. In this context and as part of international aid[33] for the Afghan refugees in Pakistan GTZ has been carrying out a series of projects since 1981 for the refugees and to relieve the regions and provinces affected in Pakistan. The projects focus mainly on the following areas:

(a) elementary education and teacher training;
(b) vocational training and instructor training;
(c) promoting income-oriented measures and employment of refugees and the affected segments of the Pakistan population;
(d) environmental protection and resource conservation, specifically promoting firewood-saving cooking stoves;

---

32 The mujahiddin joined together in a jirga (a type of exile government) in Feb. 1989 in Islamabad/Pakistan, but were unable to reach a consensus. They comprised a wide range of political movements, tribes, tribal leaders, major landowners, intellectuals and former bureaucrats, but were dominated by the political leaders and factions developed from the Sunni and Shiite clerics, who continue to provide the key potential for conflicts in present-day Afghanistan.

33 Cf. GTZ expert report, carried out under a commission of the BMZ
(a) Klein/Kruse, Project identification mission, Dec. 1980, Eschborn-GTZ
(b) Göser, Barutzki, Frommer, Knabe; Grundausbildung und Berufsausbildung für afghanische Flüchtlinge und der in den betroffenen Gebieten lebenden Pakistani, N.W.F.P. und Baluchistan, Eschborn, GTZ 1981; cf. ILO Publication, Tradition and dynamism among Afghan refugees, Report of an ILO mission to Pakistan (Nov. 1982) on income – generating activities for Afghan refugees by International Labour Office Geneva UNHCR (= United Nations High Commissioner for Refugees, Geneva).

(e) ecological housebuilding, i.e. specifically promotion of appropriate technologies for the construction of refugee camps, camp buildings and schools etc[34];
(f) health and hygiene, i.e. specifically promotion of a project to improve orthopedic technicians at the university of Pershawar;
(g) and funding and co-funding a series of projects implemented by and through the UNHCR[35] and other German NGOs and political foundations[36]

The case study chosen for this work is the Pakistan-German Technical Training Programme (PGTTP) at the Technical Training Center Peshawar in NWFP. The other projects referred to above are mentioned here simply for completeness, although where necessary reference will be made to specific links to the other projects.

3.1.3 *Pakistan-German Technical Training Programme (PGTTP) – a project for the informal sector, with model status for vocational training measures in this sector*

3.1.3.1 *The project objective, problem analysis and the target results for the project*

The Pakistan-German Technical Training Programme (PGTTP) at the Technical Training Center (TTC) in Peshawar in the North-West Frontier Province (NWFP) has been assisted by the German partner since 1982. The project is now in its fifth promotional phase. In the course of this promotion a series of studies was done on identification (1981) and planning[37] and ongoing project progress reviews[38]. Based on the

---

34 Cf. Mud Construction Training in Bost-Mason Training Centre, GTZ project, study by Cathrine Robin under a commission of GTZ, Peshawar, October 1990.
35 UNHCR = United Nations High Commissioner for Refugees.
36 In the two provinces Baluchistan and (particularly) N.W.F.P. well over a hundred NGOs, foundations and other bilateral donors (Austria, Sweden, Saudi Arabia etc) have been active since 1980. Besides international NGOs a large number of Pakistan and Afghan NGOs have been established whose existence is secure as long as there is funding. The Pakistan government is accordingly having very great difficulty controlling the activities of these organisations, some of which are not registered, and this has led to political feuds and problems in many respects in the provinces involved, not always in the best interests of the refugees affected.
37 Cf. sources, note 5 (p. 92), the internal offer documents of the GTZ to the BMZ and project planning and the German-Pakistan project agreement. The following is a brief outline of the project history:
Offer for project implementation Dec. 1981 and signature of agreement August 1982; offer with GTZ appraisal report (pilot phase) March 84; signature of agreement May 84; objectives-oriented project planning (ZOPP) report (Hurwitz) March 1986; report on project progress monitoring, G. Kohlheyer et al., June 1987; offer for project extension, Dec. 1987 and agreement May 1988; project progress monitoring, Marx/Gold, Oct. 1989; offer for

results of these studies the project was modified for the changed environmental conditions and the objectives were modified for project progress[39]. The project purpose restated in February 1993:
"The vocational training system in NWFP is more strongly oriented towards qualification concepts which lead to lasting employment or self-employment for the Afghan and Pakistan graduates of training measures."[40]

This project purpose is based on a preceding joint problem analysis[41]. It accordingly includes references to fundamental deficiencies (core problems) of the vocational training system in NWFP as listed below:

(A) *Core problems:*

(1) The vocational training system in NWFP is not oriented towards the need of the labour market in the province;
(2) The occupations for which training is offered, the training concepts and curricula in the vocational training measures implemented in NWFP do not prepare for self-employment in the informal and modern sectors.

Another important indication in the project goal is the definition of the target groups for the measures, namely the Afghan and Pakistan graduates of the training measures.

---

project extension, April 1990; objectives-oriented project planning (ZOPP), report May 1990 project progress monitoring, report: Böhm/Ebeling, Dec. 1992; objectives-oriented project planning (ZOPP), Feb. 1993, report C. Huizenga; offer for project extension April 93 and signature of agreement Sept. 93.

38 Under the agreements between GTZ and BMZ contained in the commissions, GTZ is running objectives-oriented project planning (ZOPP) workshops in consultation with and involving the local project executing agency. The results of these workshops then form the basis for further project implementation. The individual stages and partner contributions to project implementation are settled by the partners in a so-called "Plan of operation". This plan must, however, be regularly updated and adapted to project progress.

39 Cf. GTZ offer for project extension, April 93.

40 Under GTZ regulations the project goal is set so high in principle that the project can make a substantial contribution towards reaching the goal but is not directly responsible for achieving it, i.e. it is basically outside the responsibility of the project management. By definition, the project and its results accordingly make a decisive contribution towards achieving the goal.

41 The problem analysis is a step in the GTZ ZOPP procedure and leads to a corresponding hierarchical ranking of the identified problems. The causes and effects are placed in relationships to each other and dependencies displayed. The core problem here is an important problem identified as such by all those involved, and is at the centre of the problem tree. It is the centre of the problem hierarchy and the links between causes and effects, cf. Annex III, pp. 310 et seq.

(B) *The other important problems identified as leading to this core problem[42] are:*

(1) inadequate qualification of trainers and teachers;
(2) the Technical Training Centers produce skilled workers with inadequate qualifications;
(3) the concepts of the existing training facilities (TTCs, SDCs, VTCs) are not directed towards the needs of the modern and formal sectors;
(4) the concept for training in the informal sector and the curricula tested in the German-Pakistan project have not been transferred to the other institutions in the province (NWFP);
(5) the capacity for absorption of the NFWP labour market and existing system of employment is very limited;
(6) economic development and industrialisation in NFWP is stagnant and even retrograde;
(7) the links and interfaces between the traditional informal economic and employment sector and the vocational training system are inadequately explored and developed.

Consideration of the Afghan target groups integrated into the project yielded the following problem scenario:

(C) *Core problem*[43]
The German-Pakistan project for vocational qualification of Afghan target groups makes only a limited and unsatisfactory contribution towards the return of Afghan refugees to Afghanistan.

(D) *The other important problems identified which lead to this core problem are:*

(1) training concepts and curricula are inadequately oriented towards the needs of the reconstruction in Afghanistan;
(2) Afghan trainers are inadequately qualified for these tasks in Afghanistan (e.g. setting up training structures and centres);
(3) the Afghan NGO (Afghan-German Technical Training Programme[44], or AGTTP) lacks funds, staff, professionalism

---

42 Cf. internal GTZ paper and report on results:
ZOPP Workshop for the Planning of the Pak-German Technical Training Programme (TTP) in Refugee Affected Areas of N.W.F.P.-Peshawar, Pakistan by C. Huizenga, Eschborn, Feb. 1993 and Annex III, pp. 310 et seq.
43 See Annex IV, pp. 319 et seq.
44 See Annex IV, pp. 319 et seq.

and infrastructure plus assistance and recognition from the Pakistan partner;
(4) administrative problems and obstacles to cross-border activities of AGTTP reduce the efficiency and effectiveness of the repatriation and reconstruction measures for Afghans and Afghanistan;
(5) the insecure and unresolved political situation in Afghanistan hampers AGTTP in its cross-border activities and measures;
(6) the project assisted by the German partner to qualify Afghans has yet to be recognised as a model project for NFWP and has funding problems.

The project purpose cited above (see page 108) is to be achieved through the following results to be secured by the project[45] (a-h):
(a) the graduates of the SES (= "Skill for Employment and Self-Employment") training programme are qualified and promoted in line with the SES concept;
(b) the graduates of apprenticeships in bazaar establishments are qualified and promoted in line with the SES concept;
(c) the concept and model approach for securing the SES concept institutionally and organisationally in the long term have been developed and implementation is secured;
(d) monitoring and evaluation (M + E) systems for formal training (in 2 occupations) and training in line with the SES concept have been developed and are functioning;
(e) donors and sponsors for securing the SES concept financially in the long term have been identified, interested and contractually integrated into the project;
(f) graduates for the occupations of refrigeration mechanics and radio/TV electronics (maintenance and repair) are being trained in line with the needs of the market (employment and self-employment) in cooperation with the selected establishments;
(g) the teacher and trainer qualification programme adapted for results (a) – (f) and the training components and concepts has been implemented at the TTC Peshawar and is functioning;

---

45 The *project results* leading to the goal (as opposed to the project purpose) are under the direct control of the project management, and the management is responsible for achieving them. Project management is accordingly also obliged to install a special Monitoring and Evaluation (M + E) system to be able to manage the project efficiently in terms of achieving the goal (source: GTZ-Organisation Manual and ZOPP-planning documents).
Cf. also Monitoring und Evaluierung in Projekten der Technischen Zusammenarbeit, GTZ publication No. 229, Eschborn, 1992.

(h) the Afghan-German NRGO is registered and recognised in NFWP and is working in accordance with its planning in Afghanistan[46].

To date up to c. DM 15.1 million has been made available by the German Federal Government. The agreed extension requires a further c. DM 8.3 million[47]. The contract for extending the project as described here has already been placed by BMZ and it can be assumed that GTZ will implement the project jointly with the Pakistan partner in line with the planning and specifications described here.

3.1.4 *Didactical and methodological concept, project target groups and organisational structure of the Pakistan-German and Afghan-German Technical Training Programme*

Target groups
The target groups defined for the project have to be divided into two main groups by nationality[48]:

(A) Pakistani young persons, adults and unemployed women from the urban, semi-rural and rural areas of NFWP[49]:

Category 4
hired labourers and day labourers in establishments in the informal sector;

very low-paid labourers in the modern sector in NFWP;
service providers;

Category 5
apprentices employed in the traditional sector, e.g. bazaar businesses etc, or other craft establishments;

Category 6
casual labourers, day labourers or others seeking work;

---

46 Although the results cited here correspond in their content to the results of the GTZ offer and ZOPP planning papers, their language was supplemented by the author to make them easier for the reader to understand and make the concept for the approach more comprehensible. Sources: GTZ offer of April 93, ZOPP planning papers, March 93, see also note (36).
47 Loc. cit.
48 The project funds provided by the BMZ are for assistance to the Afghan refugees in N.W.F.P., and the Pakistan population and provincial government in implementing refugee measures. These political directives were/are accordingly to be taken into account accordingly in defining the target groups.
49 Tables II, III and IV, pp. 76-80 of the present work, are based on the categories presented here for target groups.

Category 7
(very) small entrepreneurs and employees of these businesses;

Category 9
underemployed and unemployed young persons;
underemployed and unemployed women.

(B) Afghanistan young persons, adults and unemployed women from urban, semi-rural and rural areas[50] Afghanistans now residing in NFWP and in the border regions of Afghanistan and Pakistan:

Category 11
refugees, political refugees and persons seeking asylum in NFWP
The special problem for this target group is that they do not form a single unit which can be allocated unambiguously to one of the categories listed under (A) but rather include members of all the categories cited[51]. It can accordingly be generally assumed that the specific measures designed for the target groups listed under (A) will also cover an adequate number of Afghan refugees. However, in designing qualification measures for refugees and the target groups cited under (A) a number of important general conditions and special features of NFWP must be taken into account:
The industrialisation policy of the NFWP provincial government can unfortunately only be described as largely unsuccessful, given that more industrial establishments in the modern production and service sector have closed down their facilities than have opened new ones. NFWP is regarded in Pakistan as an unfavourable location for modern industry, not least because of the poor infrastructure, inadequate supply of qualified labour and primarily rural, peasant and tribal cultural orientation of much of the province's population;
The steady population growth is resulting in serious deterioration in the employment situation, i.e. the ratio of vacancies to those seeking work has fallen and demand for skilled labour (skilled workers, technicians and engineers) in NFWP has decreased sharply[52];
The service sector formed by state enterprises of the provincial and central government agencies cannot be used as an unlimited

---

50 Cf. table IV, p. 80 of the present work.
51 Cf. tables I to III, pp. 74-79 of the present work.
52 Cf. Pakistan Manpower Review, Publisher, Manpower and Overseas Pakistanis Division, Government of Pakistan, Islamabad, 1989.

source of employment for unemployed and qualified graduates of the educational and vocational training institutions. This sector is already regarded as having very low productivity because of the large number of the workers in permanent employment, as confirmed by many studies on this sector which show very high underemployment leading to low salaries for many state employees, who have to take second and third jobs to survive[53];

Afghan refugees and Pakistan population groups (labourers) in the lower classes in semi-rural and rural areas, frequently have no access to employment in the modern (industrial and service) sector because they have little or no formal education or vocational qualification.

Afghans also have the problem of their nationality, i.e. government agencies and enterprises do not employ foreigners as a matter of principle.

There is a combination of a highly undifferentiated labour market with little potential for development and a vast number of potential workers, i.e. the number of those seeking work or underemployed is much higher than the number of vacancies. In addition, the training and advanced training available from private and state institutions is totally divorced from the needs of the labour market and industry, so that qualified graduates of these training facilities are frequently unable to find a job[54] and swell the ranks of the unemployed. Further, the expectations developed in these individuals by inappropriate educational and vocational training measures are completely incapable of satisfaction by the labour market.

It accordingly seems legitimate to conclude that in principle all training and advanced training measures for the target groups under (A) and (B) need to be accompanied by corresponding promotional measures, particularly where the aim is to create jobs. Here, the informal and traditional sector offers an important basis for expanding the labour market[55]. Efforts must be made to ensure that graduates of these training

---

53 Cf. Educated Unemployed, Friedrich Ebert Stiftung for Government of Pakistan, Ministry of Manpower and Overseas Pakistanis, Islamabad, 1990.
54 Op. cit. pp. 55 et seq.
55 Cf. Uwe Sturmann, Bildung, Berufsbildung ... und was dann? Verlag, Breitenbach, Saarbrücken, 1990 "The informal sector provides income-earning opportunities for a large number of people. Though it is often regarded as unproductive and stagnant, we see it as providing a wide range of low-cost, labour-intensive, competitive goods and services" (ILO 1972) "In view of the growing employment crisis in the rural area and the inability of the formal economy to absorb the growing number of unemployed workers, the informal sector appears to be a solution for the employment problem." pp. 39 et seq.

measures can find employment at an adequate income, as the available work is already being shared by too many people, and their income is shrinking steadily. As the AGTTP and PGTTP show, the informal and traditional labour market offers additional potential for appropriate concepts of income-oriented training and advanced training aimed at employment or self-employment.

3.1.5 *Conceptual and didactic considerations for project design*

The basic considerations in developing the project concept and didactic approach for implementing the PAK-GERMAN Technical Training and AFGHAN-GERMAN Technical Training Programme with its orientation towards the informal, traditional and formal sectors (TTC sector) can be described as follows[56]. First, however, it must be recognised that development of a project concept related and appropriate to the surrounding conditions and the didactic approach under the project requires us to take into account the prior analysis of the target group (see pp. 111 et seq.) and the specified target groups. Directing measures at employment and self-employment in the informal and informal sectors is another key factor of decisive importance for the didactic approach and the project concept. The aim here is to reconstruct and explain some central features of the didactic approach in the project:

(A) It is essential to ensure the *anthropocentricity*[57] of the didactic concept, addressing the following requirements:
- realistic identification of target-group specific and individual need for promotion;
- a significant contribution towards improving the situation of the target groups and individuals;

---

56 In analysing the existing reports, offers, planning workshops etc. (see note 37, p. 107) the author noted that there is no written concept or systematic presentation of the didactic approach for the project. Much that was developed and decided in the project could not be documented because of the very extensive daily workload of the team leader and his colleagues. The measures to review the project and new GTZ planning have so far not addressed this important point. This must be seen as a serious failing and is to be made good in future through scientific backstopping by the University of Bremen (see the section on scientific backstopping for AG/PGTTPs).

57 *Anthropocentricity*: an anthropocentric approach to vocational training and promotion is understood here as the need to orient measures and projects to the target-group-specific needs for promotion, realistic identification of these for designing the didactic approach and the associated promotional strategy for the target groups. The need for promotion is determined by the subjective and objective needs of these people and the environments and particularly the areas of action available to them in the informal and formal sector.
Cf. C. Lohmar-Kuhnle, Konzepte zur beschäftigungsorientierten Aus- und Fortbildung von Zielgruppen aus dem informellen Sektor, Weltforum, Cologne 1991, p. 73.

- allowance for and addressing the capability for development of the target groups and individuals in the social (political, economic, socio-cultural etc) context;
- allowance for the special situation of the Afghan refugees and Pakistan target groups in the urban, semi-rural and rural sectors (including subjective and objective conditions).

(B) The skills, competencies, knowledge and qualifications[58] must be *action oriented*[59] and relevant for utilisation. The following criteria should be taken into account in developing the didactic approach and qualification profile:
- content, teaching and learning methods, relationship between theory and practice (working environment of the informal and traditional sector) must be appropriate for the target groups and individuals;
- the qualifications must contribute to putting the target groups and individuals in a position where they can:
  (a) make an income;
  (b) expand their skills and knowledge and use them for further self-development;
  (c) develop their social personality and position.

---

58 The idea of training is introduced here to cover the complexity of the vocational pedagogical and ergonomic backgrounds of the informal and traditional sector. Although parallels and links are seen by analogy to the current debate about vocational training in the western industrialised nations and the modern sector in Third World countries, the training measures are at a low technical level and are more concerned with employment-oriented and extra-functional qualifications.

59 Cf. B. Tulodziecki, K. Breuer, A. Hauf Konzepte für das berufliche Lehren und Lernen, Naturwissenschaft, Technische Verfahren, Neue Technologien im Unterricht. Julius Klinkhardt/Handwerk u. Technik, Hamburg, 1984."The attempt to describe the phenomenon of technology cannot succeed if it aspires to cover all the dimensions of technology . . . The idea of process is present in the "Dessau" definition of technology to the extent that technology for him becomes accessible to experience "through formal design and processing" . . . As a result technical processes can be described as methods of deliberate action using technical (i.e. purposefully designed) means." P. 7 "Looking at individual studies it must be assumed that current decisions on the use of technological possibilities are already tied to issues of survival for humanity" P. 82 cf.: D. Meadows, et al.: Die Grenzen des Wachstums. Bericht des Club of Rome zur Lage der Menschheit. Reinbek, Rowohlt, 1973 "These considerations again clearly point to the need to develop criteria for evaluation in dealing with technical processes in vocational training and to establish capabilities so that vocational training in Nölker's sense does not strive through naïve rationality for the opportunity to improve circumstances ". p. 82 and p. 26.
Cf. H. Nölker, Technik und Bildung – Überlegungen zur Problematik und Begründung einer allgemeinen Didaktik der Technologie. In: B. Bonz/A. Lipsmeier (Hrsg.) 1982, pp. 18-31.
Cf. C. Lohmar-Kuhnle, note 56, and Lohmar-Kuhnle p. 82 "The primary problem for people in the informal sector is securing an economic basis for existence, . . . Anyone coming from the "informal sector" generally has a poor basis by virtue of their social origin and training in the competition for the relatively (and in some cases absolutely) declining number of jobs."

The aim is to enable the target groups and individuals to perform the jobs and tasks given to them correctly. These abilities can be measured against the following criteria:

(a) the assigned work must be performed to the usual technical standards;
(b) the assigned work must be performed with the necessary quality and precision (particularly in the case of industrial products or services);
(c) the assigned work must be done in a reasonable time and with the corresponding financial inputs (cost consciousness).

(C) The *potential for self-help*[60] and the ability to generate income through employment and self-employment of the target groups and individuals should be developed and improved. The following elements should be considered in developing the personality structure of the people (groups) in the informal and traditional sector:

The target groups and individuals must be enabled to utilise the criteria under (A) and (B) for their own interests and mobilise them for:

(a) improving the equality of opportunity of people in the informal sector;
(b) strengthening their skills and capabilities for understanding their own situation, processing information and developing their communication skills;
(c) strengthening their self-confidence and consciousness of their own value with the aim of articulating group and individual interests better and promoting these in society;
(d) improving their ability to plan funding to design economic development measures and opportunities for the group and individuals and to use the funding more efficiently;

---

60 For people in the informal sector the daily struggle is a struggle for survival. Measures in this sector must accordingly take into account the situation of the target groups or individuals and contribute to lasting change. As most people in this sector of the economy and life have major problems because of their disadvantage in drawing public attention to themselves and their situation, and mostly have no lobby to represent them in government or organised industry and politics, training measures must develop the self-help potential of those affected.

(e) developing awareness, consciousness and skills for implementing future-oriented planning and activities[61] and using these to improve the personal situation.

(D) The project concept, didactic approach and *curricula*[62] must be conceived *openly* and holistically for the situation of the group and individuals in the informal sector. The concept must have the capacity for flexible adaptation to the target group and integrate individuals and groups interested in training and advanced training or promoting employment and self-employment in the concept and didactic approach. The following aspects should accordingly be taken into account:

– target groups and individuals must be assisted through training and advanced training with the goal of promoting *income-creating employment* (including self-employment);
– the target groups and individuals must be assisted in their efforts *to save income;*
– the target groups and individuals must be assisted in their efforts *to secure their lives* as individuals and groups;
– the target groups and individuals must be assisted in their activities and efforts *to integrate* themselves in society and secure *their future position* in society (development and integration) and corresponding skills must be developed.

The following diagram shows the basic didactic structure of AGTTP/PGTTP and illustrates the relationship of these elements (A to D) to the open didactic approach with its orientation towards action and anthropocentricity and to the need to create open structures, objectives and conceptual approaches in project implementation.

---

61 This must particularly be taken into account with the Pakistan and Afghan target groups with their primarily Islamic orientation. The target groups with their Islamic orientation (lower classes) are inclined to invoke "the will of God" too often and are accordingly often hard to convince that God has also deliberately given people the ability to influence their own futures, in both the positive and negative sense (cf. sections 2.2 and 2.3).
62 Cf. W.H. Peterßen, Handbuch Unterrichtsplanung, Grundfragen, Modelle, Stufen und Dimensionen, Ehrenwirth, Munich, 1988, p. 138 "The designation ›open curriculum‹ is sometimes also applied to a curriculum which only states learning goals, ... i.e. *[if]* an effort is made to establish didactic constructive models other than on the basis of operationalised learning goals, then the terms ›open curricula‹ and ›heuristic learning goals‹ are generally used." The author supports this view and will return to with this problem in the course of the present work.

3.1.5.1: *The basic didactic structures in AGTTP/PGTTP*

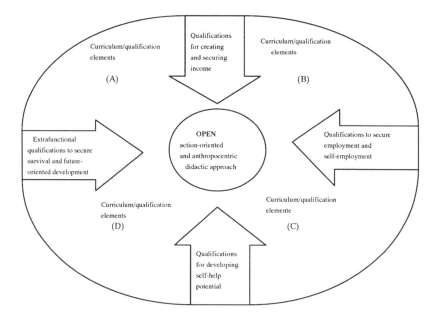

3.1.6 *Conceptual structure of Afghan/Pak-German TTP and SES Programme at TTC Peshawar*

The Afghan-/Pak-German TTP has evolved from a training and advanced training measure conceived with only isolated relevance to the needs of the Afghan refugees into an integrated promotional programme for developing vocational training in NFWP[63]. As already noted at a number of points, the special feature of this approach is its central orientation towards the informal and traditional sector in the province. Besides integrating the Afghan and Pakistan target groups into the project, it has also succeeded in extending the range of training and advanced training courses offered beyond the purely technical and craft sphere to cover the commercial and entrepreneurial content and qualification measures relevant to self-employment. In addition the project also offers graduates assistance after completing their training in the form of consultancy, financial assistance with the requirements

---

63 Cf. Gate, Questions, Answers, Information, No. 2/92 GTZ, Eschborn. Vocational Training for the informal Sector, G. Marienfeld and Jarik Lette.

for self-employment (i.e. founding small or micro businesses) and with locating jobs (employment). The established training and advanced training concept involves a didactic concept which is oriented towards the needs of the target group, is open and structured in stages and incorporates practical elements in the form of productive work, projects and production orders. The TTP/SES is concerned at every stage with giving participants maximum access to real conditions of work, employment and entrepreneurial conditions[64]. Participants in courses are systematically prepared for subsequent activity as small businessmen or employees. For this purpose preference was given to a graduated concept for training and advanced training linked with a targeted extension and entrepreneurship training concept. TTP/SES offers the following programmes:

3.1.6.1 *Basic training*

Basic training lasting c. 4 months with the following specialisations:
- *tailor* (e.g. sewing traditional garments, alterations and repairs etc);
- *construction worker* (e.g. training as a bricklayer – building traditional houses using ecological materials, modern types of construction etc.);
- *installation worker* (e.g. water and sewage mains, utility lines in housing etc);
- *welder* (e.g. oxy-gas and electric arc welding, etc.);
- *sheet metal worker.*

The curriculum for *basic training* courses (basic courses) is oriented towards production of typical products and services for bazaar businesses in urban and rural areas of NFWP and the typical qualification characteristics for the occupations in which training is offered. An effort is made to provide students in the courses with qualifications that enable them to use their certificates to find employment or self-employment in the "trade"[65] (or, better, *"specialisation"*) learned. In developing the course programmes for the specialisations listed an effort was made to ensure that the qualifications taught were primarily those which help promote the "action-oriented and anthropocentric" open didactic approach (see diagram on p. 118).

---

64 Experience in many TC projects has shown that conditions for learning and teaching are frequently light years removed from real working conditions and the graduates of public training facilities are no longer prepared to work under the conditions of bazaars and small (micro) businesses. They often prefer unemployment or a white collar job.
65 The term *"occupation"* seems overblown in the context discussed here, particularly since in Pakistan (as in most Asian countries) the European idea of an occupation is not relevant. The basic course discussed here deals only with skills and abilities.

However, at the time of preparation of the curricula and course programmes for the listed specialisations the designers of this approach to curriculum development (development committee) lacked a theory of learning based on the theoretical principles described above. As a review of the existing documentation shows, they were acting more on the basis of the needs of the informal sector for skills and knowledge and of perceptive development policy rules, namely assisting the very poorest in their struggle to survive (as refugees etc), with the aim of enabling this group to find or create income-generating employment at the end of the qualification programme.

Seen in these terms the only possible approach was to orient the curricula for the qualification measures towards the needs of the bazaar labour market as the employment environment of the informal sector and the products, services and specialisations urgently needed in the province and the huge refugee camps (some of which were settlements with over 100,000 inhabitants) (see diagram on p. 118: The basic didactic structure of AGTTP/PGTTP). Where possible the basic courses were linked with the "Practical Training Groups" (see p. 124). This has the advantage that graduates of the basic course can be introduced directly to the reality of working and commercial life and experience the temporal and qualitative conditions of work under realistic conditions, e.g. through construction orders handled by TTP/SES, thus preparing them at a very early stage for their subsequent situation in employment or self-employment.

Besides these technical and craft-related learning goals and content the curriculum for basic training also includes general subjects such as mathematics, English, sport and religion (organised by the Afghan refugees themselves). This also provides the training curriculum with the necessary background for the long-term goal of *recognition* by government agencies as an official educational course of study. So far, however, neither the ministry of labour nor the ministry of education has recognised the programmes run by TTP/SES. Even so, the real success of the measures (and graduates) speaks for itself: of over 16,000 graduates to date, some 65 % have found employment[66]. This is, in fact, striking proof of the success of the measures and a basis for further development policy, educational policy and conceptual considerations for integrating this programme into the official vocational training system in NFWP (see section 3.1.8 and diagram 3.1.9 on p. 147: Integration of vocational training measures).

---

66 Cf. project progress reports on TTP/SES, GTZ-Eschborn and U. Böhm and K. Ebeling, Berufsbildung und Kleingewerbeförderung in flüchtlingsbetroffenen Gebieten Pakistans sowie in Afghanistan, Eschborn, GTZ-1992.

3.1.6.1.1 Standard tools (tool chest) for graduates of the construction, metalworking and woodworking courses

Construction

(Photo: U. Ebeling)

Standard equipment for construction:
Spirit level, measuring tape, large steel right-angle, plumb line and various trowels, hammers and saws, hand broom and wire brush.
This equipment corresponds to the usual range owned by bazaar and building trade workers.

Woodworking

(Photo: TTP-Archive)

Standard equipment for woodworking:
Hammers, saws, vices (bazaar type, does not require workbench), hand drill, spatulas, spirit level, crowbars etc. . . .
This equipment is adequate for carrying out the woodworking orders which normally arise. It was oriented towards bazaar craftsmen.

121

3.1.6.1.2 *Standard tools (tool chest) for graduates of the metal-working, electrical and textile courses*

Electrical engineering

Standard equipment for electricians: Measuring equipment, metal tools, test lamps, pliers, hammers and other necessary small tools. No tools requiring external power sources.

(Photo: TTP-Archive)

Textiles

Standard equipment: Pakistan. manual sewing machine and bench with work table (flat table enabling working in squatting position).

(Photo: U. Ebeling)

3.1.6.1.3 *Carpenter making a (mortise and tenon) joint*

As already noted, a carpenter's equipment includes a traditional clamp, i.e. a type of vice which can be used without a workbench lying on the ground to take planks, wood blocks and rectangular material of all dimensions. This tool is found all over the sub-continent and is very skilfully used.

(Photo: U. Ebeling)

Standard equipment for metalworking

Standard equipment for metalworking: The equipment is also suitable for welders, plumbers and other metalworkers.
It comprises pliers, hammers, saws, measuring tools, pipe wrenches, spirit levels, hand drills and bits etc. Welding equipment and other special tools are provided as credits on application.

(Photo: TTP-Archive)

3.1.6.2 *Advanced Training*

Advanced Training consists of courses lasting c. 4 months, in part specially oriented towards the needs of the target groups and the labour market. This programme was also an attempt to support existing small businesses or employees in the informal and traditional sector. The aim is to support participants in acquiring the various technical and also entrepreneurial qualifications. The specialisations cover the entire technical spectrum at TTC-Peshawar, as this also enables the programmes of the training and advanced training dealing with the formal/ modern sector to be included in the service available. The specialisations involved are:

woodworking (cf. 3.1.6.1);
building trades (cf. 3.1.6.2);
metalworking (production, e.g. turning, milling etc);
automotive engineering (repair and maintenance);
electrical engineering (house, installation and industrial electrician etc);
radio/TV engineering (repair);
air conditioning, heating and refrigeration engineering (repairing air conditioning and heating installations);
entrepreneurial training (CEFE[67];)

3.1.6.3 *Practical Training Groups*

Practical Training Groups (training on building sites or production department of TTP), lasting c. 4 months. These "Practical Training Groups" consist of "Basic Training" graduates carrying out production and construction orders from TTP/SES under professional supervision and management.

These orders are carried out by TTP/SES management as subcontractors to ensure the practical relevance of the training and (in part) to refinance the current operation of the TTP/SES programme. The number of training places and capacity of the SES programme accordingly depend on the nature of orders and order book. Training places in this

---

[67] CEFE = Competency-based Economies through Formation of Entrepreneurs; cf. Brainstorm, CEFE-NEWS LETTER, 1/93, Eschborn-GTZ Target Groups in a Difficult Sociocultural Environments, Entrepreneurship Development in Pakistan`s North West Frontier Province (N.W.F.P.), by Guthier.
CEFE is a programme developed by GTZ for developing entrepreneurial skills of potential small businessmen.

programme are very much in demand among graduates of the TTP/ SES programme, as participants also share in the profit to some extent, since it is possible in some cases to pay significantly higher trainee wages. When demand is too great, selection is by lot[68]. The introduction of these "Practical Training Groups" marked the implementation in highly pragmatic form of the idea of productive training, integrating theory and practice, the world of work and an approximation to the production school[69], all in a specific manner adapted to the local environment.

---

68 Cf. U. Böhm and U. Ebeling, GTZ study "Berufsbildung und Kleingewerbeförderung in flüchtlingsbetroffenen Gebieten Pakistans sowie in Afghanistan", Eschborn (Germany), 1992.
69 Cf. H. Beyer, GTZ-Sektortagung der GTZ-Berufsbildung in Pakistan 1991, Eschborn 1991 and W.-D. Greinert, GTZ-Bericht zur Sektortagung und konzeptionelle Schlußfolgerungen, Pakistan 1991, Eschborn 1991.

3.1.6.3.1 Practical Training Groups

Hospital building site – Masons at work and training on the job

Building site: Construction by TTP/SES of a hospital with 200 beds, including administration and staff accommodation under a commission from Caritas-Deutschland-Peshawar.

(Photo: U. Ebeling)

Hospital building site – Overview of the TTP/SES building site

Building site: (For hospital see above) The commission includes development work, i.e. connection to mains water and sewerage, and interior construction, e.g. laying water pipes, installing sanitary facilities and interior and exterior painting, where required.

(Photo: U. Ebeling)

3.1.6.3.2 Practical Training Groups

Housing – Carpenters installing windows

Housing built by TTP/SES using appropriate building techniques, e.g. domed roofs = wood-saving roof design and loam construction = avoiding cost-intensive, expensive concrete construction.

(Photo: TTP/SES)

Warehouses

Warehouses built by TTP/SES for UNHCR in the refugee camps (c. 200) with pre-fabricated roofs, developed by an Australian organisation and manufactured by TTP/SES.

(Photo: TTP/SES)

3.1.6.3.3 Practical training groups

Plumbers working and training on the job

Master plumber and course participants (TTP/SES) working on the building site. This picture shows the piping for the water system and the water tank on the roof. The water tank is either on the roof or outside on a raised location to make up for the lack of water pressure for the domestic supply. In this example the water pipes were actually laid in a shaft designed for the purpose.

(Photo: U. Ebeling)

Plumbers working and training on the job

Master plumber and course participants (TTP/SES) preparing the water pipes to be laid in the building. There are no detailed construction drawings showing the supply system in the building. The supervisors and master craftsmen accordingly have to design the system on the site, improvise and ensure proper installation.

(Photo: U. Ebeling)

3.1.6.4 *Entrepreneur Training & Supervised Workshops*

Entrepreneur Training & Supervised Workshops

Supervised Workshops: these workshops are made available to graduates of the training measures listed under 3.1.6.1 to 3.1.6.6 for a limited period. They have been specifically set up for those graduates who show the potential to be independent entrepreneurs. The workshops were equipped with essential machines, fittings and tools (see the photos on pp. 121-123). Besides this basic equipment TTP/SES also provides the essential materials to start up the business. The *Supervised Workshops* are generally located in the suburbs of Peshawar or the small but commercially active settlements and villages, or even in the NFWP refugee camps (see map of Supervised Workshops, p. 151). The new entrepreneurs lease these workshops for a small fee for up to 8 months, and during this period they have to build up a stable foundation for their own small business.

TTP/SES consultancy service

The TTP/SES assists these new entrepreneurs with a specially-created consultancy service in the areas:
1. business formation
2. cost accounting, costing
3. technical questions on contract performance
4. customer service and marketing

Besides this consultancy the TTP/SES offers entrepreneurs the opportunity to purchase tools, materials and possibly machines through small credits. To date the programme has included the following specialisations:
    woodworking (carpentry);
    metalworking (welding, construction fittings and installation);
    textile processing (male and female tailoring);
    construction tradesman (mason, construction carpenter etc.).

The TTP/SES must be credited as being very successful in this area, and the number of applicants for *Supervised Workshops* far exceeds the available capacity of the programme.

Entrepreneur training

The TTP/SES offers interested graduates of the measures described in 3.1.6.1 to 3.1.6.6 special advanced training programmes for new business formation and business management. Specifically, the course elements and content are:

> questions of business formation;
> dealing with credit institutes and banks;
> how to register as self-employed or a business;
> business cost accounting and costing;
> order processing and customer service;
> product or service selection;
> technical questions on designing workshops and workplaces and equipping small (micro) businesses;
> providing training places for TTP/SES apprentices;
> personnel issues (contracting employees);
> marketing.

The elements listed here are not offered as distinct course elements or part of the specialisations by TTP/SES, but are part of the TTP/SES training consultancy service. If the project is expanded to cover even larger target groups in the entire province, the TTP/SES will quickly reach the limits of its capability, since a consultancy and training concept of this kind customised for individual needs and problems cannot be simply expanded at will. The TTP/SES will accordingly be faced by the question how far these functions could be taken over by existing trade associations or chambers. There is also the question of the need to bring together former TTP/SES graduates and entrepreneurs in corresponding associations or trade associations which could then in the long term act as multipliers or even sponsors for establishing consultancy and training measures for small (micro) business people. In any case, there is nothing in Pakistan law to prohibit such autonomous commercial organisations, given that medium-sized and large companies in the formal sector are already organised and have their lobbies to represent their interests in politics, so that these ideas or existing models could also serve as an approach for improved organisation and integration of the informal and traditional sector in the economy.

3.1.6.4.1 Supervised Workshops

Supervised Workshops for Wood and metal working for young entrepreneurs from the TTP/SES programme. The workshops shown here are located in a small suburb of Peshawar.

(Photo: Diehl)

Tailor's workshop: Supervised Workshop for a total of 6 small business persons from the SES-Programme. The workshop is located in a small suburb of Peshawar.

(Photo: Diehl)

131

3.1.6.4.2 Former TTP/SES graduates as small business people in Peshawar

Plumber

A former graduate of the TTC/SES programme for plumbers now has his own small business and works with four employed workers (plumbers).
The picture shows the typical equipment of a plumber. He received the tools and a loan which he refunded in the meanwhile.

(Photo:Diehl)

Tailor

A former graduate in front of his tailor-shop in Peshawar. He works with up to five tailors (on daily wages) which he had trained especially for his manufacture. Typical products of his workshop are traditional men's suits and women's dresses as well as head-gear. He also was able to refund the loan received.

(Photo: Diehl)

3.1.6.4.3 *Former TTP/SES graduates as small business people in Peshawar*

Welders

Welder and helper (former graduate of the TTP/SES) making cast-iron fence components. This is for an order, and the welder claims to have designed the moulds himself. He employs 2 other welders and 3 helpers. The loan and basic tools and equipment are supplied by TTP/SES. He has already paid back the loan.

(Photo:Diehl)

Products/Orders

The photo shows typical contracting for private developers, although designing fence, doors and windows generally also form part of his responsibilities. He does not work to drawings but fits or installs elements directly into the existing building on site. The entrepreneur shown here has developed a range of standard bending tools and jigs which he uses as required.

(Photo: Diehl)

3.1.6.5 *Loan Scheme*

Loan Scheme: this programme gives graduates of the training and support measures listed under 3.1.6.1 to 3.1.6.6 access to a loan for new business formation. These are smaller loans which the borrowers can repay in a reasonable period. They are in very heavy demand among graduates, as they are interest-free. According to those responsible for the project, the repayment rate among borrowers is very high, reportedly 98%. In the author's view this percentage may be overstated, since the tools, equipment and materials supplied must also be counted as loans (this applies particularly to the Supervised Workshops concept). There has, however, been no adequate reporting on this yet, or the current M + E concept[70] rules out detailed reporting on these areas.

3.1.6.6 *Apprenticeship Training*

Apprenticeship Training is another variant of the *Basic Training* described under (a). Here, self-employed master craftsmen from the informal and traditional sector are contracted at a low rate to train the contracted apprentices under contract to and in accordance with the instructions of the TTP/SES. The TTP/SES currently has c. 44 such master craftsmen (businesses) chosen throughout the province (see map on p. 152) who train local apprentices under the TTP/SES concept. No written and formal curriculum is used as many instructors are very competent at their trade but at the same time only partially literate, i.e. they are not able to follow complicated written instructions or teaching and learning regulations. The TTP/SES has accordingly developed a series of products (projects) which contain the key elements, curricular content and learning goals of the basic training[71]. This brings about a situation where training is guided by the manufacture of selected products rather than the complicated written instructions in conventional curricula. These products generally also correspond to the products and services offered by small craft businesses, so that they can be easily marketed by the training facility. The training facilities are also regularly visited by trained TTP/SES training advisers and supported in implementing the training measures. This also easily ensures monitoring and evaluation (M & E) of the funded train-

---

70 M + E = Monitoring and evaluation of the loan scheme and project overall.
71 Cf. U. Böhm and U. Ebeling, Projektprüfung und Prüfung des Vorschlages zur Etablierung einer wissenschaftlichen Begleitung des Vorhabens: TTP am TTC-Peshawar, Pakistan, GTZ 1992.

ing measures, since the TTP/SES also naturally has to account for the project funds used and other material and personnel inputs.

The curriculum integrated into manufacturing the training products (projects) corresponds to the curriculum for the full-time basic training described in section 3.1.6.1. The final examinations and certification are generally done by the instructors under the regulations of the TTP/SES and officially confirmed by TTP/SES. After completing his apprenticeship the trainee gives his instructor the traditional turban (analogous to the traditional ceremony releasing the apprentice from his indentures) and acquires a similar status to a trainee completing the long traditional apprenticeship. The turban is, as it were, the payment for his apprenticeship, and in return the apprentice is recognised by the master craftsmen as a fully-fledged journeyman. The approach established here is in line with the "ostad hargird system", the traditional apprenticeship system in Pakistan[72].

3.1.6.6.1 *Need for labour and apprenticeship training, using the example of the "Kurram Agency" and the "Dera Ismael Khan District" in the NFWP*

Under a commission from TTP/SES the Lette Consultancy[73] carried out a study in 1990 to determine the demand for labour in the traditional sector and review possibilities for expanding and introducing the "traditional apprenticeship training" described in 3.1.6.6. The study concentrated on two important rural areas in the NFWP and included four large bazaars in the "*Kurram Agency*" and "*Dera Ismael Khan*". There are around 385,000 Pakistan inhabitants (status 89/90) and c. 50,000 Afghan refugees in the "Kurram Agency". The "Agency" is a self-administered tribal area, a so-called "tribal agency"[74]. "Dera Ismael Khan" (D.I. Khan) on the other hand is one of the so-called "Settled Areas" in the NFWP, which although including tribal areas covering large parts come under the administration of the NFWP and the central government in Islamabad. The area studied borders the "*tribal agency*" of South and North Warziristan, Kohat-District and the Province of Punjab[75]. The D.I. Khan area has around 635,490 Pakistan inhabitants (status 89/90) and c. 90,000 Afghan refugees who have

---

72 Cf. Skill Generation and Entrepreneurship Development under "Ostad-Shargird-System" in Pakistan, M.A. Chaudhary, P. Azim, A.A. Burki, Islamabad 1989.
73 Cf. Jarik Lette and Ir.D. Frankefort, Survey on workshops in N.W.F.P., GTZ-Eschborn and Pakistan/N.W.F.P.-Peshawar, 1990, pp. 5 et seq.
74 Cf. Pakistan: The Social Sciences Perspective, Ed. by Akbar S. Ahmed, Oxford University Press, Karachi, 1990.
75 Cf. note 70, pp. 38 et seq.

settled here and mostly (still)live in refugee camps. The study concentrates on four large bazaars in the settlements *"Parachinar, Sadd, Shech Yousaf and Tank"*. The choice of the bazaars is logical in the author's view, since in rural areas it is the bazaars which almost exclusively provide an overview of the structure of the craft and trade economy and the technological status of small business. In addition the retail and trading houses can be used as indicators of the region's economic development capability and its supraregional importance and networking with other markets. The bazaars accordingly provide a mirror of the economic situation of the region.

In the study a total of 435 workshops and small business were visited. The owners and some employees were surveyed. The following section 3.1.6.6.2/Overview I shows in detail the businesses and workshops visited, broken down by specialisation, number and location.

A closer review of the results for the businesses visited and the overview of the businesses surveyed gives an interesting picture of the economic structure of the bazaars. The specialisations (workshops) in the bazaars also give an impression of the status of technological and industrial development of the regions studied.

Starting with the observation that the economic regions cited here have a purely agrarian structure, i.e. the major land-owning still very widespread in Pakistan with its families of agricultural families and subsistence farming alongside small farms and animal husbandry (see also the geographical sections of this work), the employment and economic potential of the bazaars also has to be estimated. The bazaars accordingly specialise primarily in the sale or manufacture of products, goods and services which serve the needs of this strongly peasant-oriented agricultural structure. To date there is a lack of innovative structural development programmes in the province and specifically in the region designed to modernise the economy and industry, and this also applies particularly to the development and need for suitably qualified labour and the structure of the labour market.

A major innovative and structure-changing role is accordingly limited to the transport, clothing and agricultural sectors, as shown very clearly in the following table (Overview II, see p. 138).

3.1.6.6.2 Overview I: *Specialisation, location and number of bazaar businesses*[76]

Location Specialisation	Parachinar	Sadda	Shech Yousaf	Tank	Total
1.0 Blacksmith		6	6	22	34
2.0 Bicycle Repair			6	8	14
3.0 Car body repair		8	1		9
4.0 Car mechanics	21	18	10	1	50
5.0 Car service		2	17		19
6.0 Carpenter	22	4	6	21	53
7.0 Charpoy maker	3	2	2	2	9
8.0 Cloth dying				1	1
9.0 Coppler			3	29	32
10.0 Dessert cooler rep.				4	4
11.0 Electrician	1	2	7	8	18
12.0 Embroidery	3				3
13.0 Fan repair				1	1
14.0 Jewelry				10	10
15.0 Lathe		5	2		7
16.0 Mattress making				10	10
17.0 Motor cycle rep.			2		2
18.0 Pipe fitter			1		1
19.0 Sewing machine rep.				2	2
20.0 Tailor	29	4	9	62	104
21.0 Tinsmith	3			7	10
22.0 Tool repair			1		1
23.0 Tractor repair	2	7			9
24.0 Tire repair	6	6	14	2	28
25.0 Upholstery			1		1
26.0 Welding			3		3
Total	**90**	**64**	**91**	**190**	**435**

---

76 Op. cit. p. 42.

Overview II[77]

Transport			
No.	Description	Number	
2.0	Bicycle Repair	14	
3.0	Car body repair	9	
4.0	Car mechanics	50	
5.0	Car service	19	
11.0	Electrician	18	
17.0	Motor cycle repair	2	
23.0	Tractor repair	9	
24.0	Tire repair	28	
25.0	Upholstery	1	
26.0	Welding	3	
	Total	**153**	

Clothing and construction			
No.	Description	Number	
6.0	Carpenter	53	
7.0	Charpoy maker	9	
11.0	Electrician	11	
13.0	Fan repair	1	
16.0	Mattress making	10	
18.0	Pipe Fitter	1	
19.0	Sewing machine rep.	2	
20.0	Tailor	62	
	Total	**149**	

77 Cf. overview I (p. 137) according to Lette-Consultant, see note 73.

In all these areas cover 302 out of 435 bazaar businesses (c. 69 %). Transport accounts for c. 33% of all businesses. This indicates that these sectors should play an important role in economic, labour and development policy in creating additional jobs and training places and modernisation of rural areas. However, the TTP/SES has so far restricted itself to textile and construction trades in its *"Apprenticeship Training Programme"*[78] in the rural areas of the NFWP, such as

   plumber/pipe-fitter
   mason
   carpenter
   tailor.

The trades listed in Overview II in the transport sector have not so far been tackled by the TTP/SES despite the demand[79].
The situation described here is confirmed again by the results of the expert team Lette and Frankefort. The team accordingly recommends expanding TTP/SES "Apprenticeship Training" to cover the following nine vocational groups:

(A) *Specialisations*[80]
   Blacksmith; car body repair; car mechanics; carpenter; lathe; sewing machine repair; tailor; tractor repair; tyre repair.

---

78 Cf. Vocational Training for the Informal Sector, by G. Marienfeld and J. Lette, in Gate: questions, answers, information, No. 2/92, GTZ-Eschborn.
79 Cf. Study: U. Böhm and U. Ebeling, see note 66.
80 Cf. note 70, pp. 29 et seq.

(B) *Absorption capacity of businesses in Dera Ismael Khan and Kurram Agency*[81]

No.	specialisation	Parachinar	Sadda	S. Yousaf	Tank	Total
1.0	Blacksmith		6	6	22	34
3.0	Car body repair		8	1		9
4.0	Car mechanics	21	18	10	1	50
6.0	Carpenter	22	4	6	21	53
15.0	Lathe		5	2		7
19.0	Sewing machine repair				2	2
20.0	Tailor	29	4	9	62	104
23.0	Tractor repair	2	7			9
24.0	Tyre repair	6	6	14	2	28
	Total	80	58	48	110	296

As the table shows, the above nine specialisations could absorb c. 296 apprentices. An expanded study showed that a further c. 1,520 apprentices could be placed in the bazaars of Kohat and Swat in the same 9 vocational groups[82].

(C) *Requirements for trainees, training pay*

The *average age* of apprentices in rural areas varies according to specialisation from 9-14 on starting their apprenticeship. Training can last from a minimum of one year to 10 years. Studies have shown that the average training period in the bazaars is c. 4 years[83]. The shortest apprenticeships (c. 1 year) are for trades like
    hairdresser
    tailor
    mason
    tanner, etc.

---

81 Op. cit. pp. 30 et seq.
82 Op. cit. pp. 30 et seq.
83 Cf. Skill Generation and Entrepreneurship Development under "Ostad-SHAGIRD-System" in Pakistan, M.A. Chaudhary, P. AZIM, A.A. BURKI, Ed. National Manpower Commission, Goverment of Pakistan Islamabad, 1989, pp. 54 fet seq.

Generally apprentices have only *very little or no formal education.* although many (c. 50%) of the master craftsmen (surveyed by the author) feel there is a need for a limited (functional) prior education. Frequently arithmetic and reading plus good language (communicative) skills are seen as desirable in apprentices. *Apprenticeship agreements* are not signed, but oral agreements have a general binding contractual status in the region.

(D) *Willingness of bazaar businesses and master craftsmen to participate in traditional apprentice training*

As the studies by Lette/Frankefort[84], Chaudhary/Azim/Burki[85] and the author[86] have shown, the bazaar businesses and master craftsmen are willing under certain conditions to participate in rural and traditional apprenticeship training. These conditions can be summarised as follows:

- the bazaar businesses must perceive some financial benefit from apprenticeship training, and a specific benefit is seen in the labour of the apprentices;
- the apprentices should be prepared to submit to the organisation and discipline of the businesses;
- the apprentices must use tools, machines and material carefully and pay for wanton damage;
- apprentices must be ready to work the expected hours (10-12 hours a day);
- the government should if possible *not* intervene in the training activities of the businesses and support the businesses financially (per apprentice);
- business owners would prefer not to be obliged to hire apprentices after they finish their apprenticeship;
- the master craftsmen and business owners would like technical support with training measures: they are prepared to release apprentices for additional theoretical training;
- business owners see problems with paying a regular wage to apprentices and entering into a training contract, which has not been customary.

---

84 See note 70, pp. 24 et seq.
85 See note 77, pp. 58 et seq.
86 The author studied some 30 businesses in the Peshawar region of former graduates of the TTP/SES and gained the impression that the businessmen surveyed entirely approved of the apprentice training, provided that the conditions cited under (D) are met.

These conditions, which have been frequently repeated by business owners and master craftsmen, show that although there is a high degree of readiness in principle to participate in apprenticeship training, there are considerable reservations about the following problem areas:

(a) not being able to live up to apprentice expectations;
(b) being overwhelmed by government influence and strict regulations;
(c) suffering financial loss from apprenticeship training or not being certain of adequate benefit (labour);
(d) inadequate theoretical and technical qualification of the businesses offering training;
(e) and a possible obligation on the business to hire apprentices after they complete their apprenticeship.

In developing apprenticeship training based on traditional conditions, this potential for conflict must be taken into account and the businesses involved accordingly.

3.1.6.7 *Admission requirements*

Admission requirements for participants in the training and advanced training measures described in 3.1.6.1 to 3.1.6.6 and special programmes under the TTP/SES programme are left entirely *open*. The TTP/SES does not require any minimum formal educational qualifications for participating in training and advanced training measures. Although this causes difficulties in running the vocational training measures, as trainers are faced with extremely heterogeneous groups, it is in the author's view a correct and logical step if the aim is to assist the informal and traditional sector effectively (cf. statistics on literacy, see table II on p. 97). If higher educational requirements are needed for training measures and specialisations, the existing formal educational and vocational training courses should be used, as this sector already has the necessary institutions, staff, funding and infrastructure. It is accordingly necessary even in developing concepts for training and advanced training measures in the informal and traditional sector to reflect the networking with the official and formal educational and vocational training system, i.e. system-building elements and activities must be incorporated in the project concept at an early stage. The following diagram recapitulates the relationships between the TTP/SES elements described in 3.1.6.1 to 3.1.6.6 and shows the links with the labour market.

3.1.7 Levels and interaction of the elements/programme components of the TTP/SES-Programme

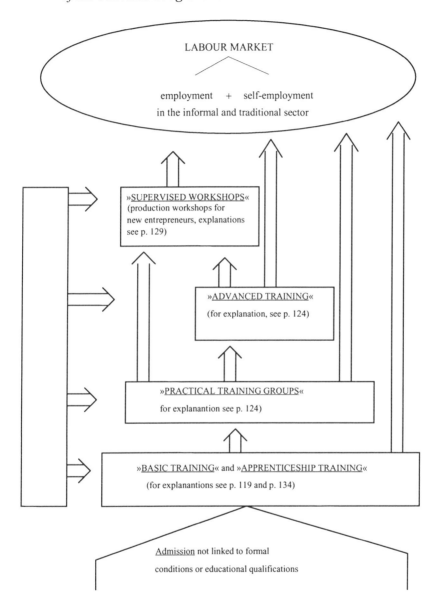

3.1.8 Integration of vocational training measures for the informal sector into the NWFP vocational training system

To achieve the project goal and ensure sustainability of the project and the didactic approach described here, it is necessary to design such a project as an integrated vocational training measure. This means it is necessary to integrate vocational training measures in the informal sector which aim at improving employability in the informal and traditional sector into the vocational training system. Diagram 3.1.9 (p. 147) shows again how the TTP/SES programme could be integrated into the system in the NWFP. To illustrate the structure of and relationships between the individual component and the systematic effect of the project as a whole on the existing vocational training system, three levels of intervention or cooperation were selected for presenting the German consultancy and project approach:
(a) the political and strategic level
(b) the functional and management level
(c) the operational and didactic level
(d) labour market

The activities with their objectives and effects operate between the three levels (a-c), which should not be seen as a rigid hierarchical structure of the training system. They could accordingly also be interpreted as levels of impact of the vocational training sector, as the formulated goals, results and activities in their hierarchical sequence are certainly intended to have an impact at all levels of intervention and cooperation. The partners generally expect cooperation in this sector to lead to a significant improvement in the employability of graduates of the vocational training sector. It accordingly appears necessary (see p. 147) to introduce another (fourth) level which represents the labour market. This is the level where the success of the project appears together with the positive and negative effects of the subsystems of the three levels of intervention and cooperation listed above.

Diagram 3.1.10 recapitulates the key elements of the Afghan-PAK-GERMAN TTP/SES in their material links with the formal vocational training system (TTC-Peshawar). Essentially, the presentation is based on three important desired areas for impact for the integrated vocational training project:
(a) improving the training available and opportunities for employment in the informal and traditional sector;
(b) improving the training available at the Technical Training Center (TTC) for the modern sector and the opportunities for employment of TTC graduates;

(c) developing the vocational training system in NWFP and disseminating the necessary approaches for improving the vocational training available.

Diagram 3.1.10 (p. 148) again shows clearly the central position of the Technical Training Center Peshawar, as in the author's view[87] implementing the project without linking it to an existing institutional and staffing infrastructure would have been significantly more difficult. It is also doubtful whether the project could have been implemented with its present success or at all without TTC Peshawar in its present form. The general question accordingly arises whether in designing such projects care should not be taken as a matter of principle to ensure that such or similar institutions form the basis for the development of small business technical promotion projects for the informal sector. Use could also be made here of specifically German historical experience[88] with the importance of the craft and trade schools of the 19th and early 20th centuries. In the context of the German history of development and industrialisation it was these institutions which took on an important progressive role in technological innovation, consultancy to small craft businesses, technology transfer (to industry and the craft trades) and training skilled labour and master craftsmen for small businesses and industry[89].

---

[87] Here the author differs very clearly from the reporting experts Böhm/Ebeling (see note 71), who are completely wrong in their estimate of the importance of the labour ministry and TTC-Peshawar for the success of the measure. This project could in the author's view never have been implemented without the agreement of the Pakistan government and the availability of the TTC-Peshawar with its infrastructure.

[88] Cf. Greinert, W.-D., Das "deutsche System" der Berufsausbildung, ed. GTZ, Studien zur Vergleichenden Berufspädagogik. Nomos Verlag, Baden-Baden pp. 80 et seq, 1993.

[89] Cf. Greinert, W.-D., et al., Das Produktionschulprinzip und Berufsbildungshilfe, ed. GTZ, Studien zur Vergleichenden Berufspädagogik. Nomos Verlag, Baden-Baden, 1993, pp. 89 et seq.

3.1.11 *Geographical overview of the individual components of the TTP/SES programme in the North-West-Frontier Province (NWFP)*

1. Basic Training und Advanced Training Centers (VTC)
    − Status Sept. 1992 −

2. PAK-GERMAN Apprenticeship Training Programme (ATS)
    − Status Sept. 1992 −

3. TTP/SES Supervised Workshops (SW) & Entrepreneur Training
    − Status Sept. 1992 −

4. Not all cross-border activities of the Afghan-German TTP/SES were taken into account in the study, as it was not possible to visit the field offices in Afghanistan for security reasons and lack of official approval. No attempt is therefore made to present these project components.

5. The graphic/geographical overviews also provide information on specific training facilities for Afghan and Pakistan women. These measures and facilities are not covered here in detail as the training programmes are generally restricted to the home environment and are not automatically or deliberately aimed at income-generating activities. The author also had great difficulty in his research activities in coming into contact with the women in question as a result of the *conditions and rules of purdah*[90]. Even so it can be said that the TTP/SES trains c. 2-300 women a year in tailoring.

---

90 *Purda* = "Compliance with the Burdah requirements (separation of the sexes) reflects a complex social phenomenon and also manifests itself in the different groups in Pakistani society. Purdah ranges from the physical seclusion of women in their four walls (home) to veiling the woman or her downcast eyes when she encounters men." In the N.W.F.P. and specifically among the Afghan refugees with their rural orientation, there is strict separation of sexes, cf. H.G. Klein, R. Nestvogel, Frauen in Pakistan, Rahmenbedingungen und berufliche Qualifizierung von Frauen in der Provinz Punjab, Eschborn, 1984.

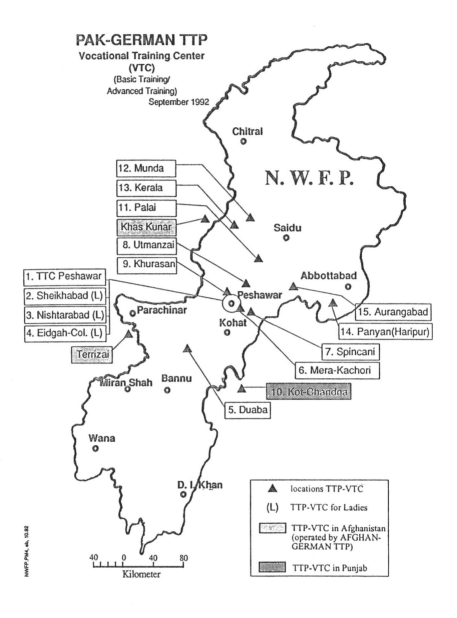

Source: Böhm/Ebeling, GTZ, Eschborn 1992

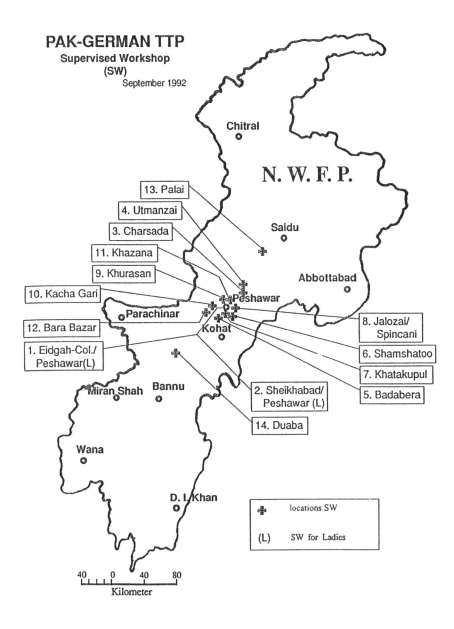

Source: Böhm/Ebeling, GTZ, Eschborn 1992

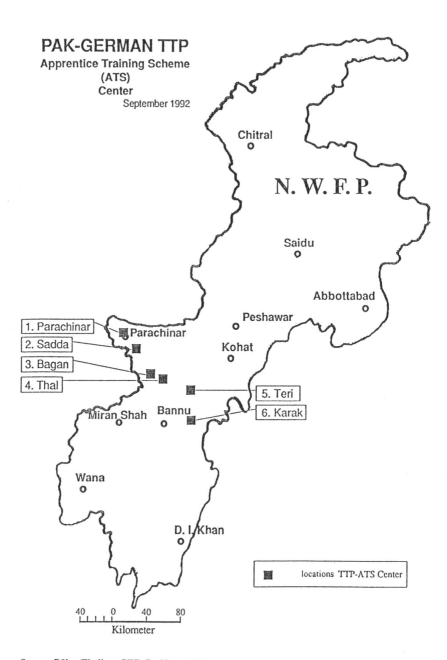

Source: Böhm/Ebeling, GTZ, Eschborn 1992

3.1.12 Analysis of the survey of former graduates and small (micro) businessmen from the TTP/SES programme

The TTP/SES have been training Pakistani and Afghan participants in the cited components since 1982. During this time over 16,000 Afghans and Pakistanis have received training and advanced training through these programme elements. To date no systematic, empirical and statistically based study has been carried out by the project on the placement of graduates. Although such a study would have been useful for the present work, it would require the formation of meaningful samples for past graduates, e.g. using the following criteria:

Dates of graduation, length of independent status;
Employment or self-employment;
Nature of employment (production, services etc);
Nature of gainful activity and number of employees;
Geographical aspects of the economic activities (rural or urban area);
Level of income and structure of the markets, nature of orders;
Socio-cultural aspects, i.e. role of the former graduates in their environment etc;
Conclusions on the validity of the results for the target groups listed in section 2.4

However, as such a tracer study requires systematic collection over a period of years and this has never been done at the TTP/SES, the study could not be done without very heavy investment of time and money[91]. Such an approach is too expensive and hence impossible for the reasons already cited of lack of funding and the time constraints for the present work. Due to the years of collaboration with the project team and the Pakistani/Afghan partners, who have shared and continue to share views openly with the author in many discussions and planning workshops, a pragmatic approach was preferred for surveying former TTP/SES students in the greater Peshawar area. With the help of the TTP/SES 30 small entrepreneurs with an average of 3-5 employees, graduates of the TTP/SES programme, were identified in the specializations:

mason; plumber; tailor; carpenter; welder and fitter.

---

[91] In his capacity as adviser for the BMZ and the responsible GTZ regional division the author recommended a scientific project-accompanying long-term evaluation lasting two years for the TTP/SES. This project is being implemented by the University of Bremen. The first results are expected (by the author) at end of 1994, so that they cannot be incorporated here.

The specialisations listed here match the current programme offered by TTP/SES under short courses for training and advanced training for target groups in the informal and traditional sector. The rural "apprenticeship training programme" is included here, and this programme as shown by the study in 3.1.6.6.1 is particularly suitable for extension to other specialisations. However, as the survey covered former TTP/SES course participants, these new specialisations were not taken into account.

The questionnaires were developed and designed to collect information on the following areas:

Information on entrepreneurs, such as:
Participation in the TTP/SES programme, personal data (on prior educational qualifications etc); national and social origins, financial situation (current loans from banks, family members or TTP/SES);

Information on businesses, such as:
Nature of business, nature of products or services, number of employees and proprietors, buildings, machines, tools, capital;

Situation of the entrepreneur, links with market, such as:
Businesses and link with markets and customers (nature of orders, customers and social structure of environment);

Requirement profile of entrepreneur, such as:
Production knowledge and qualifications; personnel management, management, marketing and customer services; social skills, pricing and costing knowledge and other important entrepreneurial qualifications and competences, social role of the entrepreneur;

Requirement profile of business employees, such as:
Practical and theoretical abilities, skills and knowledge, educational skills (reading, writing, arithmetic), social competences and specific competences, communication skills and development potential;

Selection and hiring criteria for business employees, such as:
Recruiting procedures; vocational and general educational requirements; social and religious links or obstacles; conclusion of contracts, rights and duties of employees in the informal and traditional sector, nature of work and payment;

Assessment of commercial and infrastructural situation of the business, such as:
Based on analysis of the statements of the entrepreneur and the employees and appraisal of the means of production, the quality and

nature of orders and the business's order book (i.e. plausibility check on the statements of respondents);

Assessment of the relevance of the courses and other programmes and funding contributions offered by the TTP/SES, such as:

Basic courses, courses for advanced students, entrepreneurial training, loans (tools and financial credits), consultancy and follow-up measures under the TTP/SES programme;

Assessment of the transferability of the TTP/SES approach and model nature of the project.

3.1.12.1 Analysis of the information and requirement profiles of the entrepreneurs and employees surveyed and links to local and regional markets

The analysis of the survey and accompanying observation[92] can be summarised as follows using the criteria listed above. First, it should be emphasised again that all the businesses and entrepreneurs covered by the study had either received consultancy or loans from the TTP/SES or the business founders and owners had originally attended one of the TTP/SES programme or course elements described in 3.1.6.1 to 3.1.6.6. Many of the respondents had also taken advantage of the loans offered by the TTP/SES. It should also be considered that the physical proximity to the TTC-Peshawar and hence the TTP/SES office also made possible a degree of unsystematic backstopping, depending on the demand from small (micro) businessmen. As already noted, the project has failed in this respect, in the author's opinion, as systematic backstopping and tracer studies would undoubtedly have provided the TTP/SES with valuable information on the success or need for correc-

---

92 Cf. Martin Fuchs and E. Berg, Phänomenologie der Differenz, in: Kultur, soziale Praxis, Text. Suhrkamp, Frankfurt, 1993, pp. 24 et seq.
"Participant observation" is a formula for an approach which, before it acquired significance in other contexts, was initially characteristic of modern cultural anthropology, which at the time was emerging as an independent discipline."
(a) The author is aware of the inadequate methodological derivation in the context of this study. There is, however, an advantage in using this term (by analogy with cultural anthropology as referred to earlier) as the Monitoring and Evaluation (M+E) practised in the projects is methodologically based on a concept of "participant observation".
It accordingly seems legitimate to introduce and use the term "participant observation" in describing the methodological approach described here.
(b) Besides the context described in (a) there is generally a need in contact with the target group to organise surveys using trained interviewers. The linguistic and cultural barriers basically leave no option. For this reason the person carrying out the study is relegated to a more or less passive role which reduces to participant observation. It is accordingly helpful if he prepares directly for this role and organises the survey accordingly through local interviewers.

tion to the measures or training programme. A further major deficiency in the concept for the programme described here is the failure to assist the small (micro) businessmen in the informal sector to establish self-help organisations (guilds, chambers, associations etc) to represent business owners on social, economic and political issues. In any event, consideration of these important aspects would, if accompanied by corresponding monitoring of impact and control of the programme, have given the target groups (i.e. graduates) a greater right of consultation and cooperation in designing and implementing measures[93].

The small (micro) businesses surveyed fall exclusively in the category of new businesses in the informal sector and are generally not registered as commercial establishments or recorded for tax purposes by the competent government agencies. Asked how they deal with the tax authorities, entrepreneurs replied that they satisfy the government tax officials through annual one-off payments or special services. This also avoids burdensome applications and research and the need for accurate book keeping. The government does lose important sources of tax revenue here, which are frequently tapped by corrupt officials. These are also ultimately the main reason for the tax avoidance or evasion strategy displayed here, as they are mostly not interested in legalising the relationships, which would only seal off their own additional sources of income.

Most businesses do not have suitable production facilities, good tools and suitable machines or storage facilities. The entrepreneurs solve this problem by moving production to the building sites, i.e. producing on site. If this is not possible for logistical or scheduling reasons, they generally set up their production facilities on vacant (public or private) lots, pavements, public areas or roadsides without official permission. In some cases they have succeeded in leasing premises or spaces to set up their production facilities in the existing bazaars. They all basically report enormous problems with the high cost of premises, workshops or workplaces. In addition there are high financial costs of connection to the urban electricity supply. If machinery is used most processing

---

93 Cf. Schwarz, G., Mikroindustrialisierung: Handwerk und Angepaßte Technologie St. Gallen, Verlag Rüegger, 1980, pp. 334 et seq.
The historical model is formative here. Microindustrialisation is understood here in some measure as a school for macroindustrialisation. It is accordingly a question of "creating similar conditions . . . the emergence of comparable institutions, models of behaviour and forms of production" as those which appeared earlier in western Europe. The focus is on nurturing entrepreneurs, creating local technological and innovative capacity, utilising fragmented savings potential, in other words what List characterised ›developing productive forces‹.
Cf. List, F., Das nationale System der politischen Ökonomie, vol. IV der Gesammelten Werke, ed. A. Sommer, Berlin 1930.

and welding machines require three-phase supply, which involves very high connection charges by the state electricity corporations, which treat this as an industrial connection. Many entrepreneurs cited this as a major obstacle in developing and expanding production, exacerbated by the high cost of energy[94].

On average the businesses have up to five helpers and trained (skilled) workers. Frequently these are family members or direct relatives and members of the entrepreneur's extended family or tribe. This creates a very high degree of social belonging and correspondingly great loyalty to the business. This often minimises entrepreneurial risks, and if credits are needed the family or clan help. As a matter of principle, the owners work as full-time skilled workers in the company, responsible for technical, practical, commercial and other management issues to secure current operation. Given the size of the businesses studied and the nature of the products and services, a second level of management (supervisory) is not financially feasible. The owners are accordingly responsible not only for these practical functions but also for getting new business, preparing and processing orders, cost accounting and the necessary logistics. They also need to be aware of the social problems of their employees, since as noted above these are mostly related in some way. The question on how relationships with

government agencies;

banks (private and state);

development aid programmes of bilateral and multilateral donors in cooperation with the provincial and central governments;

or other promotional programmes for small (micro) businesses (informal sector)

can be classified and described evoked a basically negative response. Those surveyed indicated that experience to date (with the exception of the TTP/SES programme)[95] has been uniformly negative, so that they avoid assistance from the above institutions, government agencies or programmes. On further enquiry the problems underlying these statements were emphasised and can be summarised as follows:

---

94 A welder-entrepreneur reported that the cost of an industrial three-phase electrical supply would be c. DM 2,000 without expediting money (bribery). This is well beyond his investment capability, particularly since he sees it as wasted money, as he still needs the corresponding welding equipment. Even so, this would be a high priority for him, as he could use industrial equipment to weld larger pieces and produce other products in better quality, i.e. he could develop his business and boost his sales and quality.

95 This reply must be interpreted in the context that the individual surveyed were assisted exclusively through the TTP/SES promotional programme. However, they made it clear that this programme was not able to supply them with adequate funds. Conversely, they are well aware of the restrictions on the resources available to the TTP/SES.

- Entrepreneurs in the informal sector have problems meeting the *formal requirements* set by the competent government agencies for integration and inclusion in small business promotional programmes;
- they do not have *any lobby* at the level of government agencies, political parties and organisations representing private industry;
- they are not recognised by *state and private banks* as potential target groups, e.g. for loans or other promotional programmes;
- they are not recognised as an important and growing sector, i.e. as *employers* and an *economic factor* by the official development policy in the countries and provinces involved and the formal sector of the economy.

The survey has shown that virtually no use was made of official credit and development programmes offered by government agencies or state and private banks. As already noted, this is due to the overcomplicated procedures, the poor social access of the informal sector target groups in question to these development programmes and to the rejection (often on traditional and religious grounds) of interest-bearing loans and bank transactions. The last factor in particular was cited by many respondents as a major reason for rejection. The following diagram presents an overview of the standard forms of financing of the businesses surveyed:

Type and opportunities for financing

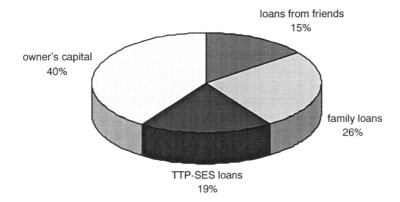

Frequently the following reasons can be identified for these objective difficulties of inadequate integration of informal sector entrepreneurs into the economic and political structures of developing countries[96]:

- The *formal educational requirements* for business owners are generally not adequate (writing, arithmetic, ability to present themselves and persistence etc);
- they are not adequately organised in their *own representative associations* (e.g. chambers, guilds, cooperatives, trade associations, political organisations etc)[97];
- Membership or social identification with the free trades and business ownership are not present given the social origins of entrepreneurs in the informal sector. It will accordingly be necessary for them to *create their own identity*. This is the only way that they can pursue their interests as a group within the state and society.
- The *shortfalls* in terms of individual abilities and belonging in the social context have adverse consequences for:
  - self-confidence;
  - communication skills in pursuing interests;

---

96 The results of the survey have already confirmed existing knowledge of the difficulties of recognition and integration into the economics and politics of the N.W.F.P., see also section 2.0 of the present work.

97 As far as readiness to become politically active is concerned, there is a growing tendency or readiness to join or at least support Islamic-integrationist (fundamentalist) movements. In future this could mean (particularly in Pakistan) even greater political destabilisation and radicalisation, and pose a danger to the democratisation of the country.

- persuasive ability in a social context;
- persistence in terms of controlling economic processes, i.e. obtaining fair prices or wages, timing in order processing and aspects of determining quality and processing criteria (contractual arrangements) in implementing orders.

This list could be expanded to include many more details. However, it is also important to avoid the impression that entrepreneurs in the informal sector are completely incapable of developing. The list of shortfalls here is not intended to do this, but rather to gather important information for developing specific programmes to strengthen these target groups.

The study produced the following profile for the surveyed entrepreneurs:

Profile of surveyed entrepreneurs in NFWP

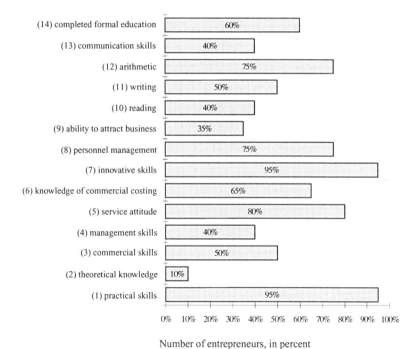

Number of entrepreneurs, in percent

The profile of the surveyed entrepreneurs reveals substantial deficits in management, business management and communication competences and in areas linked with formal education such as theoretical knowledge, reading, writing and more commercial abilities. Conversely, if we consider items (8) personnel management, (7) innovative skills, (5) service attitude and (1) practical skills we appear to be dealing with *naturally talented individuals.* This also confirms the generally-accepted hypothesis that "you can only train entrepreneurs to a very limited extent: these are a particular personality type with above-average commitment, courage to take risks and innovate and a decisive urge to improve their social and economic situation "[98]. This specific problem will be dealt with separately in chapter 4.
Most businesses are so-called "street corner jobs" or are located in semi-rural bazaars. The following figures show detailed information on target areas, i.e. direct sales markets.

Information on markets and sales areas

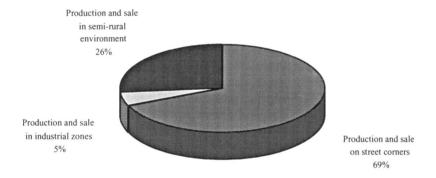

Production and sale in semi-rural environment 26%

Production and sale in industrial zones 5%

Production and sale on street corners 69%

A striking feature here is that businesses are always located near or in the immediate neighbourhood of the market or sales area. This is due to the very limited mobility of the businesses and the lack of structures for offering their products and services outside this area. The businesses surveyed here entirely lacked motorised transport. Transport is accord-

---

98 Cf. Klein, Heinz Günther, Small Business Promotion Nepal. Chapter E, Role and Functions of Entrepeneurs and Entrepreneurial Situation in Nepal pp. 110 et seq, Small Business Promotion Project (SBPP), Kathmandu, 1992- GTZ/Eschborn

ingly frequently bought in as a third-party service, using bicycle rickshaws, ox carts or human bearers etc. Information on the social status and type of customer is shown in the following diagram.

Customer type and social structure

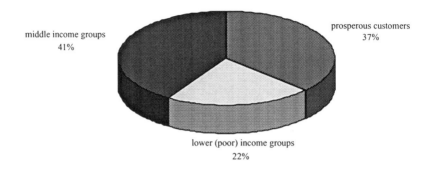

middle income groups
41%

prosperous customers
37%

lower (poor) income groups
22%

It emerges that most orders come from the upper and middle social classes. This is not surprising, since the lower groups cannot be expected to have sufficient purchasing power to buy any goods or services above the subsistence minimum. The exception here, as shown by the study, are products coming under the heading of basic needs, such as clothing, shoes, food and medication and accommodation. It is accordingly natural to conclude that there is a very great demand e.g. for tailoring and that tailors (still) have a good chance of setting up in business for themselves. Within the scope of this work it was only possible to determine demand to a very limited extent for other trades involved in satisfying basic needs, so that no final statements are possible in this area. However, it can be assumed (as shown in section 3.1.6.6) that construction, transport, textiles, agro-industry, trade and services (restaurants etc) still offer many opportunities for income-generating employment and self-employment.

As the following diagram shows, almost 90 % of customers are linked to the businesses in a fixed social context and only a very small proportion of the products and services need to be marketed. In this case these are finished products, e.g. clothing, tables, chairs, beds etc which are sold through the bazaars or other channels.

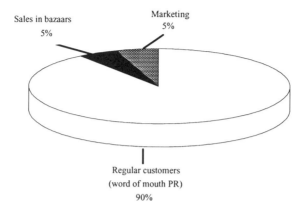

The informal sector (and this seems to be another striking characteristic) does not permit any production for stock (i.e. production of goods requiring prefinancing) because of the chronic shortage of capital. Businesses are also mostly unable to afford stocks of materials. This is partly due to the lack of finance and partly the lack of infrastructure (workshops, stores, vehicles etc). This is undoubtedly another major reason for the limited potential for development of businesses in the informal sector, since they can only offer production or services if these are demanded by the direct market (customers) and either directly paid for, or (as is normal practice) financed or prefinanced immediately[99]. This makes businesses in the informal sector heavily dependent on the state of the economy in their immediate environment (markets etc) and the surrounding conditions, and it also makes them very sensitive to competing products or services. Seen in these terms the informal sector will certainly not be able to absorb the steadily growing numbers of unemployed flooding onto the labour market, as its potential depends (as shown here) directly on conditions in local markets, i.e. their potential for development and the economic situation of the region.

---

99 The author is familiar with this from his own experience. It is thoroughly normal in India and Pakistan to pay a businessman a large part of the price demanded as an advance for the businessman to be in a position to supply the goods or services. The risk is very small, since promises once made are generally kept. However, quality and time of delivery are frequently renegotiated and are a cause of disputes and annoyance.

3.1.12.2 *Analysis of information on the businesses and employees surveyed*

The aim of the survey of entrepreneurs and employees in businesses in the informal sector was to gather information on the following areas:

requirements profile of employees;
status of employees in the business;
employer criteria for selection and hiring;
social benefits and security of employees.

The survey and accompanying observations[100] in the 30 selected businesses in the informal sector were made using the parameters listed under (a) to (g) below (see also appendices I and II). The frequency of positive statements by entrepreneurs and employees was summarised in the following diagram and shows a typical profile for the employees in the informal sector. The following parameters were specifically surveyed and checked through observations[101] at the respondents' place of work.

(a) *Vocational and general educational requirements*;
(b) *Abilities, skills and knowledge* in vocational context, i.e. for example how professionally assigned work is done;
(c) *Identification with the business* in the informal sector and *social status of employees in the business;*
(d) *Social competences* of employees, such as adaptability, ability to work in a team, readiness to work as individuals and accept changes in social situation or integration;
(e) *Competences in communicative skills*, such as mastery of informal speech, reading and writing etc;
(f) *Motivation and mobility* of employees in the informal sector, personal and family situation and expectations of employers;
(g) *Employer expectations* in the informal sector, *their role* and *relationship with employees.*

The following diagram shows an overview of the hierarchical levels and type of employee in the businesses surveyed.

---

100 Cf. note 99 on p. 163.
101 The profile shown/developed here of employees in the informal sector is based inter alia on countless project visits by the author and discussions with those involved and experts working in the informal sector for many years.

Status of employees in businesses

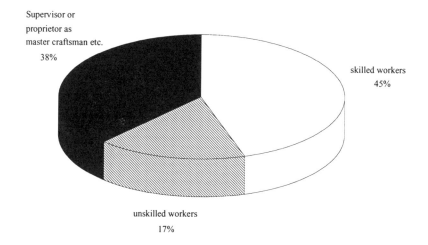

Skilled workers here means workers who have completed at least basic training or apprenticeship training under the TTP-SES programme. They have the so-called *basic skills* needed to make or provide the relevant products or services. These are by no means skilled workers as understood in Germany. As the diagram shows, c. 45 % of employees in the businesses surveyed come within this category, with supervisors and proprietors (38 %) also belonging to this category. Only c. 17 % of employees can be categorised as entirely unskilled workers and hence helpers. The supervisor level frequently coincides with business ownership. Because of their size, value of orders, lack of division of labour and turnover, the organisational structure of the small businesses does not permit complex structures. As a result proprietors and entrepreneurs are generally also the master craftsmen and manage the production process generally. They also often perform the function of the supervisor or master craftsman. This indicates that the 38 % of skilled workers at management level are for the most part proprietors. It is plausible to extend this conclusion generally to the structure of businesses in the informal sector, which allows us to say that the training measures of the type described in section 3.1.6 provide among other things the basis for establishing a business in the informal sector. This means that without technical qualifications and competences, even an individual who is suitable to become an entrepreneur will be unable to set up or run a business in the informal sector successfully in the region and economic and employment sector studied here. This is shown by the study of the informal sector in Peshawar, which basically very strongly resembles bazaar businesses in structure and performance profile[102], it is characteristic of the craft nature of the businesses and opens up the possibility of integrating the businesses into traditional economic and craft structures.

The following diagram attempts to show a profile of the *skilled workers* employed in the informal sector on the basis of the criteria in (a) to (g), using the analysis of the survey (see appendices I and II). In all 12 parameters were used, and these yielded the profile shown here as expressed in % on the basis of their frequency in the businesses and employees surveyed and the observations made in these businesses.

---

102 This observation does not apply in any way to small and medium sized businesses in the formal sector, as businessmen here are frequently not rooted in a craft trade but are active as dealers or outside investors in an entrepreneurially interesting field. They often know nothing about the products being made. In India and Pakistan what the author sees as a typical seller's market has developed in which the buyer has relatively little in the way of rights. He (the buyer) must accept whatever is offered in the way of products and services, and has little chance to protest or demand quality of the services or products. In addition there is the fact that the domestic markets have been protected for years, preventing better quality products from reaching the regional or national market legally. Recently, however, the opening up of the markets in India and Pakistan have administered a shock to local firms which are clearly feeling that they can no longer meet the quality requirements and e.g. the design etc of consumer products subject to international (world market) fashions.

Profile of employees in the businesses surveyed in the informal sector

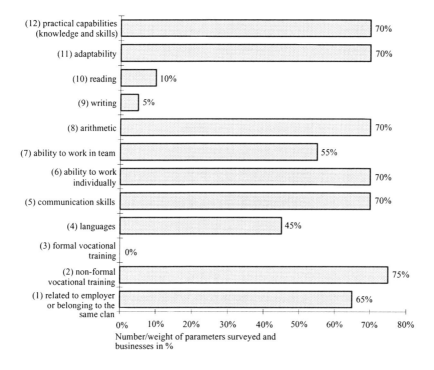

The profile of skilled workers employed in informal craft businesses shows the following key features:

No.	Parameter	Comments	Importance in %
(2)	Non-formal vocational training[a]	A significant fraction of the skilled workers employed in the informal sector have obtained the necessary training through non-formal courses. In the present case, through the TTP-SES programme.	75 %
(5)	Communication skills	These include the ability to express themselves clearly in the languages spoken in the NFWP and to communicate with the proprietor and customers. (Languages: English, Pushtu, Urdu).	70 %
(6)	Ability to work individually	This includes the skills which enable employees to perform the work assigned to them independently.	70 %
(7)	Ability to work in team	Entrepreneurs/employers expect their employees to be able to work in a team and be willing to cooperate in the division of labour.	55 %
(8)	Arithmetic	This includes the ability to perform the four basic arithmetical operations. This seems important for cutting material and determining the costs of the work performed or occasional material purchasing.	70 %
(11)	Adaptability	Adaptability of employees essentially refers to focus on customers and the ability to fit in with the operation of the business and its hierarchical structure.	70 %
(12)	Practical skills	These are concrete practical skills, abilities and knowledge. They serve primarily to perform the work (manufacture the product or provide the service) in a reasonable time with appropriate quality.	70 %

a. Non-formal vocational training = all training measures and services which are provided by unofficial agencies, including all agencies offering initial and further vocational training measures outside the education ministry. These courses are frequently not recognised by the education ministry formally as such, but they are recognised by industry and the draft trades, cf. H. Nölker, E. Schoenfeldt, Glossar: Internationale Berufspädagogik, Expert-Verlag, 1985, Sindelfingen, pp. 82 et seq.

On further enquiry the employers confirm that they rate the quality of their employees on the above criteria (2) to (12) but for recruiting (as was very often emphasised) direct social links play a role. Over 65 % of employees are directly related in some way or have other and similar social ties to the employers. Frequently employees come from the same villages or belong to the same clan. By contrast, little significance is attached to formal vocational training (e.g. graduates of the Technical Training Center-TTC etc). It should be noted here that the graduates of formal vocational training courses are frequently not available for this form of employment, as they generally try to get white collar jobs. In principle, however, bazaar businesses and small (micro) businesses are not interested in these graduates because of their very high expectations in terms of wages and salaries, working conditions and social benefits. These two groups very rarely meet in the informal sector. On the other hand, as the survey shows (see the profile of the entrepreneurs) there are many entrepreneurs with higher educational qualifications, as c. 60 % of the proprietors surveyed had formal educational qualifications (general and vocational). Respondents attached little importance to knowledge of reading and writing, i.e. only 10 % can read (or require this skill) and up to 5 % can write. In the author's view, however, this should not be taken as a rule or basis for orienting curriculum development in the informal sector, since the cultural skills reading, writing and arithmetic must be more widely disseminated in this area of Third World societies as well[103]. Everyone has the right to these skills, which form an important foundation for vocational training and job creation measures. These skills are also (as the profile of informal sector entrepreneurs shows) key qualifications which are one of the requirements for possible self-employment as a small (micro) businessman. They are also essential for improving the opportunities of the underprivileged classes and the democratisation of Third World societies[104].

3.1.13 Evaluation of the TTP/SES programme for promoting employment-oriented vocational training in the informal and traditional sector

A key indicator of the success of the TTP/SES programme is the training and advanced training provided to Afghans and Pakistanis in the past 12 years. In all, the project has provided training and advanced training to c. 16,000 Afghan refugees and Pakistani participants. According to the project tracer statistics c. 65 % were in employment or self-employment. While a critical review of the methods used and the gaps in the records of graduate placement casts serious doubt on

---

103 Pakistan specifically, as already noted, is one of the particularly striking examples of faulty educational and social policy, since over 73 % of the population are illiterate according to the latest UN statistics. Literacy must be treated as a crucial condition of change in the society, as comparative studies by the Indian government in the provinces with differing degrees of literacy (particularly among women) directly confirm, as the higher the level of literacy the lower the level of infant mortality and bacterial disease (e.g. diseases of the gastrointestinal tract).
104 Cf. World Watch Institute Report, Zur Lage der Welt 1993 Daten für das Überleben unseres Planeten, Fischer Taschenbuchverlag, Frankfurt, 1993, pp. 48-49 et seq.

this figure[105], it must be conceded that the author had no problems locating graduates in the bazaars in Peshawar and the surrounding area for his small and very limited survey of former TTP-SES students. The success of the measures can be attributed in retrospect to a few important and favourable environmental conditions and accompanying circumstances:

- The *Pakistan project executing agencies* and local implementing organisation (Directorate Manpower and Training-DMT) were at the time of the project *very favourably inclined towards measures aimed at refugees*. They gave the German partner a free hand in implementing the project;
- This *largely circumvented the state bureaucracy* and the project implementation team was also able to recruit qualified personnel from outside the state bureaucracy. It was therefore possible to pay local staff according to their performance, rather than being constrained by the excessively low government wage and salary guidelines;
- The *Deutsche Gesellschaft für Technische Zusammenarbeit*, GTZ (GmbH) assigned a project director who was (is) distinguished for his *autonomy in action* and *entrepreneurial thinking* and *outstanding commitment to the target groups* in the informal sector, and who accordingly exploited the favourable accompanying circumstances to function as an *innovative mover* for the project. The responsible departments in the GTZ and BMZ also gave the project the necessary scope for decision-making and action;
- The *Afghan refugees* were not only to poor peasants with poor qualifications, but included *very well trained experts* (teachers, trainers and engineers). These experts had mostly been trained in Germany under earlier technical cooperation, and were hired by TTP/SES, giving the project *a highly-qualified core staff*, making extensive and long-drawn-out staff training measures unnecessary, i.e. a start could be made on concrete training and advanced training without long preparation;
- The *existing buildings and infrastructure* provided by the Pakistani partner at the Technical Training Center (TTC) Peshawar were and are capable of extension and could accordingly be quickly *modified for the needs of the TTP/SES;*

---

105 A relevant scientific long-term accompanying study has since been initiated by the author and is being implemented by the University of Bremen (since July 1993). However, no results can be expected before end-1994 to mid-1995.

- *As a result of the international political context still prevailing in 1980/81 with its global division into blocs* (East-West conflict) there was *great interest in helping Afghan refugees* and particularly in helping Pakistan cope with the crisis. *Sufficient funding and material was made available worldwide for the regions affected.* It was possible for the TTP/SES approach, which – thanks to the perspicacity of the German project director – was based on productive training, to access these resources easily through the production, service and construction contracts already described and use them for the purposes of training and advanced training and employment-oriented measures;
- These "*favourable*" circumstances ultimately resulted in adequate funding being available, so that it has been possible to increase the number of students in recent years to over 4,000 a year. This was also based on the *more than DM 1 million a year for training and advanced training* provided by the UNHCR, which was used exclusively for *Afghan refugees*. These training measures were carried out by the TTP/SES *under a commission from the UNHCR* as (non-profit) reimbursable cooperation by implementing construction measures and infrastructural projects.

However, despite all the positive results, it must be noted that at the start of the project the reporting experts, project planners and project implementing team were unable to draw on any relevant experience or theoretical foundation for the design and concept of vocational training measures for the informal and traditional sector. International development policy and theoretical discussion of the informal sector and employment-oriented training and advanced training for this sector were still in their infancy at that time. There were only a few isolated voices criticising previous practice and priorities and the almost exclusive concentration of promotion on the formal economy and educational and vocational training sector. In this respect the project was a challenge for the "movers", and the situation in Peshawar (NFWP and Baluchistan)[106] required action, so that practice was forced to move ahead of the scientific literature and development policy sectoral papers. The innovation and development of the approaches described here were accordingly left almost entirely to the so-called practitioners in implementing the technical cooperation project. This applies to the entire area of income-generating and income-promoting projects, the

---

106 Deutsche Gesellschaft für Technische Zusammenarbeit (GTZ) started with two simultaneous projects in the refugee-struck provinces of Baluchistan and N.W.F.P.. These projects followed different paths, probably due primarily to the regional economic, political and socio-cultural situation. A comparative study has yet to be carried out by GTZ/BMZ.

sectors of vocational training, general education, small business promotion, environmental protection and resources conservation and dissemination and implementation of appropriate and eco-friendly technologies. Seen in this light, the cast study described here was a stroke of luck in two respects, as it was not only successful in terms of promoting the target groups but – as the present work shows – it provided sufficient approaches and experience able to develop a positive contribution to developing appropriate promotional concepts for the informal and traditional sector. Essentially, the vocational pedagogical considerations can be summarised again as follows:

The *target groups must be clearly described* in terms of the criteria identified in section 2.4 and in 3.1.4 of the case study;

The *basic didactic structure* of the vocational training and development policy promotional concepts for the target groups in the informal sector must be based on an *open, action-oriented, anthropocentric didactic approach*, i.e. the following aspects must be taken into account:
extrafunctional education to secure *survival and future-oriented development*;
education to develop *self-help potential*;
education to secure *employment or self-employment*;
education to *create and secure income*;

The *socio-cultural* and *political environment* for a project to promote target groups in the informal sector must be studied and their importance for the project recognised and given due account;

The *economic* and *development-policy environment for the local and regional labour markets* must be studied and *taken into account*;

Access to vocational training and educational measures must not be *formalised*. It must be *unconditionally available* to the identified *target groups*;

To *support systematic orientation of projects*, projects with the goal of promoting the informal and traditional sector must also *aim at moving towards or promoting openness of the formal vocational or general education sector*, i.e. integration into the formal sector should be sought (see section 3.1.8);

New measures or concepts for training skilled workers and entrepreneurs in the informal sector should *as a matter of principle take into account existing traditional training concepts or systems* and possibly integrate them (cf. traditional apprenticeships, section 3.1.6.6);

To be employment oriented, measures for training and advanced training of target groups in the informal and traditional sector must be accompanied by *flanking job-creating promotional measures*;

The informal and traditional sector requires *flexible and open promotional concepts* which are specifically oriented towards the individual conditions of *individuals and groups*. In addition, care must be taken to see that the *promotional instruments* are designed to be *simple and accessible* (without major bureaucratic obstacles) for the target groups;

The *promotional instruments and project approaches* must be integrated into *programmes for promoting the informal sector* and reflect the local and regional economic, political, socio-cultural and socio-economic structures. *As a matter of principle, individual projects must be regarded as problematic* unless they are integrated into a broader context of programmes and strategies to promote target groups in the informal and traditional sector. Sustainable impacts e.g. on the employment situation of the target groups can only be achieved through programme approaches. This is clearly shown by the example of the SES/TTP Peshawar.

3.2 The need for vocational training measures for target groups in the informal and traditional sector in India (using the example of the Federal States of Karnataka and Tamil Nadu)

3.2.1 Geographical, economic and development policy framework for India

India is the seventh-largest country on earth with a area of 3,287,590 km^2 (including Kashmir). It is nine times the size of the Federal Republic of Germany. Its north-south axis is about 3,200 km long and its east-west axis is 2,700 km long. India is bordered to the north by the Peoples Republic of China (formerly Tibet), Nepal and Bhutan. To the west India borders Pakistan and to the east Bangladesh (which is entirely enclosed by India) and Myanmar (formerly Burma). The Indian subcontinent has a coastline c. 5,600 km long, which is only economically developed and structured at a few points. There are natural boundaries to the west (the Arabian Sea), south (Indian Ocean) and east (Gulf of Bengal). The Indian subcontinent stretches southwards from the Himalayas in the north as an extended triangular peninsula, at its southernmost point almost touching the island of Sri Lanka. The country is divided geographically into the mountainous region of the Himalayas (with altitudes over 8,000 m), the plain of the Holy River Ganga (Ganges) and the southern peninsula, and the Dekkan plateau. The southern triangular peninsula (Dekkan plateau) rises on its western edge (West Ghats) to an average height of 1,000 m, with isolated peaks rising to 3,000 m, while to the east (East Ghats) the average altitude is only c. 500 m. In the southern interior of the peninsula the mountain chains reach heights of up to 1,300 m[107]. The geographical situation and landscape of India is responsible for the wide variety in the Indian climate, which ranges from the dry and cold climate of Central Asia to the dry and hot climate of the Near East and the tropical monsoon climate of south-east Asia, separated by the high mountain chains with their glaciers and the highest mountain chains on earth.

India can be categorised as a classic monsoon country: the coastal regions to the west, south and east and the broad flood plains of the Brahmaputra and Ganga are dominated by their summer rainy seasons. South Assam in the east has a distinct tropical rainy climate. The Himalayas are predominantly a highland climate, with summer rain and subtropical winter rains.

---

107 Cf. Statistisches Bundesamt, Länderbericht Indien 1991, Wiesbaden, Metzler/Poeschel, 1991 and Rouillard, H., Süd-Indien, Richtig reisen; Rouillard, H. Nord-Indien, Richtig reisen, 1981, Du Mont Buchverlag, Cologne

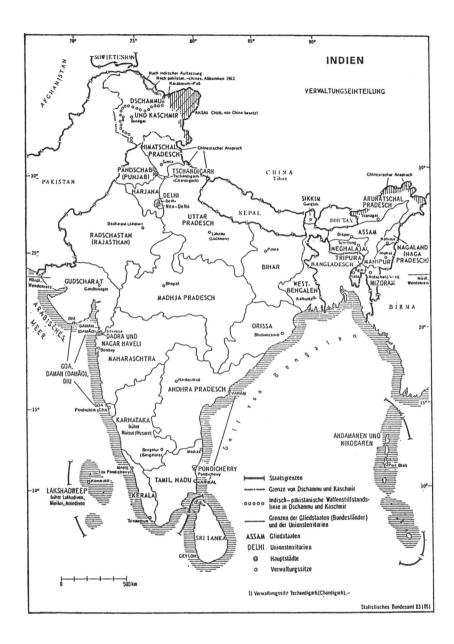

Official German language map of India.
Source: Statistisches Bundesamt.

Parts of Rajasthan and Gujarat have desert and steppe climates, reaching to New Delhi in the north, Harijana to the east as far as Madhya Pradesh and in the central Indian Dekkan plateau to Karnataka in the south. Large parts of the country accordingly have four seasons, i.e. cool, hot, monsoon and post-monsoon rainy season[108].

India's present borders date from 1947, the post-Independence partition into India and Pakistan. In 1971 eastern Pakistan split off from western Pakistan to create a new state, Bangladesh. The Indian subcontinent has been plagued repeatedly since Independence by separatist movements of individual religious or ethnic groups or even entire Federal States[109]. In addition, religious fanatics and extreme nationalists are trying to shatter the Indian unity and multicultural society. Violence against Muslims has increased since the destruction of the mosque at Ayodhya and can be regarded as an Indian identity crisis[110]. Despite its internal political problems, India still describes itself as the largest functional democracy in the world. It has a democratic constitution and is a federal republic. India consists of 25 independent Union States and 7 Union Territories. The central government is based in New Delhi. The 7 Union Territories, which are directly administered by the central government are the Andaman and Nicobar islands (in the east), the Lakschadweep islands (Lakkadives, in the west), the cities of Chandigarh and Delhi and the territories of Dadra and Nagar Haveli, Daman and Diu, Pondicherry[111]. India has 860 million inhabitants and a fertility rate of c. 4.5 %, which corresponds to annual population growth of c. 2 %. If this growth rate continues (as it is likely) India will have over one billion inhabitants by the end of the millennium[112]. Despite its declining birth rate, the Indian population will grow by 17 million a year for the next few decades, overtaking China in terms of population.

---

108 Op. cit. pp. 22 et seq.
109 See the conflicts in Jammu and Kashmir, Punjab, Assam, Tripura, etc., which partly provoked (or still provoke) military conflicts.
110 Vgl. Böll, M., Indien zur Jahresmitte 1993 in: Wirtschaftslage, Hrsg. Bundesstelle für Außenhandelsinformation (bfai), 1569, Juni 1993.
111 See note 107.
112 Cf. Guptha, B.S., Statistical Outline of India 1992-93- published by TATA Services ltd., Bombay, 1992.

Table I: *Area, population and population density by Federal State and Union Territory*[113]

Federal State/ Union Territory	Capital	Area km²	Population, 1990 (million)	Inhabitants per km²
Federal States:				
Andhra Pradesh	Hyderabad	275,068	63.51	231
Arunchal Pradesh	Itanagar	83,743	0.87	10
Assam	Dispur	78,438	24.64	314
Bihar	Patna	173,877	85.34	490
Gujarat	Ghandinagar	196,024	40.58	207
Haryana	Chandigarh	44,212	16.24	367
Himachal Pradesh	Simla	55,673	5.05	91
Jammu and Kashmir	Srinagar	222,236	7.34	33
Karnataka[a])	**Bangalore**	**191,791**	**44.83**	**234**
Kerala	Trivandrum	38,863	29.81	767
Madhya Pradesh	Bhopal	444,446	63.45	143
Maharashtra	Bombay	307,690	74.56	242
Manipur	Imphal	22,327	1.77	79
Meghalaya	Shillong	22,429	1.71	76
Mizoram	Aziawl	21,081	0.70	33
Nagaland	Kohima	16,579	1.11	67
Orissa	Bhubaneswar	155,707	31.11	199
Punjab	Chandigarh	50,362	19.65	390
Rajasthan	Jaipur	342,239	43.85	128
Sikkim	Gangtok	7,096	0.44	62
Tamil Nadu[b])	**Madras**	**130,058**	**56.00**	**430**

a. Data on the survey region Bangalore and Madras
b. Data on the survey region Bangalore and Madras

---

113 See: Statistisches Bundesamt, Länderbericht Indien 1991,Wiesbaden, Metzler/Poeschel, Stuttgart 1991.

177

Federal State/ Union Territory	Capital	Area km²	Population, 1990 (million)	Inhabitants per km²
Tripura	Aaartala	10,486	2.55	243
Uttar Pradesh	Lucknow	294,411	134.61	457
West-Bengal	Calcutta	88,752	65.18	734
Goa, Daman, Dui	Panji	3,814	1.1	225
Union Territories:				
Andaman/Nicobar	Port Blair	8,249	0.2	15
Chandigarh	Chandigarh	114	0.5	2.290
Dadra/Nagur Haveli	Silvassa	491	0.1	143
Delhi	Delhi	1,483	6.22	2.744
Lakshadweep	Kavaratti	32	0.04	937
Pondicherry	Pondicherry	492	0,60	955

The relatively good medical service and the network of healthcare facilities (doctors, dispensaries, hospitals, nurses, drug and hygiene measures etc) have reduced infant mortality and mortality generally since the 60s. This also indirectly affects the birth rate, which has fallen as a result of the improved social and medical services and the birth control campaigns[114]. The age pyramid for Indian society shows a similar breakdown to other Asian countries, with a very high proportion of younger age groups. "36.5 % of the total population were below 15 in 1990, 59 % were in the economically active years (15-65) and 4.5 % were over 65." Average life expectancy is 57.9 years, and has risen by 5 years since 1980 and 35 years since 1901-11[115]. It has not been possible to study the reasons for this in detail, but it is clear considering developments since 1947 that there has been an abrupt change in the population situation in India since the end of British colonial rule. This is also apparent worldwide in the so-called developing countries after the collapse of colonialism, where they spoke (speak) of a population explosion. Another notable development is the imbalance in genders, i.e. there is generally a surplus of men over women (107 to 100). Reasons for this are the higher infant and child mortality rate for girls and

---

114 See note 113, pp. 27/28; note 112, pp. 176 et seq and 8th Five-Year Plan, 1992-97, pub. Government of India, 1992, p. 26.
115 See Mamoria, D.B., Social Problems and Social Disorganisation in India, Kitab Mahal, Allahabad, 1961.

the higher mortality rate among women of childbearing age. The low status of girls and women in many Third World countries as productive labour and members of society (lack of equal rights and equality of treatment) may be another key reason for this imbalance[116].

The process of urbanisation is taking longer in India than in many other Third World countries. Around 28 % of the total population live in the cities or urban agglomerations. The overwhelming proportion live in c. 600,000 villages in the country[117]. This is partly due to the deliberate decentralisation policy of the Indian government, which has created regional economic centres through industrial relocation and development of the infrastructure of small and medium-sized cities. This is preventing to some extent an unrestrained migration to the major conurbations and metropolises. Even so there is no reason for celebration, since given the national population density shown in table I even the small and medium-sized cities frequently have 0.5-1 million inhabitants, and would qualify as major cities in European terms. As a multiracial state India has a large number of languages and dialects. Figures on these vary widely, according to Grierson there are 179 languages and 544 dialects in India[118]. Over 73 % of all Indians speak languages in the Aryan family, 20 % speak Dravidian languages (southern India) and 1.3 % speak Australo-Asiatic languages. There is a large number (well over 100) of other languages belonging to the Tibetan-Chinese language family, mainly spoken by smaller tribes in northern and eastern India. Officially the Indian Federal States and Union Territories recognise English, which is used as the lingua franca of central government business and commerce, and 15 other written national languages. The following table gives a more detailed picture.

---

116 This issue has been and is repeatedly addressed critically in the Indian daily newspapers, as even today boys and men have higher status in society. This goes so far that medical and technical resources in the prenatal area are being used to determine whether a foetus is male or female. If it is female, the result is frequently an abortion. This has been prohibited in India since the end of the 80s.
117 Cf. note 113, pp. 30 et seq.
118 Cf. Kingsley, Davis, The population of India and Pakistan, Russel and Russel, New York, 1968, p. 108.

Table II: *Population by selected national languages*[119]

Language	1961		1971	
	Million	%	Million	%
Indo-Aryan				
Hindi	133	31	162	30
Bengali	34	8	45	8
Marathi	33	8	42	8
Urdu	23	5	29	5
Gujarati	20	5	26	5
Bihari	17	4	21	4
Orija	16	4	20	4
Punjabi	11	3	16	3
Assamesish	7	2	9	2
Rajasthani	15	3	7	1
Kashmiri	2	0.5	2	0.5
Dravidian				
Telugu	38	9	45	8
Tamil	31	7	38	7
Malajam	17	4	22	4
Kannada	17	4	22	4

The official language is Hindi, written using the Devanagari alphabet. English is an associated language and is learned in school as the second or third language. It continues to be an important medium for intra-Indian communication, as Hindi is mainly spoken in the north and rejected as a national language by Dravidian southern India.

The majority of Indians are Hindus. Hinduism is also responsible for the hierarchical division of Indian society into castes. At the top are the "Brahmans" and at the bottom are the "casteless" or "untouchables". The "casteless" including the so-called Indian "aboriginals", the

---

119 Cf. note 113, p. 33.

"scheduled castes and tribes", represent c. 24 % of the total Indian population according to the 1981 census. Although the Indian Constitution[120] has officially abolished the castes and discriminatory social divisions and guaranteed equality of opportunity to all Indians, centuries of tradition and the actual power structures and social structures still give more power to the traditional upper classes and leadership classes. Thanks to their positions of power in government and society, these still enjoy unrestricted access to the privileges of the elite and leadership classes. This is also a reason for the recurring conflicts between castes. Recently this conflict has been extended, with the encouragement of the ultraconservative Hindu movement[121] to religious conflict between Moslems and Hindus. Besides the dominant Hindu majority, other important political and socio-cultural factors are the countless ethnic groups and the other major religious groups. The following table provides an overview of these.

Table III: *Population broken down by religious adherence*[122]

Religious groups	1961	1971	1981	1961	1971	1981
	Million			%		
Hindus	367	453	566	84	83	83
Moslems	47	62	78	11	11	12
Christians	11	14	17	2.5	3	2.5
Sikhs	9	10	14	2	2	2
Buddhists	3	4	5	1	1	1
Jainas	2	3	3	0.5	0.5	0.5
Other	2	2	3	0.5	0.5	0.5

As already repeatedly noted, the diversity of religions leads to recurrent conflicts and secessionist movements[123]. As this topic is very com-

---

120 Cf. the statements in sections 2.2 and 2.3 of the present work.
121 The largest and most politically influential Hindu party is the Bharatia Janata Party (BJP), which won 119 seats in the last parliamentary elections (1991). If elections were held today, the Hindu nationalists would get 272 seats according to the latest opinion polls in India.
122 Cf. note 113, p. 35.
123 See the: Kashmir conflict, fuelled by Muslims seeking independence. The long-lasting conflict in Punjab between the Sikhs and Hindus also aims at a separate state "Khalistan".

plex and cannot be dealt with in a few pages, it is sufficient here to note the existing potential for conflict. In planning development cooperation measures specifically aimed at promoting disadvantaged population groups or religious groups and castes, special attention must be paid to balance in external intervention. The informal and traditional sector covers large groups of the disadvantaged population groups described here, so that it can be assumed that any measures planned and implemented have the potential to encounter unanticipated socially explosive conditions and result in social conflict.

The health care system is highly developed, and since the 80s a large number of basic health services have been vigorously developed (Primary Health Care Centers). Widespread mother-and-infant care and birth control measures are also being implemented, with NGOs and charitable associations playing an important role. There has been little improvement in nutrition since the 60s. As part of the Indian population still falls short of the average required daily intake of calories the government has set up so-called "Fair Price Shops" or "Food for Work" job programmes[124]. The main problems with preventive health care are the (drinking) water supply, sanitary services (disposal of refuse and faecal matter) and parasitical, bacterial and viral illnesses such as malaria, leprosy, tetanus, diphtheria, polio, typhus, helmithological diseases, intenstinal diseases and influenzas. In the prevailing "Eighth Five-Year Plan" the Indian government makes the following statement on the health care programme. "The health facilities should reach the entire population by the end of the Eight Plan. The "Health for All" (HFA) paradigm must take into account not only the high risk vulnerable groups, i.e., mother and child (as done so far) but must also focus sharply on the underprivileged segments within the vulnerable groups." Towards Health for the underprivileged" may be the key strategy for the H.F.A. by year 2000[125]." Public spending on health care (central government and Federal States) accounted for 4.3 % of total spending in the 1988/89 fiscal year (1.4 % of GDP)[126]. However, taking into account absolute population growth there is no doubt that the situation in the social services as a whole will continue to deteriorate. The social policy goals for the year 2000 mentioned above are accordingly questionable.

Despite substantial national and international investment for the expansion of the Indian general, vocational and tertiary education sys-

---

124 Cf. Eighth Five Year Plan, 1992-97, Vol. I pub. Government of India, Planning Commission New Delhi, 1992.
125 Op. cit. p. 11.
126 Cf. note 113, p. 39.

tem, success to date in fighting illiteracy and providing access for socially disadvantaged groups to higher educational facilities can only be described as modest. The amendment (i.e. addition to) the Indian constitution in 1976 was concerned specifically with reforming education and cooperation between the central government, Federal States and Union Territories. One central statement here covered the different roles and responsibilities of the central government and the Federal States:

"While the role and responsibility of the States in regard to education will remain essentially unchanged, the Union Government would accept a larger responsibility to reinforce the national and integrative character of education, to maintain quality and standards (including those of the teaching profession at all levels), to study and monitor the educational requirements of the country as a whole in regard to manpower for development, to cater to the needs research and advanced study, to look after the international aspects of education, culture and human resource development and, in general to promote excellence at all levels of the educational pyramid through out the country[127]." These constitutional amendments in 1978 and 1992 provide specifically for integration and promotion of the disadvantaged national minorities, the castes and scheduled tribes and specific promotion of previously heavily disadvantaged women[128]. This educational policy and its consistent implementation with the goal of correcting the inequality and discrimination and improving equality of opportunity for the above target groups is the basis for future integration of this multiracial state, securing democracy and the peaceful development of the country[129]. Illiteracy continues to be one of the country's biggest problems. Although the literacy programmes are slowly starting to work, the constant population growth is still eroding the success achieved. The tables below summarise the situation discussed here.

---

127 See Ministry of Human Resource Development (MHRD), Department of Education, National Policy on Education – 1986 (with modification undertaken in 1992), New Delhi, 1992.
128 Op. cit. pp. 9-16.
129 The Indian government has been struggling for years with the conflicts between the national minorities, e.g. the Moslems and Hindus, the various castes, the "scheduled tribes", the Sikhs and Hindus and all possible separatist movements. The conflicts are constantly causing international headlines.

Table IV: *Illiteracy (men, women)*[130]

Age and sex	1971	1981	1985	1971	1981	1985	1991
	Million			%			
15 +	209.4	238.1	263.6	65.9	59.2	56.5	52.1
Men	86.3	93.9	103.4	52.3	45.2	42.8	–
Women	123.1	143.2	160.2	80.6	74.3	71.1	–

Table V: *Educational facilities (state and private)*[131]

Facilities	Units	1970/71	1986/87	1987/88	1988-89
Primary	000	408	537	544	548
Middle	000	91	137	141	144
High/higher Secondary	000	37	69	71	73
Vocational Training (ITI's)	(number)	–	831	1400	2137
General Education Colleges	(number)	4670	4151	4329	4670
Professional Colleges	(number)	1017	1547	1658	1700
Universities	(number)	93	157	176	181

As table V shows, the last 20 years have seen steady growth in the number of educational facilities at all levels. It is, however, clear (as already noted) that population growth requires even greater efforts by the Indian central government and state governments. Public spending on general education and vocational training currently amounts to c. 3 % of GDP, which is by no means sufficient to meet the future requirements of the educational system[132]. Important milestones for the development of an autonomous educational and training policy in post-colonial India were set in 1968 by the Indian parliament and the gov-

---

130 Figures were taken from the country report of the Statistisches Bundesamt (note 113), and the annual statistical digest 1992-93 of TATA, Dept. of Economics & Statistics (note 112).
131 Figures were taken from the country report of the Statistisches Bundesamt (note 113), and the annual statistical digest 1992-93 of TATA, Dept. of Economics & Statistics (note 112) and the Indian Labour Year Book 1990, Labour Bureau, Ministry of Labour, Government of India, New Delhi, 1990.

ernment in the "National-Policy-Paper on Education"[133]. Indian educational policy-makers agreed in this paper on the following key goals for educational policy:

(A) India must overcome its post-colonial social, political and economic problems and expectations.

Educational policy accordingly had to focus on national integration (multiracial state), developing a national identity (post-colonial effects) and national political and economic progress (developing the political system and the national economy).

(B) India needs a national educational policy based on national independence, aiming at high quality in all areas of education and communicating modern sciences and technology, i.e. establishes a link with international standards.

In addition educational policy should also create a link with normal daily life and contribute towards strengthening cultural autonomy. In the 1992 revision of the paper on "National Policy on Education"[134] these guidelines are still presented as correct. It is noted that Indian educational policy has achieved impressive successes to date, primarily in the following areas:

- 90 % of all Indian villages and rural areas have their own educational facilities corresponding to an agreed basic standard. These are located throughout the territory so that they are accessible within a radius of c. 1 km from the settlements;
- A national system of general education and vocational training has been implemented in almost all Union States and Union Territories (10 + 2 + 3 system);
- The curricula, length of educational and training measures and certificates have been settled and implemented on a uniform basis for the whole of India[135];

---

132 Cf. World Bank, India, Progress and Challenges in Economic Transition, Report, No. 11761- IN. The reforms recommended by the World Bank in the context of better use of existing resources, infrastructure and funding could help make optimal use of this budget. How far this happens is entirely up to the Indian government and the competent agencies. Cf. NCRT, National Council of Educational Survey Volume I + II, Government of India, New Delhi, 1992.
133 Cf. note 127.
134 Loc. cit.
135 Loc. cit.

- A dense network of instructor upgrading measures, technical colleges, polytechnics and universities has been developed and implemented[136].

However, as already noted elsewhere, the enormous population growth, internal political conflicts, stagnation in economic growth and the associated growing problems in the labour market have all lead to a serious crisis in the general educational, vocational training and tertiary education systems.

The "Fifth Indian Education Report"[137] and the "National Policy Paper on Education"[138] make the following recommendations for improving the situation in education policy:

3.2.1.2 – (A) *General and tertiary education*

(1) India should increase its educational budget: the Union States are specifically called on here to comply with the guideline of 4% of GDP for education recommended by UNESCO;

(2) Efforts to create primary and secondary schools must be increased in line with population growth;

(3) Although enrolment rates at elementary and secondary schools are relatively high at almost 100 % (elementary) and 60 % (secondary schools), dropout rates are also very high (c. 47 % for elementary and c. 63 % for secondary education). Suitable measures to improve this situation should accordingly be taken, particularly in rural areas[139];

(4) Integration of the educational system for the castes and scheduled tribes and women must be pursued more vigorously at all levels of education (e.g. students, teachers, administration and educational policy);

(5) Measures to improve literacy in youth dropouts and adults must be implemented on a widespread basis;

(6) The curricula for general schools must be reviewed and oriented more towards the needs of graduates and the labour market;

(7) The top priority must be development and expansion and reducing the drop-out rate, as this qualification is for many young Indians the final formal educational qualification giving access to the

---

136 See table V on p. 184.
137 Cf. NCERT, National Council of Educational Research and Training, Fifth All-India Educational Survey, Volume I and II, New Delhi, 1992.
138 See note 127.
139 Cf. Government of India (Planning Commission): Eighth Five Year Plan, 1992-1997, New Delhi, India 1992, pp. 284 et seq.

labour market. The curricula must be correspondingly revised and adapted to the needs of the labour market[140];

(8) The schools and their infrastructure must be reviewed in terms of these new requirements and corresponding measures for adaptation implemented;

(9) Instructors must be trained and upgraded for their new requirements and the training and advanced training facilities must be correspondingly motorised and equipped with the necessary teaching and learning materials;

(10) The polytechnic training facilities, technical colleges and universities must abandon (or limit) their mostly elitist and exclusively scientific course content and methodology and deal more with the needs of the Indian nation and economy;

(11) The above educational facilities and the primary and secondary schools must be radically opened up for the integration and needs of the lower classes, the disadvantaged classes (castes and scheduled tribes) and women;

(12) Greater attention should in future be paid to adult education at all levels and existing state and private facilities should be expanded. These include the literacy programme, distance learning, evening courses, adult education centres etc;

(13) The *private economic sector* must be even more strongly interested and integrated in education and its financial input must be improved;

(14) State, private and social (church, Islamic, Hindu and other) bodies active in education must make joint efforts to support educational facilities and educational policy so that they can meet their responsibilities and make their contribution to national integration.

The Indian government will review the success of the measures cited here every five years and make corrections if necessary[141]. Given the size of the country and the diversity and complexity of the problems to be mastered, it should be assumed that positive developments can only be achieved if India manages to preserve and advance its national unity.

---

140 In this context there is discussion in India (as in other Asian countries) of the vocationalisation of primary and secondary education, i.e. there are efforts to enrich the general educational curricula with relevant occupational content. This is intended to prepare students as early as possible for practical life and subsequent commercial environment of school graduates (similar to the work studies and polytechnic debate in the Federal Republic of Germany).
141 See the Fifth All-India Educational Report, note 137.

3.2.1.3 The general and tertiary education system in India*; competence of the Ministry of Human Resource Development

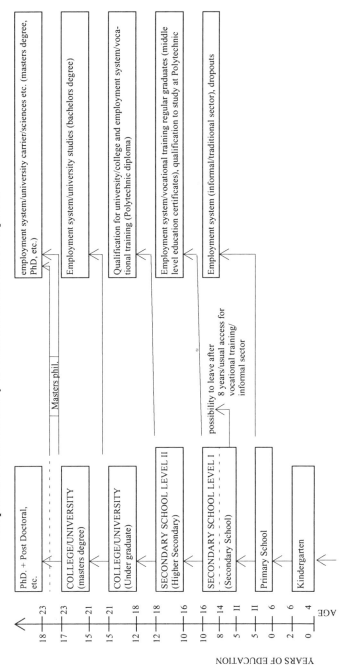

* The new structure of the educational system recommended at the 36th Meeting of the Central Supervisory Commission for Education in September 1972 (10+2+3-system), New Delhi, Ministry of HRD, India

"The future shape of education in India is too complex to envision with precision. Yet, given our tradition which has almost always put high premium on intellectual and spiritual attainment, we are bound to succeed in achieving our objectives. The main task is to strengthen the base of the pyramid, which might come close to a billion people at the turn of the century. Equally, it is important to ensure that those at the top of the pyramid are among the best in the world"[142].

3.2.1.4 – (B) *Vocational training and its relationship to human resource development*

In describing the structure and situation of the Indian labour market it is necessary first to describe the specific characteristics of the potentially active population groups. The boundaries between underemployment and employment, casual work, unpaid labour of family members and unemployment are fluid. Accordingly the statistical data collected in India has limited empirical value. In addition there are the size of the country and the variation in the professionalism of the employment centres, so that the currency and reliability of the collected data are subject to considerable doubt. The data accordingly provides only a rough picture of employment in India. The total active population[143] (employed and unemployed) is given as c. 319 million in 1992-93. In terms of the total population this gives an activity rate of c. 38.3 %. The growth in the active population is shown as c. 8.0 million a year. The official labour market reported c. 26 million jobs in 1988. The goal for the Eighth Five-Year Plan (1992-97) is to create a total of 58.0 million jobs, implying annual growth of 4.0 %. Over the entire long-term planning phase c. 94.0 million jobs will be needed, corresponding to c. 3 % growth a year in employment[144].

---

142 See note 127.
143 For a definition of economically active population see note 23 on p. 102.
144 See Government of India, Eighth Five year Plan, 1992-97, pub. Planning Commission, New Delhi, India, 1992 and Statistisches Bundesamt, Länderbericht Indien 1991, Wiesbaden, Metzler/Poeschel, 1991 and Getubig, I.; Oshima, H.T. eds., Towards Full Employment Strategy For Accelerated Economic Growth, Asian Pacific Development Center, Kuala Lumpur, 1991.

3.2.1.5 The formal vocational training system in India and the responsibility of the Ministry of Labour

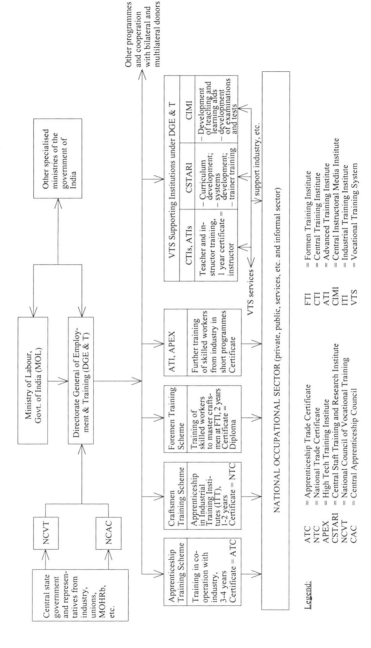

3.2.1.6 Links between general, vocational and tertiary education in India

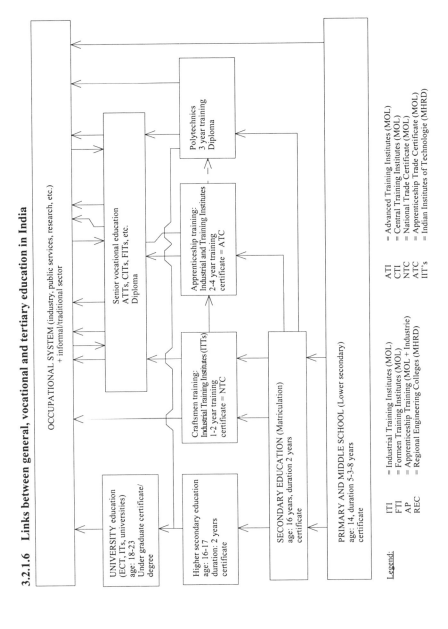

Table VI: *Active population and share in total population*[145]

Active population	Units	1961	1971	1981	1992-93
Total active population	000	188,676	180,485	244,605	319,000
Male	000	129,171	149,146	181,080	–
Female	000	59,505	31,339	63,525	–
Share in total population	%	43.0	32.9	35.7	39.0
Male	%	57.1	52.5	51.1	55.0
Female	%	28.0	11.9	19.2	21.0

However, the creation of new jobs is lagging badly behind demand. The rapid growth in population will further exacerbate this situation, as shown in table VI above. There are particular problems in agriculture, where there is increasing underemployment. The government is trying to combat this problem with employment programmes linked to corresponding training measures. These involve primarily creating income-oriented employment outside the agrarian sector.

---

145 Loc. cit. (modified).

Table VII: *Active population and activity rate by age group*[146]

Age group	1961	1971	1981	1961	1971	1981
	000			%		
< 15	14,470	10,754	13,641	8.0	4.7	5.2
15-20		17,387	26,012	8.0	36.6	40.6
20-25	93,059	21,386	31,224		49.6	54.5
25-30		23,203	31,859	66.2	56.8	62.8
30-35		41,715	28,084		60.4	66.3
35-40			26,352			67.8
40-50	68,877	32,009	43,413	73.8	62.6	68.4
50-60		19,896	26,620		59.6	63.7
60 +	12,231	14,112	17,299	49.5	43.2	40.1
unknown		38	23	102	21.8	19.6	30.6

Table VII shows that child labour (< 15) is still widespread in India: 5 % of the active population according to the 1981 census are children. Child labour is not generally prohibited in India, as the constitution states:

> "24. Prohibition of employment of children in factories, etc. – No child below the age of fourteen years shall be employed to work in any factory or mine or engaged in any other hazardous employment."[147]

However, the statistics show a trend towards a relative decline in child labour, measures against the growth in total population and particularly the younger age groups. There are also serious efforts by the Indian government to eliminate child labour in the long term in the Union States involved, and to create corresponding social services and educational facilities for this purpose.[148]

The breakdown of the active population by economic sectors in the organised and official economy can be seen from the 1981 (census) statistics:

---

146 Loc. cit.
147 Cf. Government of India, The Constitution of India, Nabhi Publication, New Delhi, India, 1992.
148 See also: Ministry of HRD, Programme of Action, 1992, New Delhi, India, pp. 40 et seq and 139 et seq.

(A) Primary sector 62.6 %; (B) secondary sector 12.6 % and (C) tertiary sector 24.8 %. Compared with older statistics there has been a shift towards the tertiary (service) sector. By contrast, employment opportunities in agriculture have declined. This is very much in line with the international trend in development. The statistics provide little information on the non-organised or informal sector. The official sector showed c. 25.8 million employees in 1981, corresponding to a share of c. 8 % of the active population (see table VI). This suggests that the non-organised sector (including the agricultural sector) employs c. 92 % of the active population[149]. This in turn suggests that the informal sector provides a substantial portion of the active population.

The results of general, vocational and tertiary education in terms of the quality and quantity of graduates conflict with the needs of the labour market. This is due partly to the inadequate quantitative capacity of the educational system. Also, there are substantial deficits in curriculum and content, particularly in vocational and tertiary education. The very high dropout rate among school and college students and trainees is just one indicator of the inadequate performance of the educational system. As has already been noted elsewhere, the massive population growth, internal conflicts and the resulting stagnation in economic development and the inadequate growth of the labour market have again thrown the educational system into crisis. The Indian government in its "Programme of Action 1992"[150] has set the following priorities and objectives for comprehensive reform of vocational training by the year 2000:

(1) The existing vocational training system must be expanded and diversified;

---

149 This matches the figures of the Indian labour ministry on the unorganised sector. Two studies on the situation in machine and manual weaving (including the cotton industry) give the following figures:
(A) The unorganised Labour (Sector) which constitutes about 90.6 % of Labour force (As per 1981 census figures) has hitherto remained a neglected part of human resources in the country. This vast majority of illiterate or semiliterate Labour force have not been able to organise itself due to various constraints. Cf. MOL, Ministry of Labour, Government of India, Report on Working and living Conditions of workers in the POWERLOOM Industry in India, New Delhi, 1988.
(B) The handloom industry, by far the largest in the unorganised sector, ranks next only to agriculture in terms of size, income and employment to about 20 million people on 3.3 million handlooms. cf., MOL, Ministry of Labour, Government of India, Report on Working and Living Conditions of Workers in the HANDLOOM Industry in India, New Delhi, 1986-87.
150 Cf. Government of India, GOI, Ministry of HRD, Programme of Action 1992, New Delhi, 1992, see also Government of India, Eighth Five Year Plan, chapter 11, Education, Culture, Sports etc., New Delhi, 1992.

(2) The requirements of the labour market must be taken into account and incorporated by vocational training facilities and programmes quickly, flexibly and in suitable form;

(3) The technological and labour market requirements must be met by technical education and vocational training;

(4) Technical education and vocational training must be broadly based enough in training skilled workers that graduates of educational facilities have adequate mobility in terms of flexibility and employment capability;

(5) Private and state enterprises and other important employers must be involved in conception and implementation of training in a way that ensures that the "world of work" is introduced to trainees during their training and is integrated into the training process;

(6) State and private sponsors of educational facilities and measures in vocational training are called on to develop and implement corresponding measures for training and advanced training in close cooperation with industry and its associations;

(7) The existing government and private systems of full-time training and advanced training facilities (ITI = Industrial Training Institutes; ATI = Advanced Training Institutes) must be modernised, instructors upgraded and the training and advanced training available adapted to the needs of the labour market[151];

(8) "Apprenticeship training"[152] should be augmented and provided in even closer cooperation with the state and private sectors and responsible facilities in training and advanced training. This applies particularly to the selection and hiring of trainees by industry, joint curriculum development, examinations and M+E measures and joint training of trainers and instructors;

(9) All vocational training measures must be opened up to socially disadvantaged groups ("scheduled tribes and castes" and girls and women). Adequate account must be taken of these target

---

151 Cf. 3.2.1.5: Diagram of the vocational training system (on p. 190).
152 Cf. Government of India (GOI), Ministry of Labour, Vocational Training in India, New Delhi, undated, p. 3, Apprenticeship Training Programme:
The Apprenticeship Training Act 1961 makes obligatory for employers in specified industries to engage apprentices. The training programme consists of Basic Training . . . On-The-Job-Floor Training . . . through-out the period of training. So far 138 Trades have been designated under the Apprentices Act, 1961 . . . In all c. 140,000 such Apprenticeship Training agreements have been concluded throughout India. Given the size of India and the uncounted number of businesses, this is a relatively trivial result. An exception here is the traditional apprenticeship system in the bazaars, which is probably considerably more successful, see also the example of Pakistan.

groups in designing training and advanced training and correspondingly involved in the development and complementation process. In addition accompanying supportive measures must be designed to promote the above-named target groups to integrate into the labour market;

(10) Implementing organisations and cooperation partners in the field of vocational training must promote the image of manual labour, i.e. skilled workers, in society. PR measures must be carried out to make the target groups and Indian parnets and other decision makers more aware of this area of education. This includes systematic development of vocational promotional measures for skilled workers and their upgrading by developing corresponding careers in businesses;

(11) The informal and traditional sector must not be neglected in efforts to create training and advanced training places. As this sector, as already shown in the example of the handloom und powerloom industry, has great potential for employment, appropriate cooperative training and advanced training models must be developed which this sector can finance;

(12) Existing training institutes such as the Industrial Training Institute, Advanced Training Institute etc and the training and advanced training facilities of other ministries and private sponsors should be persuaded to cooperate in this;

(13) The curricula, teaching and learning material, qualifications of trainers and instructors at these centres and vocational training facilities must be adapted to the changing requirements of the labour market and the needs of the trainees (target groups). This must be organised as an ongoing process integrated into the educational system;

(14) To improve employment opportunities for graduates of general education and vocational training the Indian government is implementing measures and programmes to create income-oriented employment and self-employment. These measures and strategies have been presented by the Indian government as follows[153]:
  – Promoting faster growth and geographically diversified agricultural production, which means specifically continuing labour-intensive methods of cultivation and processing;

---

153 Cf. Government of India, GOI, Eighth Five Year Plan 1992-1997, New Delhi, 1992. Chapter VIII, Special Employment Programmes.

- Promoting decentralised agro-industry and marketing strategies linked to producers and local and regional markets. Products are sold as far as possible directly by producers and processed locally;
- Promoting programmes to utilise undeveloped (waste) land for agricultural cultivation (vegetables, cereals etc) or forestry (social forestry, i.e. on a communal basis);
- Promoting programmes to protect the environment in agriculture and forestry and small and medium-sized industry;
- Promoting programmes in nonagricultural production and services, i.e. developing small and medium-sized industry in rural and village areas;
- Promoting decentralised industrial development in the production and service sectors, e.g. developing production facilities, infrastructure facilities (transport), road construction etc to promote the local, regional and national markets and infrastructure;
- Promoting special programmes to employ women and eliminate child labour in the affected areas;
- Promoting the health system, specifically in rural areas, through construction of hospitals, clinics, hiring nursing staff, doctors etc;
- Promoting the integration of the informal and traditional sector through developing better credit systems, establishing consultancy services and measures for promoting small (micro) businesses to support technical and economic development;
- Promoting the creation of sustainable economic structures in the local and regional context and securing employment;
- Adapting the general educational and vocational training system to the needs of the labour market (see points 1-14).

As shown by the "Special Programme for Employment"[154], the Indian government places special value on developing and integrating the informal and traditional sector. This economic sector still supplies over 50 % of all available jobs, and accordingly makes a very important contribution (now and in the future) to the successful functioning of the Indian economy[155].

---

154 Loc. cit.
155 See Department of Rural Development, Ministry of Agriculture Government of India, New Delhi, 1991 Manual for Integrated Rural Development Programme (IRDP) and allied Programmes of TRYSEM and DWCRA
– TRYSEM = Training of Rural Youth for Self Employment
– DWCRA = Development of Women and Children in Rural Areas.

3.2.2 Study to develop requirement profiles for small (micro) businessmen and employees in the informal sector in the southern Indian cities of Bangalore and Madras

The study concentrated on small (micro) businessmen and their employees in the informal and unorganised sector in the southern Indian cities of Bangalore and Madras.

Madras has c. 3.5 million inhabitants and with its extensive suburbs and industrial parks outside the city it probably has over 5.0 million inhabitants. The city is the fourth largest in India. It has important processing industries in chemical production, steel profile and steel production manufacture, automotive construction and automotive parts, electronic and computer industry, software development and the agro-industries. In addition Madras has many international banks, airlines and trading companies. Madras also has India's third-largest international port, after Bombay and Calcutta and is the capital of the Union State Tamil Nadu, which is one of India's most important economic states. In the past the city also produced prominent Indian political and cultural figures, such as M.G.R. Ramachandra Rao,the current president of India's Venkatarhaman etc.. It is also the centre of southern Indian Dravidian culture and preserves the traditional culture and its music, theatre and literature and produces it in the Tamil language. Illiteracy is low compared to other Indian cities. Well over 80 % of the population are Hindus, c. 10 % Christians and c. 4-5 % Moslems or other religions. So far Madras has been free from the racist or religious conflicts normal in other Indian cities, with the exception of the usual strikes fomented by politicians for or against the governing parties in New Delhi or Madras. The Tamils are regarded as a peaceful and very civilised ethnic group in India and have also played an important role in the past in implementing multicultural coexistence in India. Many northern Indians, e.g. Punjabis, Sikhs and Moslems, have found sanctuary in Madras. Climatically, Madras is very hot despite its proximity to the sea, and the dry and continental climate is often surprising. However, the rainy seasons (monsoons) are very wet (if irregular) and also necessary, since the city suffers from a chronic water shortages. Like all major Indian cities, Madras suffers from excessive growth, which is particularly evident in the steady increase in the number of slums and temporary accommodation for the rural population flooding into the city. The city is accordingly constantly changing its image: a peaceful residential area can become an overcrowded slum virtually overnight. Nevertheless the city has not lost its special southern Indian attractions and charm and it expresses an Indian lifestyle. Bangalore by contrast is a former British garrison city, because of its more favourable climate at an altitude of c. 1000 m, and is a more modern and very westernised major city. Because of the computer software and electronic industry the Indians also call this the Indian Silicon-Valley. Like Madras, Bangalore has an excellent infrastructure with an international airport, rail links and important road links. The most important industries are tools and machine tools, aircraft construction, arms factories, electrical-goods and electronics (computers and peripherals), control technology, automotive construction and automotive parts and the software production and development for which Bangalore is internationally famous. Like Madras again, Bangalore has an important technical university, colleges and a university. The literacy rate here is also considerable higher than in other comparable Indian cities. In India Bangalore ranks as a major modern city, and in contrast to Madras has little cultural or traditional importance. Nevertheless the city can be regarded as an important centre for Dravidian culture, as shown by the many important buildings and temples in its immediate environment. It also ranks as an important city alongside Mysore for the preservation of the local language, Kannada. Over 80 % of the population are Hindus, c. 15 % probably are Muslims and the remaining c. 4-5 %, are Christians or members of other religions. In contrast to Madras, Bangalore and the Union State of Karnataka are considerably more subject to political and religious conflicts. This is not least due to the endemic leadership crisis in the state going back years and the constant intervention of the Indian central government in the everyday politics of Karnataka. As developments in recent years have shown, Bangalore also has a significantly more militant integrationist Moslem movement, which has kept the city tense for several weeks in the current year as well[156].

Climatically, Bangalore is as already noted very pleasant, and under the British Raj[157] it was regarded as a spa for the harassed colonists and their families. Even today Bangalore has baths and health farms with a long history which are still used by the Indian middle classes. The rainy seasons (monsoons) provide the necessary water, although Bangalore is also coming under increasing pressure from its growing population (c. 3.5 million), with water emergencies in high summer. The growing population is also resulting in slum growth on the fringes of Bangalore. However, the inner city is largely untouched by these developments, thanks to the efforts of the city administration.

---

156 Particularly after the attacks by Muslim integrationists in Bombay and New Delhi there were militant clashes with right-wing Hindus in Bangalore in the Muslim parts of the city.
157 British-Raj = the colonial period.

Bangalore and Madras have many small businesses in the informal and traditional or non-organised sector. In part these businesses produce important cheap products such as household articles in plastic and metal, or process agricultural products (food etc), chemical products (e.g. detergents, soap etc) and repair facilities for all kinds of bicycles, mopeds, sewing machines etc or are transport businesses of all kinds and courier services. Again, it is important not to forget crafts and cotton weaving and dying which provide a significant fraction of the jobs in the informal labour market. The migration from the land and villages and the growing unemployment due to the huge population growth (which also covers the urban population) is resulting in daily growth in the slums of the two cities, which in turn causes even higher unemployment. This has also led to the constant growth of the informal sector. The reasons for the growth of the informal sector are partly the same as those in Pakistan, NFWP, but the cultural, religious, political, sociocultural and socio-economic conditions in southern India are very different. To this extent it is inappropriate to simply transfer the Pakistan results to an Indian context. The profiles of the surveyed entrepreneurs will also differ from those of the Pakistani and Afghan entrepreneurs in NFWP-Peshawar, as highlighted by the study.

This alone is a good enough reason to ensure in future project planning that the target groups are carefully surveyed and the survey results are analysed for the purposes of possible project or promotional approaches. Financial and time constraints unfortunately precluded carrying out a systematic study with a solid empirical and statistical basis which would have given a representative picture, i.e. a comprehensive description of the informal sectors of the two cities (Bangalore and Madras). Although such a study would have been desirable for the present work, the size of the informal sector would have required a substantial budget. In addition, the author believes the complexity of the structure of the informal sector would have made it impossible to quantify the representative structure of the random samples meaningfully, as the universe for the survey is not identifiable. The following survey results are accordingly presented as objectively as possible to provide an heuristic picture in the diagrams. Thanks to the author's years of local experience in the region, this can be used to some extent for the purposes of generalisation in order to formulate corresponding proposals for vocational training approaches in the informal sector in due course. The study excluded agricultural businesses and the handloom – power loom small businesses[158]. The questionnaires were

---

158 The cotton-processing industry, i.e. mechanical and manual can be regarded as a separate sector and traditional sector, as already noted in note 149 on p. 194.

developed and designed to collect information on the evolution of the profiles of the entrepreneurs and employees, and the nature of the business and market. In detail, it covered:

- **Information on entrepreneurs,** such as:
  Role in the business (e.g. proprietor etc), educational background and vocational qualifications, social background and origins, financial background (current loans from banks, family members, friends etc) relationship to employees and place in the economic sector;
- **Information on the businesses,** such as:
  Nature of business, nature of products or services, number of employees and proprietors, buildings, machines, tools, capital;
- **Situation of the entrepreneur, links with market**, such as:
  Entrepreneur and links with market and customers (nature of orders, customers and social origins etc), social structure of the environment of the business;
- **Requirement profile of entrepreneur**, such as:
  Production knowledge and qualifications; personnel management, management, marketing and customer services; social skills, pricing and costing knowledge and other important entrepreneurial qualifications and competences, social role of the entrepreneur in the business and its environment;
- **Requirement profile of business employees**, such as:
  Practical and theoretical abilities, skills and knowledge, educational skills (reading, writing, arithmetic), social competences and specific competences, communication skills and development potential;
- **Selection and hiring criteria for business employees**, such as:
  Recruiting procedures; vocational and general educational requirements; social and religious links or obstacles; conclusion of contracts, rights and duties of employee in the informal and traditional sector, nature of work and payment;
- **Assessment of commercial and infrastructural situation of the business**, such as:
  Based on analysis of the statements of the entrepreneur and the employees and appraisal of the means of production, the quality and nature of orders and the business's order book (i.e. plausibility check on the statements of respondents);
- **Assessment of the relevance of training and advanced training measures**, such as:
  Are such training and advanced training measures available, are they relevant or useful for the entrepreneurs and employees sur-

veyed, is there specific need for training and advanced training among the respondents;
- **Assessment of the importance of the informal sector for economic development and the labour market.**

3.2.2.1 *Analysis of the information and requirements profiles for the surveyed entrepreneurs and employees surveyed and links with local and regional markets*

The analysis of the survey and accompanying observations[159] using the criteria listed under 3.2.2 can be summarised as follows. First, however, some important information is needed on the context and the nature of the businesses in the informal sector selected for the survey at Madras and Bangalore.

(A) In Madras these were more the *street corner and bazaar businesses typical of the informal sector*, producing directly for their immediate neighbourhood;
(B) In Bangalore by contrast they were more small (micro) businesses located on the fringe of a major industrial estate and mostly having their market and customers there;

These specific settings had a corresponding influence on the results of the surveys, i.e. the element of random choice was constrained from the start by the choice of location and the nature of the businesses. Based on the author's years of experience in India (in the region), it was possible nevertheless to take into account industries important to the informal sector to give an impression of need, requirements and development potential of the individual segments. 50 % of the entrepreneurs surveyed in Bangalore were women in the textile and agro-product industries (e.g. flower selling, food conservation and production). The following segments of the informal sector were taken into account:

(A) Services:
- Transport businesses;
- Courier services, repair shops (automotive, metal, electrical);
(B) Production:
- Metalworking businesses (windows, doors, grills, containers etc);

---

159 Cf. section 3.1.12.1 of the present work.

- Plastic processing businesses (products for households, sub-contracting for the construction sector);
- Textile (making up men's and women's clothing);
- Wood processing (construction, furniture, carpentry etc);
- Electronic businesses (assembly of electronic components, subcontracting);
- Small (micro) printers (screen printing etc);
- Agro-industry products, such as food conservation (fruit, vegetables, chutneys etc).

Breakdown of surveyed businesses into the main segments (production, maintenance and transport) in Madras and Bangalore

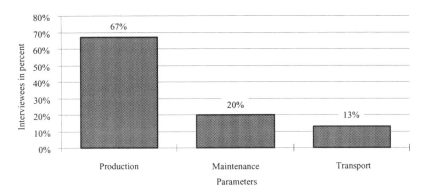

The small (micro) businesses surveyed are all new businesses in the informal (non-organised) sector, with a very few exceptions, and as such are not officially registered or listed for tax by the competent agencies. The exceptions are businesses funded (now or in the past) through state promotional programmes, but these are a minority. Answers to the question how entrepreneurs dealt with the tax authorities were similar to those in the Pakistan case study (see section 3.1.12.1): they satisfy the state tax officials through one-time annual payments or special services. This saves the businesses the burden of applications, controls and systematic book-keeping. However, this is only possible for the street corner workshops; while for small (micro) businesses working for industrial customers this approach is considerably more questionable. According to the author's opinion and experience, it is not possible in India to avoid registration and taxation, as the

Indian bureaucracy is significantly better developed in this area than is the case in Pakistan. Information on tax affairs should accordingly be treated with great caution, as the respondents (understandably) replied very carefully to questions about taxes, turnover and registration. It is, however, clear that the state is losing substantial tax revenue through the highly bureaucratic, centrally managed and very complicated procedure. To make things worse, corrupt officials deliberately obstruct this to collect the additional benefits themselves.

Businesses often lack suitable production workshops, good tools, machines, capital and – particularly in the textile segment – modern designs for products with marketing impact. This also applies in part to carpentry shops making household items, e.g. furniture. Production premises and workshops are mostly leased, and generally cannot be modified for requirements. Rents (per m^2) are very high, so that there is often a lack of corresponding storage and office rooms. This has an adverse effect on the organisation of the business and generally prevents expansion of order books and processing. Frequently the cramped premises of businesses in the informal sector also result in what the outsider sees as chaotic conditions in the workshops. Entrepreneurs are often forced to convert living space into production workshops during the day. This is particularly the case in textile processing (tailors etc) and processing agro-products (making fruit conserves, chutneys etc). The street corner workshops already mentioned move their production to the pavement and curbs where streets permit. This type of production generally forces the use of manual production methods and simple technologies which can be employed without stationary machinery and electricity. For the most part e.g. for welding or metalworking, the cumbersome protective devices have been removed from the machines and passing pedestrians are also put at risk. In other cases production is moved directly to the building site or to the customer's house or property. This avoids burdensome investment in workshops and other infrastructure. Many entrepreneurs surveyed had also succeeded in leasing a small workshop or shop in the traditional bazaar streets or, as the Bangalore survey showed, close to the industrial estate. In any event, entrepreneurs in the informal sector try to settle and produce as close as possible to their markets. This avoids additional costs for transport and seeking new business, which is mostly done by word of mouth recommendation. They are generally not listed in the post office yellow pages, but are recommended by former customers, friends and acquaintances. The informal information system is very comprehensive and reliable in terms of the entrepreneur's abili-

ties, reliability, price and quality. If an entrepreneur makes serious mistakes or is too expensive, he will get very few new orders.
Another far-reaching problem for the development of entrepreneurial potential is the high investment and energy costs if machinery and electricity are required for production. Many technological processes require these, as products e.g. in metalworking and wood processing, require a certain shape and precision which can only be achieved efficiently by using at least a degree of mechanical processing. Welding equipment and for textiles sewing machines, irons, and lighting also require electricity. State or communal power utilities demand a great deal of money for professional or industrial mains connections. Entrepreneurs complain about these costs which also often involve heavy bribery to get connected at all. This also applies to telephone connections[160]. Many entrepreneurs simply cannot afford a telephone and use local facilities if necessary. These are only the most important obstacles and cost factors which can block the establishment and development of a business in the informal sector[161].
On average the businesses have up to five helpers, 3-4 skilled workers and often have a manger or supervisor in addition to the entrepreneur. A striking feature here is that the social origin and position of entrepreneur, helper, skilled worker and supervisor are not determined as in Pakistan by extended families and tribal ties: in southern India caste plays a very important role in recruiting. This results in a very strong sense of social belonging and correspondingly high level of loyalty among employees, and also ensures a lack of labour conflict. Entrepreneurs in the businesses surveyed mostly had very high educational qualifications and often were members of the higher social classes (castes). Family relationships generally help minimise risk for the individual. If loans are needed or financial or other problems arise, the family steps in as a matter of course and problems are solved jointly. In contrast to Pakistan, proprietors mostly do not work as skilled workers[162], but concentrate on management, getting new business, customer support and staff management. They often regard their function as

---

160 In India connections can cost up to 20-50,000 Rupees with waiting times of 3-10 years.
161 Frequently the necessary sanitary and hygienic facilities are also lacking, to say nothing of water supplies, sewerage or even disposal of the toxic substances occurring in production. Here, the street has to serve, which often leads to an extremely filthy, slum-like environment. The government or the local authorities do not even do the minimum necessary to ensure regulated growth in an environment fit for humans. Most politicians and office-holders simply collect their "extra incomes".
162 This does not apply to all industries, e.g. in the modern technological sectors (textile design, electronics, computer technology etc) highly-qualified entrepreneurs (mostly engineers, designers etc) also work in the daily operation of the business.

managerial (making money) rather than technical. Entrepreneurs also have to deal with the private problems of their employees, as this is their obligation under the system of caste relations (higher and lower and between casts) particularly typical of India. Most (or all) entrepreneurs in India are terrified by the unions, so that they try to restrict businesses to a certain size. They prefer to set up a new business to reduce the risk of unionisation of employees, since it is easier to keep 10-15 employees under control than 50. Even so there is a strong trade union movement in India, although this focuses mainly on the organised sector where it causes many social conflicts and strikes and works vigorously to improve the working conditions of employees. In the author's view this is an important contribution to the functioning of the "biggest democracy on earth". The informal or non-organised sector has little or no union activity, since employees live on the brink of survival, their income and social awareness and their social role are too low or poorly developed because of their low caste or casteless status. These target groups are primarily concerned with survival first and foremost. This does not apply to the entrepreneurs, so to this extent there is a qualitative difference from the Pakistan case study. However, in terms of relations with

- government agencies;
- banks (private and state);
- development aid programmes of bilateral and multilateral aid organisations and cooperation with government agencies;
- or other government-organised promotional programmes for the informal sector and small businesses

the response of those surveyed was basically negative. Past experience is described as basically a problem, although use of bank loans and participation in development programmes are present in around 40 % of cases in Bangalore and Madras. This is significantly higher than in the Pakistan case, and the reason for this is undoubtedly the higher than average educational background (and qualifications) of the entrepreneurs surveyed. The statements of the entrepreneurs can be summarised as follows:

- entrepreneurs in the informal sector with inadequate *formal education* and *belonging to the lower social classes* have basically poor prospects of being included in the craft and small business promotional programmes of national and international development banks;

- entrepreneurs in the *informal sector* have *no lobby* with the political parties and competent government agencies. They also have *no representative organisations* generally, such as guilds, chambers, associations etc to represent their interests;
- They are frequently *not recognised as important target groups* by state and private banks, and accordingly do not count as potential customers for loans or other promotional programmes; mostly the loans are also too small for banks and are *uneconomical from the point of view of the banks;*
- The informal sector is *not regarded as an important and expanding economic sector*, i.e. as an important *employer and economic factor* under the official development policy of the countries, regions and institutions etc.

The following diagrams show an overview of the current types of financing in Madras and Bangalore for the entrepreneurs surveyed. The comments on the diagrams correspond to those in section 3.1.12.1. Further explanation of the diagrams is accordingly omitted.

Type and potential for financing, Madras

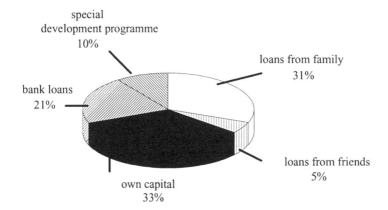

Type and potential for financing, Bangalore

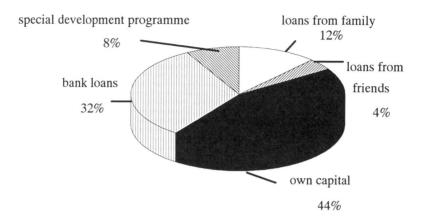

Profile of surveyed entrepreneurs in Madras and Bangalore

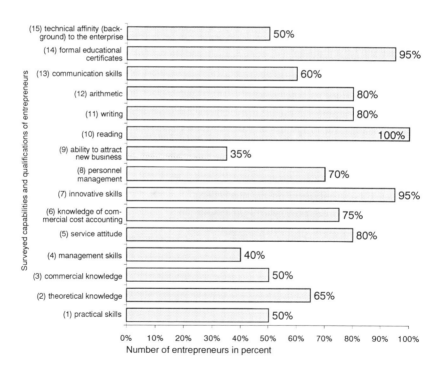

The profile of respondents shows serious shortfalls in the areas practical skills (1), theoretical knowledge (2), commercial knowledge (3), management skills (4), ability to attract new business (9), communication skills (13) and the entrepreneur's technical background (15) for the entrepreneurs surveyed. In contrast to the Pakistan case study, these entrepreneurs attached strikingly high value to knowledge and skills from formal education, such as formal educational certificates (14), arithmetic (12), writing (11), reading (10) and knowledge of commercial cost accounting (6). These results show that the entrepreneurs can be assigned to a different social class than in the Pakistan case study, and it is also clear that the significantly higher degree of schooling and generally better educational qualifications in southern India also influence the educational structure in the informal sector in this region. Specifically, it is clear that a different type of entrepreneur has evolved here, one who does not become an entrepreneur exclusively from a craft and technical background and motivation, but rather from the drive to earn money through the work of others. This also partly explains the lack of technical affinity (15) to the products manufactured evident or implicit in the profile. This suggests that the target group for promoting entrepreneurs in the informal sector should not be identified exclusively in terms of the technical profile, but that the purely entrepreneurial characteristics shown in the profile can also be extremely important. A requirement is, however, that the person or applicant in question should show the outstanding characteristics of the entrepreneurial type, such as.:

- courage to take the risk of starting a business;
- above-average readiness to act in an entrepreneurial way and corresponding commitment;
- delight in new ideas and innovations;
- drive to achieve a decisive improvement in his social and financial position in society;
- lack of inhibitions about breaking through the social and political barriers set by the caste system;
- responsibility towards other people and willingness to do the work and carry out the orders in line with the normal criteria in the market.

Many of these characteristics, skills and competences cannot be developed or inculcated exclusively at school. They are often present as natural talents, which only have to be activated at the right moment and under the right circumstances. The majority of the businesses surveyed are in the urban areas of Madras and Bangalore and accordingly have their markets and customers in this area.

Information on market and sales areas

Madras

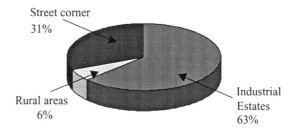

Street corner 31%
Rural areas 6%
Industrial Estates 63%

Bangalore

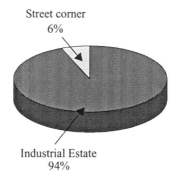

Street corner 6%
Industrial Estate 94%

A striking feature is (as the Pakistan case study also showed) that the businesses are located in the immediate proximity of their markets and customers. This is partly due to the lack of infrastructure, financial resources and mobility of small businesses which would be required for small businesses to offer and market products and services over longer distances. There is also often a lack of suitable support structures, cheap transport facilities and communication facilities for dealing with longer distances. Information on the social status and type of customer is shown in the following diagrams.

Type and social structure of customers

Madras

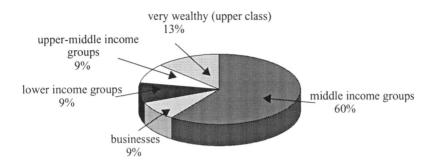

Type and social structure of customers

Bangalore

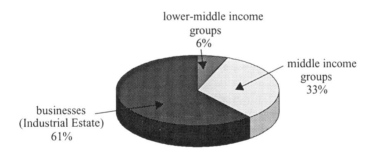

The diagrams show that in Madras the businesses surveyed in the informal sector draw c. 74 % of their customers from the upper income groups in society. In Bangalore by contrast (due to the proximity and nature of businesses) c. 61 % of customers are businesses from the nearby Industrial Estate. These are accordingly mainly service or sub-contracting businesses for the larger companies on the Industrial Estate. Another proportion (c. 33 %) of orders comes from the nearby residential areas, i.e. from middle income group customers.

Type and relationship to customers in Madras and Bangalore

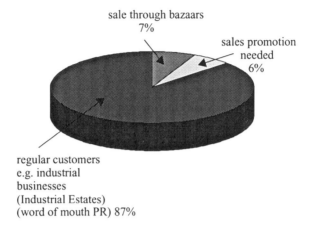

This diagram again shows the type of link between businesses in the informal sector and their customers. A very small fraction of products is sold through bazaars and/or marketing activities by the businesses. Most of the goods, services and production orders are for regular customers (industrial businesses) as subcontractors. The relationship shown here is naturally not representative of all businesses in the informal sector in Bangalore and Madras but reflects only the businesses surveyed. This area of the development of markets and products and services customised for markets is, in the author's view, still completely unresearched, "specifically as far as the opportunities of the informal sector are concerned". In future, when promotion of projects in the informal sector is an issue, studies should pay particular attention to this area. Further comments on this issue are made above in section 3.1.12.1; and these can broadly be transferred to the situation in India.

3.2.2.2 *Analysis of information on the businesses surveyed and their employees (requirement profile in Madras and Bangalore)*

The survey of entrepreneurs in the informal sector and their attitude to their employees was intended to provide information on the following key issues:

- requirement profile of employees;
- status of employees in the business;
- selection and hiring criteria;
- social benefits and security of employees.

The survey and accompanying observations of a total of 60 businesses surveyed in the informal sector in Madras and Bangalore were carried out using the following parameters (a-g):

(a) *Vocational and general educational requirements*;
(b) *Abilities, skills and knowledge* in vocational context, i.e. for example how professionally assigned work is done;
(c) *Identification with the business* in the informal sector and *social status of employees in the business;*
(d) *Social competences* of employees, such as adaptability, ability to work in a team, readiness to work as individuals and accept changes in social situation or integration (requirements going beyond caste membership);
(e) *Competences in communicative skills*, such as mastery of informal speech (reading and writing etc) and other important commercial languages (such as Tamil, Talugu, Kannada, Hindi or English);
(f) *Motivation and mobility* of employees in the informal sector, personal and family (caste) situation and expectations of employers;
(g) *Employer expectations* in the informal sector, *their role* and *relationship with employees.*

Status of employees in businesses in Madras and Bangalore

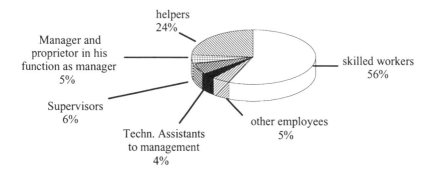

Skilled workers have mostly completed an apprenticeship in the informal sector (on-the-job training) or have corresponding non-formal or formal vocational basic training. This basic training can be obtained at ITI (Industrial Training Institutes) through a 1-2 year full-time training after graduating from the 8th-10th class. Alternatively the technical knowledge and craft skills are acquired in the business in question and the worker works up from helper to skilled worker. 57 % of workers clearly come under the category of skilled worker[163], supervisors and technical assistants representing 11 % can also be assigned to this category, so that a total of c. 68 % skilled workers are employed in the businesses surveyed. Around one-quarter (24 %) of employees of these businesses are helpers and can be regarded as totally unqualified. In contrast to the Pakistan examples the businesses selected and surveyed in Bangalore and Madras have developed a supervisory and management level. This may be partly due to the fact that many of the entrepreneurs surveyed do not have a craft and technical background, and in some cases also have very high educational qualifications. In addition there is the socio-cultural and traditional context of southern Indian society, which still very strongly favours and follows the caste hierarchy, as craft and manual work is reserved for lower social classes. If the entrepreneur can finance this in any way, this automatically makes necessary a technical management level in the businesses[164].

---

[163] Skilled worker = must not be confused with the equivalent German term. He has only a certain basic knowledge and is able to perform the tasks assigned to him independently up to a certain point. These requirements are determined essentially by the production processes and division of labour in the businesses.

[164] See note 102 on p. 166.

Profile of employees in the business surveyed in the informal sector in Madras and Bangalore

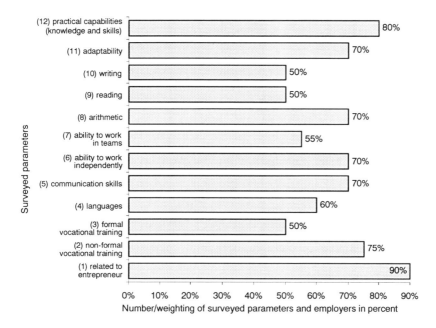

Comments on the profile of the skilled workers employed in the informal sector, which shows the following key features:

No.	Parameter	Comments	Importance in %
(1)	Hiring features	A very large proportion of employees in the informal sector are recruited through direct family relationships or other direct relationships to the proprietor. Abstract standards or requirements are very seldom applied.	90 %
(2)	Non-formal vocational training	Many employees have acquired their knowledge, skills and abilities in the businesses and outside the formal educational system.	75 %
(4) (5)	Languages Communication skills	India as a multicultural and multinational society often requires knowledge of more than two languages. This is the basis for being able to communicate with customers coming from the various Union States.	70 %
(6)	Ability to work independently	This means technical and extrafunctional qualifications which enable employees to carry out the assigned work independently.	70 %
(8)	Arithmetic	This means mastery of the four basic arithmetical functions. This is important for a wide range of responsibilities.	70 %
(11)	Adaptability	Adaptability of employees essentially refers to focus on customers and the ability to fit in with the operation of the business and its hierarchical structure.	70 %
(12)	Practical skills	These are concrete practical skills, abilities and knowledge. They serve primarily to perform the work (manufacture the product or provide the service) in a reasonable time with appropriate quality.	80 %

On further enquiry the employers confirm that they rate the quality of their employees on the above criteria (1) to (12) but for recruiting the qualitative features in the profile play a subordinate role, as most employers state that they hire employees almost entirely on the basis of relationship, acquaintance, recommendation by trusted individuals, caste membership or other social links important to them. The aim is essentially to prevent *"trouble makers"* from getting into the business.

As a result the formal and technical qualifications of applicants are initially of secondary importance, as the social ties with the employer are more important. This must in any case be taken into account as an important factor in all promotional programmes, i.e. the social network and informal links between potential target groups must be studied in detail and taken into account. This inevitably also leads to the need for intensive involvement in planning and implementing the measures of both wage earners and the entrepreneurs involved in the promotion (see also the recommendations on p. 169).

3.2.3 *Evaluation of the studies carried out in Bangalore and Madras*

The socio-cultural, socio-economic and political conditions in the region have shown that the experience collected in the Pakistan (regional) context of the NFWP cannot be transferred without further consideration. It is clear that the informal sector is developing in parallel with the formal sector and can primarily develop in the economic sectors and areas of employment where the formal sector needs cheaper products and services. Alternatively, it can grow through gaps in production of consumer goods, services and other areas of production (specifically agro-production) where the formal sector leaves the informal and traditional or non-organised sector enough scope to develop. In the Indian context it is important not to overlook the traditional cotton and carpet small (micro) industry (handloom and power loom) and the Khadi industry[165] founded by Gandhi. These economic segments of the so-called "unorganised sector" represent a vast potential for employment in the informal sector[166]. In southern India the tanning and leatherworking industry also offers an important field for the development of small (micro) businesses and widespread home based industries. Leather products and textiles are major export areas (the Federal Republic of Germany in particular is an important market for these products) for southern Indian small (micro) businesses and medium-sized companies. Under some circumstances this can also be

---

165 Khadi-Industries = cotton production, weaving and spinning and making the material up into mainly traditional garments. This is a major market, since traditional Hindus only wear natural products, which are also increasingly preferred in the western industrialised nations.
166 Cf. Government of India, Eighth Five Year Plan 1992-93, New Delhi, India 1992, p. 132
"One of the areas of priority of the Eighth Plan is generation of adequate employment to achieve near full employment level by the turn of this century ... It's possible to dovetail programmes of khadi, village industries, handlooms, sericulture and handicrafts to integrated local area development programmes for selects villages poverty alleviation through increase in employment ... and the informal sector will be made free of innumerable rules, regulations and bureaucratic controls."

viewed as an example of how whenever the informal sector (cotton production, textile products and leather goods) becomes a factor through home-based industrial production and also gains indirect access to the world market, it becomes exposed to and required to meet the quality standards of the world market. This in turn requires a certain allocation of resources to training and advanced training measures for the crafts involved in production, if these standards are also to be met in the output of small businesses and home-based groups and families. It is important in this context to recognise the joint responsibility of customers, as child labour is particularly apparent in these sectors in India. As noted elsewhere the Indian government is trying to reduce this evil through corresponding promotional policies, but this can only be successful if income-generating occupations can be created for adult family members and the international community refuses to accept products (primarily) manufactured using child labour. This means developing the willingness among consumers in the western industrialised nations to pay more than in the past for products from these countries (carpets etc). It is accordingly a matter of principle not merely to support or assist uncritically and irresponsibly the expansion of the informal sector and employment in this sector. Instead, the promotional strategies of bilateral and multilateral donors must focus on the exploitation and socially unjustifiable conditions and poor living conditions of these people. The following aspects should accordingly be taken into account in identifying, planning and implementing promotional measures

- *Target groups* must be clearly identified and described in accordance with the criteria developed in section 2.4;
- The target groups *absolutely* must be *adequately involved* in identifying measures to promote these groups;
- The *socio-cultural, socio-economic, traditional* and *social environments* must be studied and duly *taken into account* in developing and implementing projects in the informal sector;
- The *economic and development policy goals of bilateral and multilateral* donors must be reviewed for their promotion of local and regional labour markets and corrected if necessary;
- Promotion of the informal sector *includes designing measures to promote small (micro) businesses* and creating *appropriate training and advanced training measures for entrepreneurs and skilled workers*;
- Promotion in the above sectors must, however, be combined with measures to develop *labour markets* and *employment* in the areas of *self-employment and employment*;

- Measures in the informal sector must as a matter of principle be designed so that they make a *long-term contribution towards the integration* of the informal *economic and employment sector* into the formal economic sector;
- *Access to promotional measures* must *not be formalised* and must be *unconditionally available* to the *target groups and individuals in the informal sector*;
- The *basic didactic structure* of the vocational training and development policy promotional concepts for the target groups in the informal sector must be based on an *open, action-oriented, anthropocentric didactic approach*, i.e. the following aspects must be taken into account:
  - *extrafunctional education to secure survival* and future-oriented development
  - *education* to develop *self-help potential*;
  - education to secure employment or self-employment
  - *education* to *create and secure income*;
- To *support systematic orientation of projects*, projects with the goal of promoting the informal and traditional sector must also aim at *moving towards or promoting openness of the formal vocational or general education sector*, i.e. integration into the formal sector should be sought (cf. section 3.1.8);
- *New measures or concepts* for training skilled workers and entrepreneurs in the informal sector should *as a matter of principle take into account existing traditional training concepts or systems* and possibly integrate them (cf. traditional apprenticeships, section 3.1.6.6).

3.2.4 Photo documentation on the informal sector in southern India

Traditional blacksmith
Family business, manufacture and repair of domestic and farm equipment

(Photo: Sigrun Neumann)

Traditional backsmith
Family business and mobile business, manufacture and repair of domestic and farm equipment.

(Photo: Sigrun Neumann)

Traditional blacksmith
Family business and mobile business, manufacture and repair of domestic and farm equipment, shoeing draught animals.

(Photo: Sigrun Neumann)

Traditional wheelwright
Family business for manufacture and repair of ox carts and wagon wheels

(Photo: Sigrun Neumann)

Traditional wheelwright
Family business for manufacture and repair of ox carts and wagon wheels

(Photo: Sigrun Neumann)

Traditional ropemaker
Family business for manufacture of rope

(Photo: Sigrun Neumann)

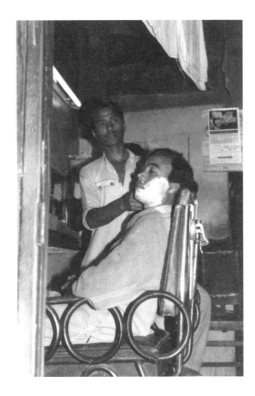

Traditional hairdresser
Family business with two employees

(Photo: Sigrun Neumann)

Traditional fish market
Fisherman sells his catch
family business

(Photo: Sigrun Neumann)

Traditional weaver
Manufacture of cotton
cloth and carpets

(Photo: Sigrun Neumann)

Street vendor
and production of sugar cane juice (beverage)

(Photo: Sigrun Neumann)

Street vendor
Sale of dried legumes etc.

(Photo: Sigrun Neumann)

Motorised rickshaw waiting for passengers

(Photo: Sigrun Neumann)

Bicycle rickshaw
waiting for
customers

(Photo:
Sigrun Neumann)

*Collecting firewood
for sale*
a typical activity for
women

(Photo: Sigrun Neumann)

4 Employment-creating training for target groups in the informal sector – Approaches to holistic, target-group centred vocational pedagogics

4.1 *The context and need for vocational pedagogics oriented towards the informal sector*

The preceding chapters have shown the need for and importance to development policy of including the informal sector as a special area for promotion in vocational training aid. Far-reaching changes will be needed to existing promotional policies of bilateral and multilateral donors and the ministries responsible in the countries of the Third World. Vocational training aid has to develop and implement new concepts and strategies for achieving these goals. The new *sectoral concept* of the BMZ[1] is an important step in this direction, as this is the first time that the informal sector has been explicitly cited as one of the key areas for promotion in the context of vocational training aid. The World Bank in its new Policy Paper[2] has also emphasised the informal sector in connection with employment-creating vocational training as having future importance as a key point for promotion. A major reason for the past neglect of the informal sector in bilateral and multilateral vocational training aid is a faulty evaluation by the donor nations, which assumed that the informal sector would develop in the wake of the modern and industrial sector. The basic assumption was that the economically advanced sectors would develop sufficient self-sustaining economic development which would then trickle down to the other (less successful) sectors of the economy and labour market, so that in the long term sufficiently broad impact could be achieved[3]. However, developments in the past 30 years have shown that this assumption was illusory, as demonstrated by the case studies from India and Pakistan in the present work.

The informal sector has not disappeared as hoped – instead, it has expanded in most Third World countries. If the current global economic crisis intensifies, it is likely that this sector will also become an

---

1 Cf. BMZ, Sektorkonzept: Berufliche Bildung, BMZ, Bonn 1992.
2 Cf. World Bank, Vocational and Technical Education and Training, The World Bank, Washington D.C., 1991, chapter 1, pp. 11 et seq.
3 In this connection the expression "trickle-down-effect" has often been used.

emerging factor in the industrialised nations. The former communist nations (Eastern Block) are already experiencing uncontrolled development and expansion of the informal sector. Criticism of the past one-sided orientation of vocational training aid is prompted by the following inaccurate assessments in bilateral and multilateral aid.
- industrialisation of Third World countries is essential for social and economic development and progress generally in these countries;
- industrialisation and modernisation of national economies are the key to overcoming the underdeveloped state of Third World countries;
- a crucial barrier to the emergence or success of industrialisation is the lack of strategies to develop adequately qualified skilled workers, middle-level technical management potential and top management;
- the industrialisation process can only be effective and sustainable if the technical and institutional requirements for ensuring training and advanced training of skilled workers and management are met and secured in the long term;
- demand for skilled workers and technically-qualified managers is more or less unlimited, justifying high investment and spending on development aimed exclusively at the modern sector;[4],[5]
- given the anticipated technological progress and technology transfer to the Third World countries, training and advanced training for skilled workers and middle-level technical managers requires a very high technological standard of qualification for these individuals, justifying extensive promotion of elites;
- these skilled workers and managers can accordingly only be trained in multi-establishment or external training facilities with correspondingly modern equipment and in co-operation with the relevant establishments; in this process the required practical and theoretical qualifications must be taught and acquired.

4　Cf. note (13) paper by W.-D. Greinert: Instrumente und Strategien der Systementwicklung/Systemberatung. "Greinert supports this thesis by reference to the economic dualistic relationships in an analysis by Lutz, B. (6). Based on an analysis of the European example of historical and economic developoment, this reference argues that the modern sector has a relationship of positive interchange with the traditional/informal sector and functions effectively as a locomotive for development (in both a positive and negative sense). This would then also justify concentrating promotional resources on the formal sector of the economy." In the author's view this argument is correct but difficult in that the formal sector in many Third World countries only functions in this way because it receives corresponding support from the informal sector. This is why European experience based on extensive industrialisation can only be applied to Third World countries which have similar development trends.
5　Cf. also: Lutz, Burkhart: Der kurze Traum immerwährender Prosperität. Eine Neuinterpretation der industriell-kapitalistischen Entwicklung im Europa des 20. Jahrhunderts, Frankfurt/New York, 1989

Such an approach to vocational training aid assumes that the modern sector will follow the pattern of western industrialisation and be able to employ the mass of school leavers and others seeking work. However, the experience of the past 30 years of development co-operation shows that this trend has followed or will follow in very few countries[6]. In addition, we know that vocational training without the corresponding economic development in a country will not be able to solve the problem of employment, let alone offer a secure job. Further, experience with vocational training projects under German Technical Co-operation with Third World countries has shown that the modern sector is incapable of absorbing the vast number of school leavers and that the technical colleges (full-time educational facilities) often provide an education which is not aligned to the needs of the labour market[7]. Mostly, these graduates are not looking for work in the informal sector, nor are the employers in this sector interested in graduates of these facilities: the products of conventional vocational training facilities The graduates of conventional vocational training facilities are not suited to employment in the informal sector by virtue of the social status attaching to their formal educational qualifications and the resulting view of themselves and their entitlements. A system of vocational pedagogics which accepts the informal sector as part of the existing system of employment would accordingly also have to acknowledge the specific problems of this sector and contribute to removing the artificial divide between the formal, non-formal and informal educational sectors. It would have to take a holistic approach which puts people back at the focus of vocational pedagogical thinking and concepts. This is particularly true of vocational training aid, since it is vital to avoid a situation where this is used exclusively for developing the modern and industrial sectors in Third World countries. It is accordingly an important responsibility for the donor nations and specifically for German vocational training aid to develop instruments and vocational pedagogical concepts which give greater emphasis to promoting informal sector in development policy key programmes and strategies. This will meet particular resistance from the elites and decision-makers in many Third World countries, where the informal sector is frequently regarded and presented as neither attractive nor worthy of promotion.

6   However, this is only partly true: the so-called "new tigers" in south-east Asia give new hope, as a number of countries here have clearly succeeded in making the breakthrough into the world economy. Countries like Thailand, Indonesia, Singapore, Malaysia, Korea etc have high economic growth and have clearly established themselves as modern industrialised societies.
7   Cf. Thiel, R.E., Berufsbildung – nur für Eliten ?, in BMZ (pub.), Entwicklung und Zusammenarbeit, No. 2, Bonn, 1985.

Many countries here adopt a posture of studied ignorance, treating this sector as non-existent. This situation is not helped by suggestions like those of Greinert/Wiemann that experts in developing countries are more appropriate to help this sector autonomously and with their own resources. It is undoubtedly true that vocational education projects have little prospect of success without links to other projects such as regional development projects and craft promotion programmes. However, it is doubtful (and experience with Technical Co-operation bears this out) that the proposed division of labour between donor and developing countries is feasible (see quote) or helpful.

"The vocational training required for the informal sector can only be an element in integrated promotion with key points which are specific to regions, crafts and social groups. In implementing such programmes the developing countries themselves are much more expert and capable of adaptation, externally-managed and specialist vocational training aid can achieve nothing here as the requirements for such a concept are not met at all. Vocational training aid by the industrialised nations must accordingly focus on improving the expert capability in developing countries and promoting the creation of vocational training systems in order to support infrastructural improvements."[8]. Vocational training aid – as now reflected in the BMZ sectoral concept (1992) – gives developing countries access to international and German experience in implementing vocational training projects in the formal, non-formal and informal sectors and assist them with issues systems development. We should, however, beware of specifying areas in co-operation between development aid organisations and the developing countries where they are subsequently held responsible for non-implementation of specified key promotional programmes but at the same time given a ready-made excuse for failure because they are able to pass on responsibility for failures to the developing countries themselves. While there is no suggestion that this was the intention of the authors quoted above, donor countries must not be relieved of their political responsibility to make a serious effort to give greater priority to the informal sector and the poor population groups in the Third World in their promotional key areas. It is also not apparent why vocational pedagogics should not take up this difficult issue, given the absence in many Third World countries of suitable research facilities, qualified scientists or corresponding funding, as financial resources are frequently budgeted and spent

---

8   Cf., Greinert, W.-D., Wiemann, G., Produktionsschulprinzip und Berufsbildungshilfe, Baden-Baden, 1993, 2nd edn, p. 17, and Arnold, R., Burk, H.: Der Streit um die Berufsbildungshilfe in Entwicklung und Zusammenarbeit, No. 12., 1987, pp. 14-17.

exclusively in the modern, strategic sector. This is yet another reason for the established vocational pedagogic system in Germany and official government development aid to contribute concepts and scientific and financial resources for developing vocational pedagogics in connection with integrating the needs of the informal sector. A modest start has already been made by the BMZ through the frequently-quoted study by C. Lohmar-Kuhnle[9] (1991). The goal of the study was to identify the need for promotion of the informal sector in terms of training for target groups within the framework of future vocational training measures. The study puts human beings at the centre of future promotional approaches, and Lohmar-Kuhnle talks of human-centred approaches to vocational training aid in the informal sector. These approaches (as shown in chapter 2.0) require relating to the culture, tradition and specific concept of work in the partner countries. They also require *complex* and *multidimensional identification of target groups*[10], as developed in section 2.4 of this study. For classic vocational training aid this means initiating a transformation in vocational training strategies, given the worldwide growth of the informal sector and the need to abandon the notion of this sector as a temporary phenomenon of disrupted development in favour of understanding it as a permanent. "As a result of these developments the social policy pressure on the governments of the developing countries is increasing. This also means rising expectations of vocational training's ability to help resolve the general problem, i.e. to create training vacancies for an annually increasing number of young people. In this situation we can see a distinction or a shift in vocational training strategies, replacing or supplementing the "classic" system-oriented training approach ("development of widespread, formal, systematically-organised vocational training systems") by flexible approaches to integrated training measures for the informal sector which have relevance to life."[11] Vocational training must accordingly be expanded to cover target groups in the informal sector and convey competencies, skills and knowledge which are oriented towards the living environment and employment."[12] "The focus here is firmly on knowledge and competencies in self-organisation, and establishing and running firms."[13] According to C.

---

9 Cf. note 42 (on p. 33), p. 32.
10 Cf. loc. cit.
11 Cf. Arnold, R., Interkulturelle Berufspädagogik, BWP 8b, Oldenburg 1991, p. 99.
12 Cf. Arnold, R., Neue Akzente der internationalen Berufsbildungs-Debatte-Impulse für eine künftige Entwicklungszusammenarbeit im Bereich der beruflichen Bildung ?
13 In: Biermann, H., Greinert, W.-D., Janisch, R. (pub. GTZ, Eschborn) Systementwicklung und Systemberatung in der Berufsbildungshilfe (Berichte, Analysen, Konzepte), Nomos, Baden-Baden, 1994.

Lohmar-Kuhnle[14] and Arnold[15] there are essentially four model approaches to promoting this sector through vocational training aid which can promote employment:
- individual training and advanced training oriented towards the (labour) market and/or subsistence;
- training and extension work to promote economic independence;
- complex approaches to employment-oriented[16] training and social education of rural target groups;
- basic education as an element in employment-oriented training and advanced training.

As also confirmed by the case studies in the present work, vocational training aid can make an important contribution towards securing the livelihood of individuals and entire groups through specific promotion of target groups which have been carefully selected in advance. The insecure jobs and sources of income in the informal sector have to be made more secure through measures providing vocational qualifications. Specifically, this means that measures providing vocational qualifications in the informal sector must contribute towards securing basic needs. Greater economic security is accordingly a crucial prerequisite. Creating additional jobs which provide a source of income and new areas of employment in regions with rural structure through new forms of vocational training can counter the flight from the land."[17] In contrast to traditional vocational pedagogics which are firmly focused on the defined sectors of the economy in question (e.g. occupation profiles, requirement profiles, curricula etc), vocational pedagogics directed at the target groups and promotional approaches described here would have to be conceived in open and holistic terms. They would also (as very clearly shown by the case studies in the present work) have to be combined with other important promotional elements, such as promotion of small businesses, job creation programmes, regional development programmes and similar employment-creating or income-creating measures. It should, however, be noted that there would probably be no significant difference between traditional vocational pedagogics and vocational pedagogics oriented towards the need of the informal sector in terms of conveying relevant vocational qualifications. In fact, the concept of qualification ought in this context to provide a suitable basis for understanding between the formal and informal sector.

14 Loc. cit., cf. note 42 (on p. 33), p. 32.
15 Cf. note (15).
16 Cf. note (13).
17 Cf. Möller, S., Schlegel, W., Schleich, B. and Waltenborn, M., Wie kann man durch Berufsbildung den informellen Sektor fördern ? DSE-ZGB/Mannheim 1986.

4.2 *Target group orientation and developing a didactic basic structure for vocational training in the informal sector*

This section returns to the conceptual and didactic considerations in designing the TTP/SES Peshawar. An attempt is made here to transfer the analyses and experience presented in the case study to a didactic basic structure with general relevance for the informal sector which could then serve as a basis for designing income-oriented vocational training appropriate to the target groups. The first step is to recapitulate the central features (see sections 3.1.5 and 4.2) of the approach to vocational training measures in the informal sector:

(A) *Anthropocentricity*, i.e. *target group specific* orientation of the didactic approach must be ensured.

The following aspects, criteria and content must be taken into account in this:

- Careful target group analysis must determine the realistic needs for promotion;
- Training and advanced training measures or other relevant measures must make a significant contribution towards improving the situation of the target groups and the individuals affected;
- The capacity for development of the target groups and individuals must be taken into account with due regard to the political, socio-economic and socio-cultural aspects and contexts, and an effort made to induce a positive change;
- The specific situation of the target groups and individuals in the urban, semi-rural and rural setting must be taken into account along with their subjective and objective situation (learning attitudes etc), so that favourable and lasting changes can improve their situation in life.

(B) The *action orientation* and *relevance for application* of the qualifications to be transferred (skills, abilities, knowledge and extrafunctional qualifications) must be ensured and must make a contribution towards income-oriented employment.

The following criteria, aspects and content must be taken into account in this:

- Curriculum, methods of teaching and learning, relationship between theory and practice, i.e. the reflection of the world of work in the informal and traditional sector must be taken into

account and be appropriate to the basis of experience of the target groups;
- The qualifications taught must contribute towards enabling target groups and individuals to:
  - earn an income;
  - expand their abilities, skills, knowledge and extrafunctional qualifications and develop them autonomously;
  - improve their character and social position in society.
- The target groups and individuals should also have their specialist and technical qualifications improved so that they can perform the work assigned to them better and more efficiently. These abilities can be estimated and developed using the following criteria:
  - The assigned work and tasks must be performed in line with the conventional technical standards;
  - The work and tasks assigned must be performed with the necessary quality and accuracy and in accordance with their functional importance. This seems particularly critical and important in the performance of technical production and repair work and in the service sector;
  - The work and tasks must be performed within a commercially acceptable period and with correspondingly economical use of resources.

(C) *The self-help potential* and ability of the target groups and individuals to earn an income from employment and/or self-employment should be developed and improved.

The following elements should be taken into consideration in order to develop the personality and self-confidence of the people (and groups) in the informal and traditional sector:

- The target groups and individuals must be enabled to apply the criteria and qualifications listed under (A) and (B) in order to achieve their own interests or to mobilise them in accordance with their abilities. Specifically, the following areas should be cited for this, e.g.:
  - Improving equality of opportunity for people in the informal sector.
  - Strengthening their abilities and competence in perceiving their own situation, analysing and digesting the necessary information, and developing their communication skills.

There is also a need here to overcome traditional and society-specific obstacles[18].
- Strengthening their feeling of self-worth and their self-confidence with the goal of articulating their own interests and the interests of the group better and if necessary being able to assert these in dialogue with the society (employers, customers, representatives of local state structures etc.).
- Improving knowledge and abilities in economic and possibly entrepreneurial contexts in order to be able to analyse, plan and act in their own interests and the interests of the group. This is intended to secure the developmental capability of the individual and the group in an economic context, and also to contribute towards decision-making competence and rationality in utilising the opportunities for development (for both the individual and the group).
- Developing the perception, awareness and ability to plan for the future and implement these plans in a way which strengthens and develops the individual (interests etc) or group (family, caste etc)[19].

(D) The concept of *vocational training aid*, the *didactic structure* of projects, the *curriculum elements* and development of the *necessary qualifications* must be conceived *openly* and *holistically* for developing the situation of group and individual in the informal sector. There must be the ability to adapt flexibly to the direct needs of target groups. Individuals or groups interested in training and advanced training or promotion for employment or self-employment must be involved in the process of developing curriculum elements and integrated as correspondingly active partners in the concept and the didactic structure of the projects.

The following aspects of content and methodology should be taken into account in developing measures and vocational pedagogic concepts for promoting the target groups in the informal sector:

---

18 Cf. specifically the problems due to the caste structure of the lower classes in India and other traditional forms of coexistence in so-called tribal societies.
19 Future-oriented action is essentially a luxury which the poor in all societies have great difficulty in imagining or even affording. They are forced by their personal and economic situation to focus on daily problems of survival. This is not enough to break out of this vicious circle, which only a fixed determination to improve their lot can help to do. People need a vision or dreams and these have to be supported for the necessary motivation to be generated.

- Appropriate and individual approaches and programmes must be developed with *(labour) market* and/or *subsistence orientation*.
- These training and advanced training programmes must have the goal of promoting *income-creating employment or self-employment*.
- The training and advanced training offered must be combined with *consultancy* to promote *commercial independence* and *new small business formation*.
- The target groups and individuals must be supported and promoted in their efforts *to save income*.
- Complex approaches must be developed and implemented for *employment-oriented training and advanced training and social education* of rural and urban target groups and individuals.
- The target groups and individuals must be supported and promoted in their efforts to *secure their lives* as individuals and groups.
- The target groups must be *given* the opportunity to access facilities for *general basic education* and they must be *supported and promoted* in *obtaining* a corresponding *general basic education* (arithmetic, reading, writing etc).
- The target groups and individuals must be supported in their activities and efforts *to integrate* themselves into the society and to secure their *future position* (development, integration, recognition) and corresponding qualifications must be developed.

The following diagram attempts to place what has been said so far and the structural elements of the approach to vocational pedagogics within a didactic basic structure for measures to promote the informal sector.
Didactic basic structure for income-creating vocational training projects in the informal sector
The purpose of the didactic structure is to establish a basis for a promotional vocational pedagogics approach which is action-oriented and anthropocentric (target group centred). As explained in section 2.4, a detailed analysis of the target groups is required to identify their areas for action. This analysis will also provide adequate information on existing deficits. The advisable participative approach, i.e. the active involvement of those affected (target groups, individuals) in this analysis, will also give a correspondingly reliable and authentic impression of the need for promotion of the target groups and individuals. The key elements for ensuring *open, action-oriented and anthropocentric* didactic approaches are:

Didactic basic structure for income-creating vocational training project in the informal sector

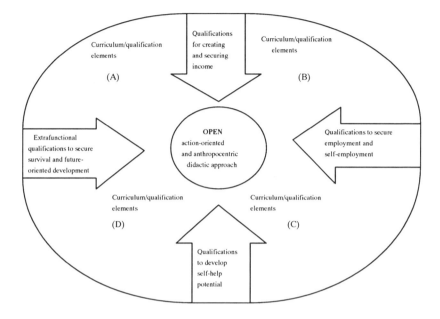

(A) the *extrafunctional qualifications* to ensure *survival* and *future-oriented development* of the target groups and individuals;

(B) the qualifications for creating and securing income, i.e. here specifically including the development of abilities, skills and knowledge for *saving income*;

(C) the *qualifications* for securing *employment* and *self-employment*, including technical and entrepreneurial skills, knowledge and abilities (commercial, management etc) and general education;

(D) the *qualifications* for developing *self-help potential* of the target groups and individuals, i.e. abilities, knowledge, skills and socio-psychological changes in forms of behaviour must be developed which strengthen or develop self-help potential and behaviour in these groups and individuals.

The approach to target group analysis presented in section 2.4 has showed that the informal and traditional sector displays particularly marked inhomogeneity in its target group structure. As already noted (section 4.1) vocational pedagogics with its more or less internationally established structure of professions, vocational profiles and curricula, is unable to operate. Complex curriculum development methods which are oriented towards formalised training and advanced training also appear inappropriate for these sectors. Here it is more a question of the conception and development of measures, courses, training and advanced training programmes etc which follow the didactic approach described here and which are characterised by a correspondingly great openness[20] in terms of the need and participation of the identified target groups and individuals. This *openness* of curricula for training measures did, however, also require correspondingly flexible and unbureaucratic organisational structures on the part of the responsible implementation institutions and organisations. In addition such measures must also be supported and accompanied by corresponding job-creating promotional instruments. This in turn requires co-operation going beyond the sector of vocational training between the responsible implementation organisations for such programmes. It is also necessary (as shown by experience with the informal sector) for teachers, trainers and consultants to have both training specifically related to this sector and adequately interdisciplinary knowledge. In addition to teaching qualifications they should also have the motivation of a social educator.

4.3 *The concept of training in the context of job-creating vocational training in the informal sector*

A vocational pedagogics for the informal sector which is job-creating, action-oriented and anthropocentric[21] must be based on the actual working, living and social conditions of the potential target groups. As the conditions that people in the informal sector have to live under are

---

20 Cf. Nölker, H., Schoenfeldt, E., Berufsbildung: Unterricht, Curriculum, Planung, Expert Verlag, Grafenau, 1980, pp. 84 et seq. "Open curricula by contrast have a chance [compared with closed ones: author] of being taken seriously by the instructors. The instructors able to adapt to them because of the alternatives available in detail, the administration [school bureaucracy: author] has greater assurance that their guiding ideas will be complied with and implemented. "Another important reason for an open structure for curricula, if these can be formulated at all for short courses, is the need for and goal of matching the needs of the target groups [author].
21 Cf. C. Lohmar-Kuhnle, note 42 (on p. 33), p. 25.

alarming in every respect, all promotional measures must have a direct relationship to this situation with the goal of initiating or directly achieving an immediate and perceptible improvement in both qualitative and quantitative terms for the target groups. However, this is just one aspect, i.e. direct intervention with the goal of improving or ameliorating the living conditions of the target group directly and immediately through *crash measures*. It is, however, not sufficient to try and tackle the problems of the informal sector with such very short-term objectives. This would ultimately mean that the target group would relapse into its old situation after the measures were completed or the funding ran out. Or – and even more of a problem, as seen in the past with more charity-oriented aid measures – these groups can develop a charity-recipient mentality, losing all independent initiative and self-confidence and crippling the drive to self-help. It is accordingly important to understand the informal sector as a part of the social and economic system and to ensure that this sector receives the corresponding social policy, economic and development policy attention in the national and international context of "technical co-operation" or "development aid".

For vocational training aid this means that the approaches presented in sections 4.1 and 4.2 to employment-creating training of target groups in the informal sector with their complex diversification (see section 2.4) can most effectively be developed by identifying and analysing the necessary training structures, which can then be used as a basis for designing the corresponding promotional programmes. In contrast to the formal educational sector, which is sanctioned by government and social requirements mostly operating through the agreed official curricula, the informal and traditional sector is entirely unstructured. The informal sector also generally lacks any binding requirements relating to the implementation of the training and promotional programmes and other structural requirements, e.g. curricula, training courses and diplomas or concrete socio-political and development policy requirements for the development of this sector. Even so the vocational pedagogics approach involving identifying demand for training and advanced training jointly with detailed target group analysis identifying training requirements and qualification profiles appears to be the more appropriate methodology for the need of the target group. This avoids a situation where – similar to experience in the formal vocational training sector – training and advanced training is offered which is unrelated to the needs of the employment system. "The link between (vocational) training and employment is the vocational qualification. At the macro level, at the level of society or the economy, vocational training qualifications are the social medium of exchange in the labour market."[22] This applies to both the formal and the informal-traditional sector. The definition offered by Alex, L. for the concept of qualification again illustrates the transferability of this approach to employment or the labour market in the informal sector:

"Qualification means the totality of knowledge and abilities (including behavioural models and skills) acquired in the processes of socialisation and education. Acquisition of qualifications promotes the active shaping of life not only as a worker but also as a citizen and family member A qualification accordingly also has not only a vocational but also a social dimension. The latter applies specifically to abilities which enable individuals to satisfy social requirements arising out of a working democracy, i.e. particularly the demands of participation at all levels[23]. Assuming that this definition of vocational qualification can also be applied in the informal sector, we still need to take into account certain specific features of this sector. The employment system (businesses etc) in the informal sector is essentially characterised by the following specific features:

- The production and repair and maintenance businesses are *mostly organised like bazaar businesses*, i.e.:
  - they specialise narrowly on a few products and services;
  - they have minimal depth of production and service;
  - they mostly repeat these products and services over the entire lifetime (existence) of the business;
  - they have little or no flexibility in adopting new products and services into their range;
  they mostly have a very low standard of technology;
  - in organisational terms they are very simply structured and their operations are based on craft production or services;
  - they have a traditional-hierarchic organisation, with the owner retaining all the decision-making powers;
  - employees often have a very constricting working relationship with their employer with little participation;
  - employees have very low wages and no social security, they bear the full risk of bad entrepreneurial decisions.
- *The work processes* in most businesses in the informal sector are *mostly performed manually* because of the low level of technology

---

22 Cf. Alex, L., Berufliche Qualifikationen heute – Entwicklung und Akteure, in: Berufsbildung in Wissenschaft und Praxis, vol. 2/1991.
23 Cf. Alex, L., Qualifikationsforschung – eine Zwischenbilanz, in: Berufsbildung und Wissenschaft und Praxis, vol. 1, 1979.

in production techniques or services. The use of machinery is mainly limited to equipment which does not rely on external energy and very low-cost processes;
- The *investment costs* for *setting up work areas* are very low;
- *Businesses have very little in the way of financial reserves* for new *investment* or *expanding* their range of products and services;
- *Businesses are directly tied into their local markets* and have *little knowledge of the development potential* of their activities or markets;
- *Many economic activities* in the informal sector fall into *the category of employment securing subsistence*;
- The d*evelopment potential* for entrepreneurs in the informal sector is *very small without external financial inputs, consultancy, entrepreneur training* and *training and advanced training for their employees.*

These features accordingly constitute further influences on the development of the qualification profiles for entrepreneurs and employees in small businesses and microbusinesses in the informal sector. In developing training and advanced training programmes aimed at improving the performance profile, efficiency and development potential of small businesses and microbusinesses in the informal sector, it is important to develop and offer specific and customised programmes aimed at the target groups and entrepreneurs. A distinction must be made here between the entrepreneurs and the employees of small businesses and microbusinesses, as the qualifications needed to manage a business and to carry out orders in the operating area of a business are entirely different in their nature and also require different competencies, strategies and didactic concepts for developing them. Experience has shown that transferring theoretical and practical qualifications is not enough to develop entrepreneurs. Otherwise, for example, management studies would have to create a significantly higher proportion of entrepreneurs than is the case[24]. The approach of creating model or demonstration businesses in various industries and then releasing these for duplication has also failed. It is impossible in practice to duplicate businesses, and successes are the exception[25]. The key to success is accordingly identifying individuals who are suitable for forming and managing small businesses and microbusinesses in the informal sector or assisting entrepreneurs who are already successful and further developing

---

24 Cf. GTZ, CEFE-Competence based Economies by Formation of Entrepreneurs, Eschborn.
25 Op. cit.

their competencies and qualifications. For entrepreneurs in this sector the following key qualifications[26] (see also the requirement profiles in section 3.0) or competencies can be stated as a basis for training measures and entrepreneurial ability[27])

Entrepreneurial ability =
– technical competence; – methodological competence; – social competence; – learning competence; – communication competence; – entrepreneurial competence.

(for further explanation see the figure: Entrepreneurial (key) qualifications for successful management of a business in the informal sector (on p. 244).

The "key qualifications" cited here and their effectiveness in close connection with the cultural and traditional social conditions (see chapter 2) and the development potential of the business to be promoted in the informal sector, i.e. entrepreneurial training etc, are still not enough to make a successful business. To succeed in the informal sector a business accordingly requires review and co-ordination of three important areas, specifically:

– the market for the products and services;
– the suitability of the entrepreneurs;
– the environment (economic, political, legal etc).

The relationships shown here demonstrate clearly the complexity involved in describing the requirements and competencies for entrepreneurs. This also applies to businesses in the informal sector, particularly if the aim is to integrate this area into the informal economy on a long term basis. It is not, however, intended to go further into these specific problems and issues here: instead, the aim is to look only at the important aspects of training and systematic development of qualifications for entrepreneurs and employees in the informal sector. These approaches will or are intended to serve as a basis for developing appropriate and culture-specific curricula (for short and long courses).

---

26 Cf. Mertens, D.: Schlüsselqualifikationen, in: Mitteilungen aus der Arbeitsmarkt- und Berufsforschung, 7, 1974, pp. 36-43.
27 Cf. Frenz, A. and Kohlshorn, R.: Existenzgründungen fördern, in: GTZ-Info, 5, 1987, pp. 16 et seq.

The following figures show paradigmatic structures for
(A) the qualification profile for entrepreneurs and
(B) the qualification profile for employees
in the informal sector.

The relationships between commercial and entrepreneurial competence[28]

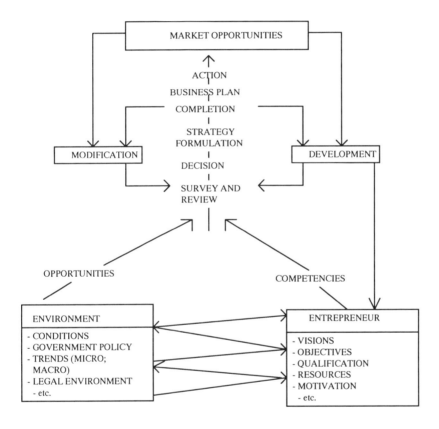

---

28 Based on a diagram in GTZ-CEFE-Konzept zur Förderung von Unternehmen im informellen Sektor und der Kleinindustrieförderung.

Entrepreneurial (key)qualifications for successful management of a business in the informal sector

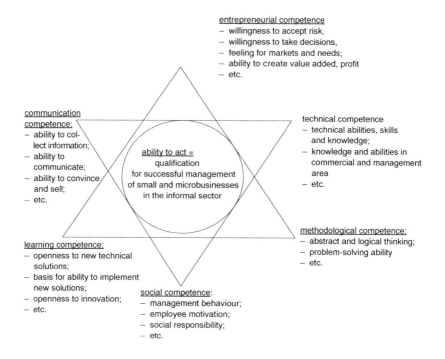

The "(key) qualifications" for employed individuals (employed and self-employed) in the informal sector have their specific origin in the differing areas of employment in this sector (see also section 4.2). These fields can be categorised as follows:
– the *formal labour market* of the traditional and informal sector;
– the *subsistence economy employment areas*, (obscure segments of the labour market) e.g. in agriculture, animal husbandry, family businesses etc;
– the *income-saving employment areas* in the informal sector (rural, urban, semi-rural, semi-urban etc);
– *other areas of employment* still *to be defined* or *to be replaced* in the informal sector (e.g. income from drug cultivation, prostitution, smuggling and other illegal activities).

Generally, however, the following (key) qualifications can be identified for developing open curricula for training and advanced training measures:

Ability to act =
qualification to perform the assigned tasks successfully and the ability to attain their own interests

=

- social competence;
- methodological and learning competence;
- technical competence.

The following diagram recapitulates the relationships between the competencies listed here and the context for action, the environment and the employment system.

(Key) qualifications for employees in the informal sector[29]

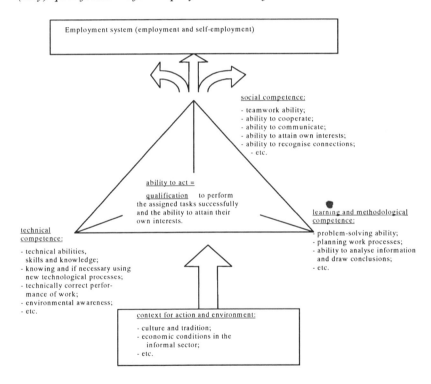

[29] This diagram was developed by analogy with the concept of key qualifications for the BFZ-Essen department of modern technologies developed by Norbert Meyer. Cf. Government of India Workshop on Vocational Hi-Tech Training 2000 AD, pub. Central Instructional Media Institute, Madras, 1990.

4.4 Approaches to employment-oriented learning in the informal sector

In the case study "TTP/SES at the Technical Training Center-Peshawar, N.W.F.P.-Pakistan" presented in section 3.1, four successful approaches to vocational and job-creating learning were developed and implemented. The case study showed very clearly that vocational training and advanced training in this sector cannot succeed without accompanying job-creating promotional measures, since the absorption capability of the existing labour market is very limited.

Essentially, the following approaches to training were introduced in this project:

- *systematic short and long training courses* (short or long courses of study in defined occupations or areas of employment);
- *traditional apprenticeships* (initial vocational training in bazaar businesses);
- *training together with production* (training integrated into execution of production orders);
- *training and consultancy in supervised workshops* (combination of production orders, training and consultancy with the aim of promoting self-employment and promotion of small-scale enterprises).

The *central orientation* of all the didactic and methodological approaches described above is connected with the aim of "an open action-oriented and anthropocentric didactic approach" to "employment-oriented learning in the informal sector. These approaches to the training of skilled workers, however, represent only a fraction of what should be possible in the informal sector. W.-D. Greinert[30] distinguishes in his study "Methods and arrangements for qualifications in vocational training in the developed industrialised nations" between five basis models of vocational learning". These models are presented in the following overview[31].

---

30 Cf. Greinert, W.-D., Instrumente und Strategien der Systementwicklung/Systemberatung in: Biermann, H., Greinert, W.-D., Janisch, R.; pub., GTZ-Eschborn, Systementwicklung und Systemberatung in der Berufsbildungshilfe (Berichte, Analysen, Konzepte), Nomos, Baden-Baden, 1994.
31 Loc. cit. slightly modified by the author.

Basic models of vocational learning:		
	Models	Methodology/didactics
1	Learning in the real work process	training under economic pressures; e.g. craft apprenticeship
2	Learning through apprenticeship method	artificial "didactic" models; training outside the production process.
3	Learning through holistically structured training methods	artificial "didactic" models; training outside the production process.
4	Learning in simulated working/production process	training and production; attempt at systematic (didactic) linking of working and learning
5	Learning in working process according to didactic criteria	training and production; attempt at systematic (didactic) linking of working and learning

The following aspects are important for successful design and implementation of training measures in the informal sector:
– selection of the sites for learning;
– length of training measures;
– organisational form of the measures;
– qualification of trainers and instructors;
– methodological-didactic concepts;
– technological appropriateness of teaching and learning materials and the upgrading facilities;
– integration into widespread and intersectoral promotional programmes.

Learning at work:
Learning on the job or training on the job is a decisive element in successful learning, particularly for training measures in the informal sector. Learning at work tracks the *real conditions* of the informal sector, and is accordingly *realistic* and almost always *true to working life*[32]. *This learning* site is particularly important to the employer, who given the size of the business, the nature of the procedures and the importance of every employee being productively occupied (i.e. earnings his or her keep) will not agree to any other arrangement. Any

---

32 Loc. cit. and Franke, G./Kleinschmitt, M. et al.: Der Lernort Arbeitsplatz (Schriften zur Berufsbildungsforschung, vol. 65, pub. Bundesinstitut für Berufsbildung), Berlin/Cologne 1987.

change in learning location is only conceivable for a short period and specific training measures, e.g. in connection with technological innovations or even courses with a general educational nature. These are most likely to be acceptable if they are offered outside working hours.

Length of the training measure:
If carried out at work the length of the training measures must be arranged wherever possible with the employer. Traditional craft training in the informal and traditional sector tends to last a very long time and is associated with poor payment and great dependence. The length must be in an acceptable relationship with the requirements of the occupation or the work to be performed. In the case of training and advanced training at special government or non-government centres etc, the length must be kept as short as possible and possibly reduced to an acceptable length for participants in the form of courses, courses of study etc. The important thing is to recognise that the target groups are not available for training measures covering an extended period of time or for systematic and full-time training and advanced training, as they have to earn a living directly alongside training and advanced training – or at least make a major contribution towards this.

Organisational forms of training measures:
Training and advanced training in the informal sector can be organised and carried out in a very wide range of forms. However, particularly in the informal sector it is important to prevent the training processes becoming an end in themselves by removing training and advanced training from the small businesses and microbusinesses and hence of the actual production processes. This would cast doubt on their appropriateness and need-orientation and hence put at risk acceptance by future employers. Promotion and training programmes for entrepreneurs must also be carried out as close as possible to the entrepreneur in the informal sector. Two target groups must be take into account here in principle:

– *existing* small (micro) entrepreneurs
– *those wanting to become entrepreneurs*.

For small and micro entrepreneurs, training and advanced training programmes can only be organised if they do not disrupt production etc. Programmes must take the form of on-site consultancy or be run as weekend seminars or evening events. In any event these programmes must be developed and implemented in close consultation with the participants. For target groups to be prepared for their role as small (micro) entrepreneurs a large number of different concepts have been developed, particularly in the promotion of small-scale businesses. These concepts and programmes can also be used for target groups in the informal sector. It should be recalled here that the entrepreneur training and promotion concept developed at TTP/SES-Peshawar (e.g. the creation of supervised workshops) has proved its value and is still operating successfully.

Qualification of trainers:
The qualification profile for trainers in the informal sector ranges from the specialist with good technical qualifications who plays the role of the master craftsman to the specialist responsible for designing the training and advanced training programmes. However, the learning site, length and form of organisation of courses and the content and methodological-didactic standards of the training and advanced training measures must be taken into account here. Generally trainers from government and private vocational training facilities are not able to take on these responsibilities without additional training measures. They are, however, the most suitable experts in formal terms, as far as their previous education and experience as trainers is concerned. Experience has, however, shown that they have great difficulty in adjusting to the conditions in the informal sector. Qualified trainers from the formal vocational training system regard working in the informal sector as social discrimination because of the low standard of technology and the specific role of the informal sector in society and the social role of the target groups. This situation results in a major problem in finding experts with adequate technical qualifications for the informal sector and using them as teachers, social workers and management consultants. This experience is not limited to the developing countries, as it is difficult even in Germany to attract teachers or other specialists to work with so-called marginal social groups. This suggests that specific qualifications programmes need to be developed in Third World countries for training and advanced training for experts (trainers etc) for the informal sector, as these experts make a major contribution to the success of projects in this area.

Methodological-didactic concepts and approaches to training and advanced training:
Training and advanced training measures for job-creating vocational upgrading in the informal sector must (as already repeatedly noted and explained) have an anthropocentric and action-oriented focus. Four

model approaches have been identified for promoting this sector (see section 4.1):
- individual training and advanced training oriented towards the (labour) market and/or subsistence;
- training and consultancy to promote economic independence;
- complex approaches to employment-oriented training and social education of rural target groups;
- elementary education as part of employment-oriented training and advanced training.

In designing training and advanced training and accompanying job-creating promotional programmes, two specific types of target groups and individuals must be taken into account

(A) independent persons (self-employed, small (micro) entrepreneurs etc);
(B) employed persons (skilled workers, hired labourers etc in small (micro) businesses.

For the group of *self-employed* or those aiming at this status, the following (key) qualifications were identified (see section 4.2):
- entrepreneurial competence;
- technical competence;
- methodological competence;
- social competence;
- learning competence;
- communication ability.

The corresponding short courses and consultancy concepts must be evolved to develop these qualifications. These courses can be offered in the following form as:
- institute-based, short *standard courses* whose content must be worked out in close co-operation with those involved;
- courses and consultancy activities carried out *directly* in the small (micro) businesses as:
  - standard programmes;
  - tailor-made programmes;
  - individual measures;
- courses with the help of *mobile* training and advanced training facilities, e.g. *"Didaktomobile"* or *Mobile Training Units*.

In terms of content and methodology these courses can be developed and offered as standard programmes, special courses, modules, study courses and tailor-made courses. The important thing here is that the content must match the need of the target groups and contribute towards improving the ability to act of the small (micro) entrepreneurs and their development skills.

For the group of *employed* individuals or school-leavers or drop-outs (see target groups, section 2.4) etc looking for employed status the following (key) qualifications were identified (see section 4.2):
- learning and methodological competence;
- technical competence;
- social competence.

Vocational training for these specific target groups generally takes the form (as shown by studies) of:
- *traditional apprenticeship* in bazaar businesses or small (micro) businesses in the informal sector;
- *dual/co-operative* forms, i.e. the mainly practical part and basic skills in bazaar businesses or small (micro) businesses and the theoretical parts of the training in government or private vocational training facilities;
- *productive training* in government or private training facilities as basic training with occupational relevance and subsequently as vocational advanced training programme;
- *local training and advanced training* with the help of *mobile training facilities* such as Mobile Training Units, "Didaktomobile" or direct training in bazaar businesses or small (micro) businesses in the informal sector.
- *specific vocational special training measures* in the context of small-scale business promotion, rural regional development programmes or programmes to promote the informal sector.

In terms of content and methodology these training measures can be assigned to the category of vocational training and advanced training. These are generally developed and offered as standard programmes, courses of study or in modular forms. The important thing here is that the content, training methods, vocational and qualification features (fields) should match the demand and the organisation of work or division of labour of the employment system in the informal sector. The businesses affected should be involved in a leading capacity in developing the curricula for training and advanced training (e.g. for courses, courses of study etc). The aim here is to ensure acceptance of training and advanced training measures among participants and employers.

Technological appropriateness of training and advanced training measures:
The institutions and executing agencies for vocational training measures involved in measures to promote training and advanced training of target groups and individuals must ensure that:

(A) the technologies used are easy to operate and fit in with the natural living and economic environments of the informal sector;
(B) improvements are made which do not create dependence on investment and foreign currency through new technologies;
(C) the technologies do not impose additional burdens on the environment and people dealing with them but have a correspondingly innovative and conservative impact on the environment.

Employment-oriented vocational training must accordingly draw primarily on available resources which are either already known, available or easily producible. It also has an innovative function, and can transfer recent results on using technology or revive long-forgotten (appropriate) technology and make it available again to the production or service process[33].

Integration of widespread and intersectoral promotional programmes:
Vocational training for the informal sector can only be successful if it is planned and implemented in the context of job-creating promotional programmes. Although it creates the prerequisites for employment through training, this itself does not create any significant number of new jobs, which are limited to the direct area of implementing these training and advanced training measures. It is accordingly necessary to link measures for vocational training in the informal sector with e.g. small-scale business promotion, regional development programmes and other infrastructural and economic promotional measures.

4.5 *Integration of employment-oriented vocational training in the informal sector into the formal vocational training system or systemic aspects of projects in this area*

The practical experience presented in section 3.0 has shown that certain parallels can be drawn between the development and historical importance of the traditional sector of the economy in Germany up to the mid-20th century and in the informal sector in the Third World. W.-D. Greinert shows this in his book on the history of the "Dual System" on the basis of B. Lutz's "Reinterpretation of the develop-

---

[33] There are innumerable examples of this. TTP/SES for example has revived long-forgotten dome construction methods in housing in Pakistan and Afghanistan. The goal was to save building wood, as virtually no wood is needed for ceiling construction in domed structures.

ment of industrial capitalism in Europe in the 20th century". These observations are helpful in understanding the context and the importance of the link between the informal/traditional sector and the modern industrial sector. They have the following comments on this specific relationship (Greinert/Lutz):

> "Most rural businesses, the craft trades, retail outlets (including primary services) and domestic services retained the typical features for their sector of a traditional economy, namely:
> - the predominant focus of work on meeting demand rather than profitability (= market);
> - the dominance of small businesses with a family business nature;
> - the secondary importance of hired labour in employment."
>
> The authors also note that "a key feature of the economic duality is that the "interchanges" (Lutz) between the two sectors are limited to a few very clearly defined exchanges:
> - The traditional sector is the most important reservoir of labour for the modern industrial sector, particularly as long as it remains the major source of the population surplus.
> - The hired labour in the industrial sector meets its direct living needs primarily from goods and services from the traditional sector.
> - Income of families and businesses in the informal sector from the modern industrial sector has a primarily investment nature (capital goods or indirect taxes, levies used to fund public infrastructural measures)."

Lutz and Greinert further note that there is a "positive feedback" (Lutz) mechanism with prosperity effects: if the modern industrial sector grows more dynamically, the traditional/informal sector also experiences positive economic stimulation. The intersectoral behaviour is similar if the modern industrial sector is subject to economic "depressions", in which case the informal/traditional sector experiences negative economic feedback. This is also apparent in Third World countries. Specifically, in the countries (Pakistan and India) discussed in the present work, such economic dependencies between the informal and formal sector can manifest themselves as a result of their developed modern industrial sector. In periods of economic growth in the modern sector there is accordingly automatic growth in demand for labour (unskilled, semi-skilled and skilled), which is met primarily from the reserves in the informal sector. In the informal sector there is growth in both need and demand for cheap products and services, resulting in growth in the need for labour. A further consideration is that this sector is providing additional labour, which leads to the conclusion that the businesses in the informal sector play a not unimportant role in vocational training of labour for the formal sector. To this extent the question arises as to the systemic connection between vocational training in the informal sector and the formal vocational training system.

The case study in section 3.0 of the TTC-TTP/SES Peshawar has shown that employment-oriented vocational training measures can be attached to training and advanced training facilities in the formal vocational training system. This has the advantage that the existing infrastructure, training facilities, training staff, teaching and learning aids and existing finance (budget) can be used as infrastructure and services to the informal sector. Figures 3.1.9 (p. 146) and 3.1.10 (p. 147) show how the individual training courses oriented towards employment in the informal sector can be linked with the formal vocational training system. It is useful here for clarification and understanding of the systemic relationships to subdivide the vocational training system into levels of effect, as done in this example:

(A) the political and strategic level;
(B) the functional and controlling level;
(C) the operational and didactic level;
(D) the labour market and the employment system.

Using these four levels of effect (which should not be taken as representing the strict hierarchical structure of the training system) it is possible to analyse and identify the points of contact between the vocational training measures aimed at the formal or informal sectors. This should not lead to the imposition of formal admission requirements for employment-oriented training measures aimed at the informal sector: this would be an obstacle on balance for the potential target groups in the informal sector, as most of them (as already adequately demonstrated) lack any formal educational certification. It would, however, be possible for institutions in the formal training system to develop and offer e.g. special courses (evening courses etc) which are open to individuals interested in training and advanced training measures in the informal sector. It would also be possible e.g. through training passes (similar to the electronics pass of the H. Piest Institute or the welding examination to DIN of the SLVs etc.) to provide participants in training and advanced training events with written documentation of the qualifications acquired. This would also lead to a situation where the formal/modern sector would be able to offer more skilled positions to workers from the informal sector.

In the long term the aim should be to upgrade and integrate the informal economic and training sector, as this will have a favourable effect on the development potential of this sector and also improve the employment situation for groups which have previously been disadvantaged.

4.6 *Summary and review of approaches to holistic vocational pedagogics for the informal sector*

4.6.1 *Holistic vocational pedagogics*

The present work has identified and demonstrated the need for and urgency for development policy of adopting the informal sector as a special area for promotion in vocational training aid. The criticism of the present one-sided orientation in vocational training can be attributed to the following mistaken judgements in bilateral and multilateral development co-operation:
- industrialisation is an essential precondition for social and economic development and progress;
- a key obstacle to accelerating this process is the shortage of skilled labour;
- the industrialisation process can only be successfully pursued if the deficiencies in the field of vocational training are eliminated and the corresponding facilities and institutions are created;
- the need for skilled labour has been assessed as more or less unlimited;
- the technological standard of the industrial modern sector has been assessed as very high and the training of skilled workers accordingly had to match this standard;

These judgements and the vocational training aid devised and developed in this context resulted in a very one-sided focus on the modern industrial sector and rejected the steadily expanding informal sector. However, the lack of economic growth in the formal sector has resulted in a situation where graduates of the training facilities in the formal vocational training system in these countries also have been or are unable to find jobs in the modern sector. Graduates of these training facilities are, however, seldom prepared to work in the informal sector, unless forced to do so by necessity.

However, a vocational pedagogics which would accept the informal sector as part of the existing employment system would have to open itself to the specific problems of the sector and make a contribution towards eliminating the dividing line (which in any case is unclear and artificial) between formal, non-formal and informal training. It would have to adopt a holistic approach. Above all, the people and their problems will have to be restored to the focus of vocational pedagogical efforts. This is also particularly true of vocational training aid as it is currently practised, which is far too focused on the narrow modern industrial sector of Third World countries and which ignores the broad

masses of the underemployed and unemployed. The change or reorientation of vocational pedagogics and vocational training aid requires the adoption of the "anthropocentric action-oriented concepts and multidimensional target group identification" called for by the present work as the decisive basis for developing new approaches and promotional concepts. Employment-creating vocational training in the informal sector must accordingly be based on four model approaches:
- individual training and advanced training oriented towards the (labour) market and/or subsistence;
- training and extension work to promote economic independence;
- complex approaches to employment-oriented training and social education of rural target groups;
- basic education as an element in employment-oriented training and advanced training.

In contrast to the traditional vocational pedagogics, which is firmly focused on the defined areas and sectors of the prevailing economic system (e.g. occupational profiles, curricula, requirement profiles etc), a vocational pedagogics oriented towards the target groups and promotional approaches identified here would have to be conceived in open and holistic terms. To have an effect on employment, such a vocational pedagogics would also have to be co-ordinated with other promotional areas and instruments in development co-operation (e.g. small-scale business promotion, regional development, job-creation programmes etc).

4.6.2 *Target-group orientation, didactic basic structure and the concept of qualification in the context of employment-effective training and advanced training*

Target group orientation:
The following approaches to vocational training have decisive importance for training and advanced training measures. They also provide the basis for the basic didactic structure of the vocational pedagogic concept of training in the informal sector. The following individual principles must be taken into account here:
(A) *Anthropocentricity,* , i.e. *target group specific* orientation of the didactic approach must be ensured.
(B) The *action orientation* and relevance for application of the qualifications to be transferred (skills, abilities, knowledge and extrafunctional qualifications) must be ensured and must make a contribution towards income-oriented employment.

(C) *The self-help potential* and ability of the target groups and individuals to earn an income from employment and/or self-employment should be developed and improved.
(D) The concept of *vocational training aid*, the *didactic structure* of projects, the *curriculum elements* and *development* of the necessary *vocational* and *extrafunctional* qualifications must be conceived openly and holistically with the goal of improving the situation of group and individual in the informal sector.

The possibility of adapting flexibly to the direct needs of target groups must be ensured. Individuals or groups interested in training and advanced training or promotion for employment or self-employment must be involved in the process of developing curriculum elements and integrated as correspondingly active partners in the concept and the didactic structure of the projects. This participation is a crucial requirement for ensuring the openness called for here.

The basic didactic structure:
The key elements in ensuring an *open and action-oriented* didactic approach are:
(A) the *extrafunctional qualifications* to ensure *survival* and *future-oriented development* of the target groups and individuals;
(B) the *qualifications* for creating and securing income, i.e. here specifically including the development of abilities, skills and knowledge for *saving income*;
(C) the *qualifications* for securing *employment* and *self-employment*, including technical and entrepreneurial skills, knowledge and abilities (commercial, management etc) and general education;
(D) the *qualifications* for developing the *self-help potential* of the target groups and individuals, i.e. abilities, knowledge, skills and socio-psychological changes in forms of behaviour must be developed which strengthen or develop self-help potential and behaviour in these groups and individuals.

The concept of qualification in employment-oriented training and advanced training in the informal sector:
"The link between (vocational) training and employment is the vocational qualification. At the macro level, the social or macroeconomic level, vocational qualifications are the social medium of exchange in the labour market" (Alex, L., Vocational qualifications today, 1991). This applies to both the formal and the informal sectors. The definition of the concept of qualification supplied by Alex, L. again shows its

applicability and usefulness for developing a concept of qualification in the informal sector:
"Qualification means the totality of knowledge and abilities (including behavioural models and skills) acquired in the processes of socialisation and education. Acquisition of qualifications promotes the active shaping of life not only as a worker but also as a citizen and family member A qualification accordingly also has not only a vocational but also a social dimension. The latter applies specifically to abilities which enable individuals to satisfy social requirements arising out of a working democracy, i.e. particularly the demands of participation at all levels." (Alex, L. Vocational qualifications today, 1991). Assuming that this definition of vocational qualification can also be applied in the informal sector, it is still necessary to interpret it for the purposes of this sector. First, two fundamentally different target groups have to be specified:

(A) *self-employed persons*, e.g. subsistence economy businesses, bazaar businesses or other small (micro) entrepreneurs;
(B) *employed persons*, e.g. skilled workers in bazaar businesses and small (micro) businesses, hired labourers, family members helping out etc.

– The most important (key) qualifications for *self-employed* and *entrepreneurial activity* can be summarised as follows:

Entrepreneurial ability to act	=

| – technical competence, |
| – methodological competence, |
| – social competence; |
| – learning competence; |
| – communication competence |
| – entrepreneurial competence. |

These (key) qualifications and interconnections cited here are closely related to the cultural and traditional social conditions and the specific development opportunities of the target groups. Their establishment lays the basis for successful promotion of businesses in the informal sector. They are also the basis for developing training and advanced training courses, programmes and other promotional measures.

The most important (key) qualifications for employment and *non-entrepreneurial work* can be summarised as follows:

Ability to act = *qualification* to perform the assigned tasks successfully and the ability to attain their own interests	=

– social competence;
– methodological and learning competence;
– technical competence.

4.6.3 *Employment-oriented learning in the informal sector*

Employment-oriented learning in the informal sector occurs in the context of the central methodological-didactic approach, i.e. an open, action-oriented and anthropocentric concept vocational pedagogic and approach. The following aspects are important for successful design and implementation of training measures in this sector:
– selection of the sites for learning;
– length of training measures;
– qualification of trainers and instructors;
– technological appropriateness of teaching and learning materials
– the training facilities;
– integration of the training measures into widespread and intersectoral promotional programmes which include job-creating components.

Vocational training for the informal sector can only be successful if it is planned and implemented in the context of job-creating promotional programmes. Although it creates the prerequisites for employment through training, this itself does not create any significant number of new jobs, which are directly linked with the implementation of these training measures. It is accordingly necessary to combine these vocational training measures in the informal sector with other promotional measures as described above and implement these jointly.

4.6.4 Vocational training measures in the informal sector and the need to combine these with the formal vocational training system: systematic aspects of development

Experience with the informal sector has shown that a key feature of the relationships between the informal sector and the formal (modern industrial) sector is the *economic duality*. The "interchanges" (Lutz, The brief dream of lasting prosperity, 1989) between the two sectors are limited to the following areas:

- The traditional/informal sector is the most important reservoir of labour for the modern industrial sector,
- The hired labour in the industrial sector meets its direct living needs primarily from goods and services from the traditional sector (cheap products, services etc),
- Income of families and businesses in the informal sector from the modern industrial sector has a primarily investment nature (capital goods, taxes etc).

These specific relationships show that the informal sector does better when the prosperity of the formal sector is ensured. Conversely, however, the economic situation in the informal sector is likely to have little direct influence on the success of modernisation and industrialisation in Third World countries. This dualism is only found in a marked form where corresponding industrialisation has already taken place (e.g. India, Pakistan, Indonesia etc). The relationships between the two sectors shown here does, however, justify the conclusion that the informal sector plays a not insignificant (indirect) role in vocational training of labour for the modern and industrial sector. To this extent there is also a link here in developing vocational training measures for the informal sector. While the present work did not permit adequate treatment of the problem of integration and the system-shaping character of vocational training measures, the author feels it is necessary to investigate this specific relationship between the two sectors and consider the development of an integrated vocational training system. A mutually exclusive treatment of the two sectors involves the danger of further political, social, economic and development policy marginalisation of the informal sector. This is something to be avoided at all costs.

5 Summary and conclusions

5.1 *Vocational training for the informal sector: context, definitions and interfaces with the formal sector*

Vocational training aid under technical co-operation with Third World countries is generally seen in the context of the desired socio-cultural, socio-economic and technological development potential of the modern manufacturing and service sector. Project-specific and didactic approaches accordingly also focus primarily on the parameters forming the environment and context for the methodological, didactic and curricular conclusions for creating training measures, institutions and vocational training systems.

The training institutions and vocational training systems and approaches to system building which have been promoted in the past under technical co-operation with Third World countries have accordingly – and despite all efforts to avoid this – been oriented towards the so-called formal sector of the economy (i.e. the modern, organised sector). Growing urbanisation and resulting emergence of giant slums in the industrial and rural areas of the Third World have ultimately given rise to what we now call the informal sector. This term first appeared in international debate on development policy in May 1972 in an ILO study on Kenya (ILO, employment, incomes and equality: A strategy for increasing productive employment in Kenya, 1972). Nevertheless, the innumerable contributions to the debate and scientific studies since then have been unable to describe or define this term clearly and unambiguously. In the author's view, such success is highly unlikely, as the so-called informal sector has too many facets and different dimensions to be captured in a single definition. However, the informal sector is becoming increasingly important in development policy debate and activities, as further demonstrated by the present work. If we consider the facts – a situation where a growing part of the active population (over 50% in many developing countries) in Latin America, Asia and Africa belong to the informal sector – the social relevance and potential explosiveness of this issue become clear. This is also a major reason behind the inclusion of the informal sector as a development policy goal for promotion in the new BMZ "Sectoral concept for vocational training". The new World Bank Policy Paper also favours promoting the informal sector. The revision of the basis for promotion of vocational training measures was needed, as public international criticism of projects, i.e. the objectives and the one-sided focus on specific target groups in technical co-operation, had been growing in weight and volume since the mid-Eighties. The key points of this criticism can be summarised as follows:

- Concentration of promotion on so-called elites in the Third World, i.e. exclusively or primarily promoting projects in the modern industrial sector and hence mainly training skilled workers for this sector.
- Focusing on industrialisation policy and simultaneously neglecting the rural and informal sector.
- Inadequate flexibility in vocational training aid and lack of constructive promotional approaches in the face of growing unemployment among graduates (i.e. of the training facilities being promoted) and of the growth of the informal sector.
- No conclusions drawn for the development of new concepts, strategies and projects in vocational training aid, and inadequate link between vocational training and the needs of the labour market.
- Growing impoverishment of sections of the urban and rural population, i.e. failure to connect with the relevant target groups in the informal sector.
- Inadequate networking of existing promotional instruments and sector-related promotional approaches in terms of promoting training for employment and self-employment in the informal sector, i.e. inadequacy of existing approaches for promoting measures which create income and secure survival.

The BMZ has, as already noted, drawn the consequences from this controversy, not least under the pressure from development policy debate and public opinion. In the new sectoral concept the informal sector is clearly named and emphasised. The following key orientations are enunciated for development co-operation:

- "Demand from target groups in the informal sector, and specifically of disadvantaged population groups for improving their opportunities for earning and their living situation should be addressed by special services in vocational training. These must target the learning capability of the participants, their circumstances and the concrete demand for training arising out of these. The services should open up additional or improved opportunities for employment, for

self-sufficiency or for effective self-employment in the subsistence economy" (Sectoral concept, 1992, BMZ).
- "Particularly in promoting target groups in the informal sector, and specifically disadvantages population groups ... should use intersectoral concepts for ... combating poverty through helping self-help movements (e.g. NGOs etc) as partners in development co-operation and the promotion of women in developing countries" (Sectoral concept, 1992, BMZ).
- The idea of the informal sector as understood by German official development aid (BMZ) accordingly covers all economic activities of the target groups which have not been covered by the formal economy so far. This is what is meant by the "variety and diversity of activities by small (micro) businesses and single proprietors on the fringe or in the shadow of the modern sector which are obviously economically relevant but can hardly be subsumed under the conventional macroeconomic categories" (see Sectoral concept, 1992, BMZ).

Closer consideration of the economic activities of the target groups and individuals coming under the informal sector will require extension to a broad spectrum. The field of activity ranges from traditional handicraft and agricultural services of the informal sector through services aimed at the modern industrial sector to the countless nonspecific services. The activities and necessary qualifications for providing the range of services of the informal sector accordingly involve or require a very wide range of technological, commercial and organisational standards among the target groups. Generally, all areas of economic and social life in the formal sector and the modern economy are affected by the informal sector, although this often happens at a very low economic, technological and organisational level (cf. C. Lohmar-Kuhnle, Cologne, 91). As a result of the previously badly underestimated commercial and value-added significance of the informal sector for the national economy, the entrepreneurs in the informal sector lack access to the lending, marketing, information and decision-making systems. In addition, they lack influence on the local and national economic and political environment. Exceptions here are the social forces which have recently developed (particularly in the Islamic and Asian cultures), often based on traditional bazaars and also religious and political protest movements. These forces are frequently underestimated by domestic leadership elites and international politics and business in terms of their political relationships and influence on the poor groups in these countries (see for example the Islam-integrationist movement, particularly in Algeria, Egypt, Iran, and Pakistan and India). These developments do not in any event make co-operation (bilateral and multilateral) easier with the potential target groups in the informal sector, since traditional and culture-specific conditions prevail here to a particular extent which are frequently only accessible to insiders. The consequence is that measures for the informal sector can only be successful with strategic involvement of the target groups, with the agreement of the leadership elites emerging in this sector (where these are present) and taking into account the traditional and cultural context.

It is virtually impossible to determine exactly the interfaces between the informal and formal sectors of the economy. Often it is impossible to assign the members of the target groups in the informal sector in Third World countries clearly to these sectors, as their second or third jobs take them into the informal sector while at the same time they earn part of their income as salaried staff or employees e.g. in the public service of the country in question. Particularly in urban or semi-urban areas, this makes it difficult to assign them unambiguously. In rural areas, by contrast, the modern and traditional sectors are much more distinct and separate, to the extent that there are stable opportunities for earning. Here again, however, expansion of the informal sector is evident in a situation of growing impoverishment. The labour market is accordingly an important tie and interface between the informal and formal sectors. It should be noted here that the two sectors share a major problem, in that the labour market is unable in both sectors to offer adequate employment for the great majority of the unemployed.

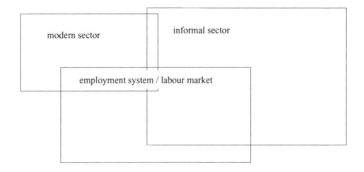

5.2 The importance of culture, tradition and the need to develop a concept of work intrinsic to the cultures

The importance of work as a concept and in its own right is understood in all cultures and in all human eras on the basis of its socio-cultural, socio-economic, historical, religious, political and ecological relationships and its background. Work is accordingly linked directly with people and their existence – without people there would be no work and without work there would certainly be no people, who are at the same time the subject and object of work.

In its significance and its assignment to the different levels of the society under consideration (and also in assignment of the specific activities or even entire vocational groups) work can accordingly reflect the socio-cultural, socio-economic and social and political structure of these societies (H. Marcuse, Suhrkamp, 1967).

For technical co-operation in the field of vocational training aid to the informal sector, it is accordingly particularly important to recognise our own western notion of work (with its Judaeo-Christian flavour) and to place it in relation to the value systems of our own and foreign cultures and societies. Only in this way can we avoid serious misunderstandings and inappropriate behaviour, particularly at the level of the informal sector target groups with their often traditional orientation. Project work accordingly has to take into account the following important issues:

- The background of the local concept of work must be clarified.
- The cultural and social context of the partners in Third World countries must be studied and the goals (including ethical, moral and religious etc) must be discussed and understood. This understanding is an important basis for future co-operation and success.
- Egocentric and "western" self-seeking and career-oriented approaches, which in some cases degenerate into Eurocentric missionary activity, have to be avoided. This requires a high level of absorption and acceptance of the foreign culture, tradition and society.
- Where technical co-operation on training is being sought with Third World societies, the partners must be clear about the religious, traditional, social and ideological goals for education and training.
- Education and vocational training are defined in terms of pedagogical methodology and didactics arising inter alia out of the social and cultural relationships in the target societies. The concepts for advisory projects in technical co-operation on vocational training must accordingly be formulated and implemented inter alia in terms

of the existing relationships in the target societies and their relationships with work.
- Vocational pedagogics, the instruments for formulating approaches to solutions, implementation of studies and the groups of experts commissioned to carry these out must all free themselves from their own approaches, which are frequently excessively influenced by the solutions, and strive for realistic and appropriate solutions which are acceptable in terms of the problems and systems, without however having to abandon the drive for innovation.
- Vocational pedagogics must find new culture-specific approaches (in terms of the informal sector) which are oriented towards the environment of the target groups, taking into account the concept of work or ideas about work of the target society and target groups and the aid measures for system building approaches in the vocational training sector, and also taking into account the employment situation and prospects of the national economy.
- Changes in the understanding of work should basically orient themselves towards the potential for change and development of the prevailing and culture-specific division of labour. Such an approach must also ensure that the target groups and target societies have an opportunity to preserve or further develop their own identity.

5.3 *Importance of culture and tradition for technical cooperation in the informal sector*

5.3.1 *Tradition*

The question of the importance of culture and tradition is no mere hypothetical issue in this context, but rather one with a concrete and reciprocal link with the relationship under development aid and technical co-operation between the countries offering aid and the countries receiving aid. This relationship is generally very strongly shaped by the colonial past of these countries and their relationship with their former colonial masters. The western industrialised nations (Europe, the USA and Japan and the former Soviet Union) still have a very strong influence on the modern sector, the middle classes, the leadership elites and the politicians in these countries. The so-called Third World countries are accordingly frequently subject to a strong ethnocentricity originating in the donor countries which often has post-colonial characteristics and engenders dependency.

This particularly strongly affects those key areas of development policy which are heavily dependent on cultural, traditional, social-policy and to some extent also ideological factors. If we consider the social and political importance our society generally attributes to education as a whole and to vocational training, this inevitably also applies to technical co-operation in this sector. Frequently, however, vocational training is regarded here as having a less political role. The fact that this cannot be the case is shown by the educational policy controversies in the Federal Republic of Germany. Experience in technical co-operation in the sphere of vocational training aid in connection with the attempted transfer of typically German approaches to vocational training, such as the "Dual system", is increasingly showing the political delicacy of this area. These questions are extremely important in the context of the debate about the transfer and model nature of the German vocational training system and the development of vocational training systems in Third World countries. However, knowledge of cultural and traditional models of behaviour of the potential target groups is even more important in connection with the elaboration of promotional concepts and strategies for the development of the informal sector. Frequently a double problem emerges here, since the target groups are not only wrongly assessed and advised by the donor organisations but also very remote from the local decision-makers. In fact, they are frequently even more remote from these groups than the foreign advisers, who as a result of their modern interactive research and planning methodology often have a much more target group oriented and participative approach than their local partners. In addition there is also the question of the individual attitudes of the target groups involved, who mostly come from the lower and smallholder classes and are relatively conservative. As a result of what is often a socially hopeless situation together with poor experience in the past, these groups are generally unreceptive to development projects with a highly innovative nature. Experience has shown that the behaviour of these social groups can be characterised as follows:

- Decisions on innovation or non-innovation for small farmers, self-employed craft workers and micro businessmen are complex processes. Cultural value systems play a selective and productive role in these. Such decisions have to supply tried and tested methods of securing income and survival.
- Rejection of untried innovations frequently appears sensible in poor societies, as mistakes can endanger the survival of entire groups or small businesses.

- Conversely, successes with innovation can under some circumstances disrupt the economic equilibrium and consequently endanger the communal solidarity. This can lead to new and dangerous or undesired dependencies for the group.
- Traditional forms of behaviour must accordingly also be understood as protective measures for these communities against undesired changes and even as risk minimisation. They produce "efficient poverty".

For vocational training projects this means that it is necessary to ensure that the target groups are as closely involved as possible in the process of identification, planning and implementation of projects in the informal sector. It is necessary to identify and develop action-oriented, anthropocentric approaches.

5.3.2 *Culture*

In connection with the discussion about achieving sustainable and qualitative changes and inducing open development processes for target groups in the informal sector, the question of vocational pedagogical approaches is very important. The decisive question in this context is how participants, i.e. those who are making available their knowledge and skills and those who are the targets for and recipients and initiators of the desired changes can make joint use of their "can" and "will" for change so that the desired changes (goals) ultimately happen? It is accordingly necessary, if such a situation arises, to create an atmosphere of great openness in co-operation and allow the participants the maximum scope for decision-making and protect them from bureaucratic red tape and obstacles. If this is not done, it will be virtually impossible to achieve the necessary positive effects with the target group and exercise an integrative effect on the informal sector (cf. G. Lachmann, Berlin 1988).

The BMZ framework concept for taking into account socio-cultural criteria for projects in development co-operation proposes observation of the following "key factors":

1. Legitimacy (acceptance)
2. State of development reached
3. Socio-cultural heterogeneity.

In detail these "key factors" have to be reviewed as concrete individual cases and separately considered and elaborated in their relevance for the sectors and sub-sectors.

For projects in the area of vocational training aid, this can look as follows:

- Document and review the social will and legitimacy of individuals, groups, ideas and institutions active in vocational training policy and providing vocational training. The question is, what do the target groups and those involved in implementing projects in vocational training and job-creation measures wish to achieve and what role do they play in this.
- Implementation of situation analyses with the goal of identifying the state of development achieved in terms of the capability of the target groups and those involved. The situation, i.e. the prevailing state of the system of vocational training (formal, non-formal and informal) is analysed to permit formulation and elaboration of approaches based on the existing potential which seek evolutionary change.
- The diversity, i.e. the socio-cultural heterogeneity of the target groups and those involved in such vocational training and employment systems, complicates the planning and implementation of measures in these areas. It is accordingly necessary to establish adequate clarity right from the project planning stage regarding the diversity of the target groups, those involved and the existing social roles and power structures. A particular point to bear in mind is that the measures can contribute towards a possible shift in existing power structures or contribute to their stabilisation.
- The diversity of the impacting cultures (the so-called "donor" and "recipient" countries) which cannot be expressed in the major categories of intercultural communication "language" and "socialisation" can have a seriously adverse effect on the above points and doom joint projects. It is accordingly particularly important to ensure with projects for vocational training aid that adequate expertise is available in the expert teams right from the analytical and planning phase. These teams should accordingly be assembled on a multidisciplinary basis by this stage. (M. Schürmann, Bonn, 1990)

5.4 *Potential target groups for measures to promote the informal sector*

In section 2.4 the potential target groups for measures in the informal sector were presented in a synoptic table. The following groups were identified by their social status and their dependencies within the local or regional economy:

(A) *Groups independently creating income and hence jobs for employees:*
   - small (micro) entrepreneurs with few (up to 10) employees;
   - individual entrepreneurs without employees or self-employed;
   - small (micro) entrepreneurs in increasingly sophisticated technology and service areas.

(B) *Groups with income from employment in urban and rural economies:*
   - wage earners and day labourers in the informal sector;
   - wage earners and day labourers in establishments in the modern sector;
   - wage earners and day labourers in the service sector;
   - apprentices and child workers in establishments in the informal sector;
   - casual labourers, day labourers, street children;
   - prostitutes and people earning a living by illegal methods;
   - slave-like employment (bonded labour, c. 100 million people worldwide: source ILO statistics);

(C) *Groups in rural areas who have recently become employees performing their original activities and occupations as employees:*
   - small (micro) entrepreneurs and employees from these establishments, generally traditional craft and service establishments unable to make an adequate income due to turnover problems;
   - small (micro) farmers and family subsistence farms which (as above) are unable to make an adequate income;
   - underemployed and unemployed young persons;
   - landless rural labourers;
   - underemployed and badly paid labourers in public services and other medium-sized companies.

(D) *Special groups in rural and urban areas who have lost their employment and traditional living area as a result of displacement and flight:*
   - refugees, victims of political persecution and asylum seekers.

Given the diversity of the target groups and their problems in the informal sector, it will not be possible to establish a uniform and overarching vocational pedagogic system of programmes or courses for training and advanced training. Educational and vocational training policy approaches must accordingly be formulated and conceived in terms of the specific situation of the target groups. To ensure the success of promotional measures in this sector the following important elements must accordingly be taken into account in identifying, planning and implementation.

Careful and comprehensive analysis of the target groups, the integration of general educational and vocational training measures into the project are required. Improving incomes and living conditions for these groups in the informal sector is the priority objective of measures.

- Definition and description of clear targets, i.e. conceived measures, must correspond with and cover the specific needs and problems of the target groups. Care must be taken here to take into account the specific conditions of target groups in the informal sector in:
  a) rural areas
  b) urban areas
  c) rural-urban areas.
- The context for the measures for the informal sector must be investigated closely and reviewed for favourable impact of the projects in political, economic, social and cultural terms and other elements important to the target groups for ensuring sustainable success.
- Involvement of the beneficiaries, i.e. the target groups, responsible government offices and other important associations and groups associated with the project must be ensured at all stages of identification, planning and implementation of measures.
- The role of women, men and children in the informal sector must be taken into account in designing the projects and planned and implemented in accordance with the principles of equality of men and women and the international statutes and regulations on the protection of children and young people.
- In planning and implementing measures in the informal sector, it must be assumed that the informal sector already has its own microeconomic structures and generally already operates according to free market rules. Care is accordingly required in developing concepts for promotional measures to ensure that these structures are not disrupted by promotion from outside. The goal must be to improve on existing aspects, where acceptable, and to move in the direction of integration.
- The measures must accordingly focus on the people in the informal sector and the goal must be action-oriented, anthropocentric projects. Projects accordingly provide stimuli complementary to the

existing structures in the informal sector and represent a concentration of various measures, e.g.
  d) general education and vocational training measures
  e) measures to promote trades and crafts
  f) health and hygiene measures
  g) measures for the protection of children and young people
  h) job-creation programmes etc.
- Training and advanced training projects in the informal sector need to develop flexible concepts which permit ongoing adjustment to employment and economic structures, i.e. contents, methods and didactics must be oriented to demand.
- Projects must show quick successes and need expert and flexible management and committed staff trained in the needs of the informal sector.
- Measures must be planned and funded with an adequate horizon in order to ensure sustainability of the desired success. In addition there must also be corresponding follow-on and backstopping services to ensure long-term prospects for development.
- Projects in this sector should be followed using specially adapted scientific methods in order to collect and analyse project experience, errors and successes. This is intended to ensure reproducibility and multiplier effect in the field of development co-operation.

With regard to the last point specifically it should be repeated that in addition to the elements needed for successful project implementation in the informal sector listed here, there are two other very important considerations:
a) Ongoing participation of the target groups is absolutely essential at every stage of project identification, planning and implementation, and
b) It is very important to develop willingness of the relevant agencies in the local government to develop commitment to the informal sector. It must be ensured for the long term that the informal sector is credited with the political, economic and development-policy importance that it deserves on the basis of its size and relevance for employment policy.

5.5 *Results of the study on TTP/SES Peshawar, Pakistan*

The results of the study on graduate placement and potential target groups for Pakistan (TTP/SES Peshawar) can be summarised in the following recommendations.

- The target groups must be clearly identified using the criteria developed in section 2.4 and exactly described as in 3.1.4 of the caste study
- The basic didactic structure of the vocational training and development policy promotional concepts for the target groups in the informal sector must be based on an open, action-oriented, anthropocentric didactic approach, i.e. the following aspects must be taken into account:
  - extrafunctional education to secure survival and future-oriented development;
  - education to develop self-help potential
  - education to secure employment or self-employment
  - education to create and secure income.
- The socio-cultural and political environment for a project to promote target groups in the informal sector must be studied and their importance for the project recognised and given due account.
- The economic and development-policy environment for the local and regional labour markets must be studied and taken into account.
- Access to vocational training and educational measures must not be formalised. It must be unconditionally available to the identified target groups.
- To support systematic orientation of projects, projects with the goal of promoting the informal and traditional sector must also aim at moving towards or promoting openness of the formal vocational or general education sector, i.e. integration into the formal sector should be sought (cf. section 3.1.8).
- New measures or concepts for training skilled workers and entrepreneurs in the informal sector should as a matter of principle take into account existing traditional training concepts or systems and possibly integrate them (cf. traditional apprenticeships, section 3.1.6.6)
- To be employment oriented, measures for training and advanced training of target groups in the informal and traditional sector must be accompanied by flanking job-creating promotional measures.
- The informal and traditional sector requires flexible and open promotional concepts which are specifically oriented towards the individual conditions of individuals and groups. In addition, care must be taken to see that the promotional instruments are designed to be simple and accessible (without major bureaucratic obstacles) for the target groups.
- The promotional instruments and project approaches must be integrated into programmes for promoting the informal sector and

reflect the local and regional economic, political, socio-cultural and socio-economic structures. As a matter of principle, individual projects must be regarded as problematic unless they are integrated into a broader context of programmes and strategies to promote target groups in the informal and traditional sector. Sustainable impacts e.g. on the employment situation of the target groups can only be achieved through programme approaches.

5.6 Review of the studies carried out in Bangalore and Madras

The socio-cultural, socio-economic and political conditions in the region have shown that the experience gathered in the Pakistan (regional) context in the NWFP cannot be simply transferred. It is clear that the informal sector is developing in parallel with the formal sector and is able to develop primarily in those economic areas and employment contexts where the formal sector needs cheaper services and production (products). Alternatively, it does so through gaps in consumer goods production, services and other areas of production, specifically agricultural products (agro-production) where the formal sector leaves the informal/traditional and unorganised sector enough space to develop. In the Indian context it is important not to forget the traditional cotton and carpet small-scale (micro) industries (handloom and powerloom) and the khadi industry founded by Gandhi. These areas of the so-called "unorganised sector" represent vast potential for employment in the informal sector. In southern India the tanning and leather industry is another important area for the development of small (micro) businesses and widespread home-based industries. Leather products and textiles are major export areas (the Federal Republic of Germany in particular is an important market for these products) for southern Indian small (micro) businesses and medium-sized companies. Under some circumstances this can also be viewed as an example of how whenever the informal sector (cotton production, textile products and leather goods) becomes a factor through home-based industrial production and also gains indirect access to the world market, it becomes exposed to and required to meet the quality standards of the world market. This in turn requires a certain allocation of resources to training and advanced training measures for the crafts involved in production, if these standards are also to be met in the output of small businesses and home-based groups and families. It is important in this context to recognise the joint responsibility of customers, as child labour is particularly apparent in these sectors in India. As noted elsewhere, the

Indian government is trying to reduce this evil through corresponding promotional policies, but this can only be successful if income-generating occupations can be created for adult family members and the international community refuses to accept products (primarily) manufactured through child labour. This means developing the willingness among consumers in the western industrialised nations to pay more than in the past for products from these countries (carpets etc). It is accordingly a matter of principle not merely to support or assist uncritically and irresponsibly the expansion of the informal sector and employment in this sector. Instead, the promotional strategies of bilateral and multilateral donors must focus on the exploitation and socially unjustifiable conditions and poor living conditions of these people. The following aspects should accordingly be taken into account in identifying, planning and implementing promotional measures:

- Target groups must be clearly identified and described in accordance with the criteria developed in section 2.4.
- The target groups absolutely must be adequately involved in identifying measures to promote these groups.
- The socio-cultural, socio-economic, traditional and social environments must be studied and duly taken into account in developing and implementing projects in the informal sector.
- The economic and development policy goals of bilateral and multilateral donors must be reviewed for their promotion of local and regional labour markets and corrected if necessary.
- Promotion of the informal sector includes designing measures to promote small (micro) businesses and creating appropriate training and advanced training measures for entrepreneurs and skilled workers.
- Promotion in the above sectors must, however, be combined with measures to develop labour markets and employment in the areas of self-employment and employment.
- Measures in the informal sector must as a matter of principle be designed so that they make a long-term contribution towards the integration of the informal economic and employment sector into the formal economic sector.
- Access to promotional measures must not be formalised. They must be unconditionally available to the identified target groups.
- The basic didactic structure of the vocational training and development policy promotional concepts for the target groups in the informal sector must be based on an open, action-oriented, anthropocentric didactic approach, i.e. the following aspects must be taken into account:

- extrafunctional education to secure survival and future-oriented development;
- education to develop self-help potential
- education to secure employment or self-employment
- education to create and secure income.

• To support systematic orientation of projects, projects with the goal of promoting the informal and traditional sector must also aim at moving towards or promoting openness of the formal vocational or general education sector, i.e. integration into the formal sector should be sought (cf. section 3.1.8).
• New measures or concepts for training skilled workers and entrepreneurs in the informal sector should as a matter of principle take into account existing traditional training concepts or systems and possibly integrate them (cf. traditional apprenticeships, section 3.1.6.6)

5.7 *Summary and presentation of approaches for a holistic vocational pedagogics for the informal sector*

5.7.1 *Holistic vocational pedagogics*

The present work has identified and demonstrated the need of and importance for development policy of the informal sector as a special area for promotion in vocational training aid. Criticism of the one-sided orientation of vocational training aid to date can be ascribed to the following misjudgements in bilateral and multilateral development cooperation:

Industrialisation is a vital condition for social and economic development and progress.

- A key constraint on this process is the shortage of qualified skilled workers.
- The industrialisation process can only be successfully pursued if the shortfalls in the field of vocational education are removed and corresponding facilities and institutions created.
- Demand for skilled workers has been estimated to be more or less unlimited.
- The technological standard of the modern industrial sector has been estimated as very high, with the consequence that education of skilled workers had to meet this standard.

These judgements and the vocational training aid formulated and developed on this basis led to a very one-sided focus on the modern industrial sector and neglect of the steadily-growing informal sector. However, the lack of growth in the formal sector resulted in a situation where even graduates of the formal vocational training system in these countries were or are unable to find jobs in the modern sector. Graduates of these training facilities are, however, seldom ready to work in the informal sector unless forced to by circumstance.

However, a vocational pedagogics which accepts the informal sector as part of the existing employment system would have to open itself for the specific problems of this sector and contribute towards eliminating the dividing line (which in any event is unclear and artificial) between formal, non-formal and informal training. It would have to be oriented towards a holistic approach. Above all, the people and their problems must be returned to the focus of vocational pedagogics. This is also (and particularly) true of vocational training aid as currently practised, which is far too strongly oriented towards the narrow modern industrial sector in Third World countries and ignores the broad mass of the underemployed and unemployed. Modification or reorientation of vocational pedagogics and vocational training aid requires that the "anthropocentric and action-oriented concepts and multidimensional target group identification" championed in the present work become the decisive factors in developing new approaches and promotional concepts. Four model approaches should accordingly be used for employment-creating vocational education in the informal sector:

- Individual (labour) market oriented and/or subsistence oriented training and advanced training
- Training and consultancy to promote economic independence
- Complex approaches to employment-oriented training and social education of rural target groups
- Elementary education as part of employment-oriented training and advanced training.

In contrast to traditional vocational pedagogics which are firmly focused on the defined sectors of the economy in question (e.g. curricula, occupation profiles, requirement profiles etc), vocational pedagogics directed at the target groups and promotional approaches described here would have to be conceived in open and holistic terms. To impact employment, they would also have to be combined with other promotional areas and instruments of development co-operation (e.g. promotion of small businesses, job creation programmes, regional development programmes etc).

5.7.2 Target group oriented basic didactic structures and the idea of education in the context of employment-promoting training and advanced training

Target group orientation
For training and advanced training measures the following approaches are decisive for vocational training. They also provide the basis for the basic didactic structure of vocational training concepts in the informal sector. Specifically, the following factors must be taken into account:

(A) Anthropocentricity, i.e. target group specific orientation of the didactic approach must be ensured.
(B) The action orientation and relevance for application of the qualifications to be transferred (skills, abilities, knowledge and extrafunctional qualifications) must be ensured.
(C) The self-help potential and ability of the target groups and individuals to earn an income from employment and/or self-employment should be developed and improved.
(D) The concept of vocational training aid, the didactic structure of projects, the curriculum elements and development of the necessary qualifications must be conceived openly and holistically for developing the situation of group and individual in the informal sector.

There must be the possibility to adapt flexibly to the direct needs of target groups. Individuals or groups interested in training and advanced training or promotion for employment or self-employment must be involved in the process of developing curriculum elements and integrated as correspondingly active partners in the concept and the didactic structure of the projects. This involvement is a key condition for ensuring the openness called for here.

The basic didactic structure
The key elements for ensuring an open, action-oriented didactic approach are:

(A) the *extrafunctional qualifications* to ensure *survival* and *future-oriented development* of the target groups and individuals;
(B) the qualifications for creating and securing income, i.e. here specifically including the development of abilities, skills and knowledge for *saving income*;
(C) the *qualifications* for securing *employment* and *self-employment*, including technical and entrepreneurial skills, knowledge and abilities (commercial, management etc) and general education;

(D) the *qualifications* for developing *self-help potential* of the target groups and individuals, i.e. abilities, knowledge, skills and socio-psychological changes in forms of behaviour must be developed which strengthen or develop self-help potential and behaviour in these groups and individuals.

The concept of training in the context of job-creating vocational training in the informal sector
"The link between (vocational)training and employment is the vocational qualification. At the macro level, at the level of society or the economy, vocational training qualifications are the social medium of exchange in the labour market." This applies to both the formal and the informal-traditional sector. The definition offered by Alex, L. for the concept of qualification again illustrates the transferability of this approach to employment or the labour market in the informal sector:
"Qualification means the totality of knowledge and abilities (including behavioural models and skills) acquired in the processes of socialisation and education. Acquisition of qualifications promotes the active shaping of life not only as a worker but also as a citizen and family member A qualification accordingly also has not only a vocational but also a social dimension. The latter applies specifically to abilities which enable individuals to satisfy social requirements arising out of a working democracy, i.e. particularly the demands of participation at all levels" (Alex, L. Berufliche Qualifikation heute, 1991). Assuming that this definition of vocational qualification can also be applied in the informal sector, it still needs to be interpreted in terms of this sector.

(A) *self-employed persons*, e.g. subsistence economy businesses, bazaar businesses or other small (micro) entrepreneurs;
(B) *employed persons*, e.g. skilled workers in bazaar businesses and small (micro) businesses, hired labourers, family members helping out etc.

The most important (key) qualifications for *self-employed* and *entrepreneurial activity* can be summarised as follows:

Entrepreneurial ability to act	=

– technical competence, – methodological competence, – social competence; – learning competence; – communication competence – entrepreneurial competence.

The (key) qualifications and interconnections cited here are closely related to the cultural and traditional social conditions and the specific development opportunities of the target groups. Their development lays the basis for successful promotion of businesses in the informal sector. They are also the basis for developing training and advanced training courses, programmes and other promotional measures.

The most important (key) qualifications for employment and *non-entrepreneurial work* can be summarised as follows:

> *Ability to act =*
> *Qualification* to perform the assigned tasks success- =
> fully and the ability to attain their own interests

> – social competence;
> – methodological and learning competence;
> – technical competence.

5.7.3 *Employment-oriented learning in the informal sector*

Employment-oriented learning in the informal sector occurs in the context of the central methodological-didactic approach, i.e. an open, action-oriented and anthropocentric concept vocational pedagogic and approach. The following aspects are important for successful design and implementation of training measures in this sector:
– selection of the sites for learning;
– length of training measures;
– qualification of trainers and instructors;
– technological appropriateness of teaching and learning materials
– the training facilities;
– integration of the training measures into widespread and intersectoral promotional programmes which include job-creating components.

Vocational training for the informal sector can only be successful if it is planned and implemented in the context of job-creating promotional programmes. Although it creates the prerequisites for employment through training, this itself does not create any significant number of new jobs, which are directly linked with the implementation of these training measures. It is accordingly necessary to combine these vocational training measures in the informal sector with other promotional measures as described above and implement these jointly.

5.7.4 Vocational training measures in the informal sector and the need to combine these with the formal vocational training system: systematic aspects of development

Experience with the informal sector has shown that a key feature of the relationships between the informal sector and the formal (modern industrial) sector is the *economic duality*. The "interchanges" (Lutz, The brief dream of lasting prosperity, 1989) between the two sectors are limited to the following areas:

- The traditional/informal sector is the most important reservoir of labour for the modern industrial sector,
- The hired labour in the industrial sector meets its direct living needs primarily from goods and services from the traditional sector (cheap products, services etc),
- Income of families and businesses in the informal sector from the modern industrial sector has a primarily investment nature (capital goods, taxes etc).

These specific relationships show that the informal sector does better when the prosperity of the formal sector is ensured. Conversely, however, the economic situation in the informal sector is likely to have little direct influence on the success of modernisation and industrialisation in Third World countries. This dualism is only found in a marked form where corresponding industrialisation has already taken place (e.g. India, Pakistan, Indonesia etc). The relationships between the two sectors shown here do, however, justify the conclusion that the informal sector plays a not insignificant (indirect) role in vocational training of labour for the modern and industrial sector. To this extent there is also a link here in developing vocational training measures for the informal sector. While the present work did not permit adequate treatment of the problem of integration and the system-shaping character of vocational training measures, the author feels it is necessary to investigate this specific relationship between the two sectors and consider the development of an integrated vocational training system. A mutually exclusive treatment of the two sectors involves the danger of further political, social, economic and development policy marginalisation of the informal sector. This is something to be avoided at all costs.

Reference Literature

Author	Title	Year of publication
Abdel-Malek, Anouar	La Pensèe politique arabe contemporaine, Seuil, Paris	1970
Adorno, Th. W.	Ohne Leitbild. Parva Aesthetica, Edition Suhrkamp, Frankfurt/M.	1968
Ahmed, Akbar S.	Pukhtun economy and society, Traditional Structure and economic development a tribal society, London	1980
Ahmed, Akbar S.	Pakistan: The Social Sciences Perspective, Ed. by Akbar S. Ahmed, Oxford University Press, Karachi	1990
AL-Attas, S.N. (Ed.)	Aims and Objectives of Islamic Education, Aufsatz von A.K. Brohi: Education in an Ideological State, Hodders and Stoughton, K.A. University, Jeddah	1979
Alex, L.	Berufliche Qualifikationen heute – Entwicklung und Akteure, in: Berufsbildung in Wissenschaft und Praxis, Heft 2	1991
Alex, L.	Qualifikationsforschung – eine Zwischenbilanz in: Berufsbildung in Wissenschaft und Praxis, Heft 1	1979
Ali, M. Muhammad	The Religion of Islam, Cairo	
Arnold, R.	Der Streit um die Berufsbildungshilfe – Berufsbildung für die Dritte Welt im Widerstreit von Konzeptionen, Baden-Baden	1989
Arnold, R.	Interkulturelle Berufspädagogik, BIS-Oldenburg	1991
Arnold, R.	Berufliche Bildung und Entwicklung in den Ländern der Dritten Welt, Nomos, Baden-Baden	1989
Arnold, R.	Neue Akzente der internationalen Berufsbildungs-Debatte. Impulse für eine künftige Entwicklungszusammenarbeit im Bereich der beruflichen Bildung?	

Author	Title	Year of publication
Arnold, R., Burk, H.	Der Streit um die Berufsbildungshilfe in E+Z, Heft 12	1987
Axt, H.J/Karcher, W./ Schleich, B. (Hrsg.)	Ausbildungs- und Beschäftigungskrise in der Dritten Welt?, Frankfurt	1987
Beyer, H.	GTZ-Sektortagung der GTZ-Berufsbildung in Pakistan 1991, Eschborn	1991
bfai	Pakistan-Wirtschaftsentwicklung 1989, Bundesstelle für Außenhandelsinformationen, Köln	1991
Biermann, H., Greinert, W.-D., Janisch, R.	Systementwicklung und Systemberatung in der Berufsbildungshilfe (Berichte, Analysen, Konzepte), Nomos, Baden-Baden	1994
Blankertz, Herwig	Theorien und Modelle der Didaktik, Grundfragen der Erziehungswissenschaft, Juventa Verlag, 10. Auflage, München	1977
BMZ	Grundlinien der Entwicklungspolitik der Bundesregierung, Bonn	March 1986
BMZ	Sektorkonzepte: Förderung der Sektoren, Grundbildung, ländliche Entwicklung, Armutsbekämpfung und zur Förderung der Frauen, Bonn	
BMZ	Sektorkonzept: Berufliche Bildung, BMZ-Referat 310, Bonn	Jan. 1992
BMZ	Journalisten-Handbuch Entwicklungspolitik 87, Bonn	1987
BMZ	Grundbedürfniskonzept, Bonn	1978
BMZ	Sozio-kulturelle Kriterien für Vorhaben der Entwicklungszusammenarbeit – Rahmenkonzept –, Bonn	1992
Böhm, U. and Ebeling, U.	Berufsbildung und Kleingewerbeförderung in flüchtlingsbetroffenen Gebieten Pakistans sowie in Afghanistan, Eschborn	1992
Böll, M.	Indien zur Jahresmitte 1993 in Wirtschaftslage, Hrsg. Bundesstelle für Außenhandelsinformation (bfai)	June 1993

Author	Title	Year of publication
Bollnow, O.F.	Pädagogische Forschung und philosophisches Denken, in: Erziehungswissenschaft und Erziehungswirklichkeit, edited by H. Röhrs, S. 229 aus: W. Klafki, Aspekte kritisch-konstruktiver Erziehungswissenschaft, Beltz, Weinheim	1976
Borsutzky, Dieter	Die Industrialisierung im informellen Metallsektor: Das Maschinenkleingewerbe in Penang/Malaysia, Saarbrücken	1992
Braun, G.	Vom Mythos des Traditionalismus, in: E+Z 8/9	1986
Buchmann, Michael A.	Berufsstrukturen in Entwicklungsländern, Erdmann, Tübingen	1979
Capra, Fritjof	The Tao of Physics, New York	1984
Caroe, Sir Olaf	The Pathans, Oxford University Press, Karachi	
CDU/CSU	Berufsbildung als Schlüssel zur Armutsbekämpfung, Reihe Argumente, Neue Wege in der Entwicklungspolitik, Bonn	1986
CEFE	Competency based Economies through Formation of Entrepreneurs, Eschborn	
Chaudhary, M., Ali, P., Azim, Burki, A.A.	Skill Generation and Entrepreneurship Development under »Ostad-Shagird« System in Pakistan, Publ. National Manpower Commission, Government of Pakistan, Pakistan	1989
Department of Rural Development	Ministry of Agriculture, Government of India, New Delhi, Manual for Integrated Rural Development Programme (IRDP) and allied Programmes of TRYSEM and DWCRA – TRYSEM = Training of Rural Youth for Self Employment – DWCRA = Development of Women and Children in Rural Areas	1991
Diehl, M.	Die Naturwissenschaften in Pakistan, Eds. S. Laik Ali, W. Voelter, Z.H. Zaidi, Deutsch-Pakistan. Forum e.V., Mayen	1986
Diehl, M.	Die berufsbildende Schule, Probleme beim Transfer des dualen Systems in die Länder der Dritten Welt	March 1993

Author	Title	Year of publication
Dubois Abbe, J.A.	Hindu Customs and Ceremonies, Asian Educational Services, New Delhi	1985
Edwards, David Busby	The Marginal Identity of Afghan Refugees – in: Frontier, Boundaries and Frames, Akbar S. Ahmed (Ed.); Pakistan, The Social Sciences Perspective, Oxford Press Karachi	1990
Employment Promotion Unit, Technical Wing	Manpower Employment and Training Services in Pakistan. Islamabad	1990
Ende/Steinbach	Der Islam in der Gegenwart, C.H. Beck, München, III. Auflage	1991
FES	The Regional Workshop on Development and Utilization of Human Ressources: Issues and Policies, Islamabad, Pakistan	1988
FES (Friedrich Ebert Stiftung)	Educated Unemployed, Friedrich Ebert Stiftung and Government of Pakistan, Ministry of Manpower and Overseas Pakistanis, Islamabad	1990
Fluitman, Fred	Training for work in the informal Sector . . ., ILO, Geneva	1989
Fluitman, Fred	Strategien Selbsthilfefördender und Beschäftigungsinitiativer Berufsbildung in der Dritten Welt; Ausbildung für den informellen Sektor: Ein Tagungsordnungspunkt für die Neunziger Jahre, S. 32 ff, Berlin, Expertentagung Juni 89, DSE-ZGB, Mannheim	1989
Frank, Manfred	Was ist Neostrukturalismus, Suhrkamp, Frankfurt	1984
Franke, G./ Kleinschmitt, M.	Der Lernort Arbeitsplatz (Schriften zur Berufsbildungsforschung, Bd. 65, Hrsg. vom Bundesinstitut für Berufsbildung), Berlin/Köln	1987
Frenz, A., Kohlshorn, R.	Existenzgründungen fördern, in: GTZ-Info, 5	1987
Frey, K.	Berichte und Reprints aus dem Institut für berufliche Bildung und Weiterbildungsforschung (IBW-Berichte), TU-Berlin, Nr. 7	1991
Friedeburg, Ludwig von	Bildungsreform in Deutschland, Kapitel Bildungsgesamtplan, Suhrkamp, Frankfurt	1992
Fuchs, Martin and Berg, E.	Phänomenologie der Differenz in: Kultur, soziale Praxis, Text. Suhrkamp, Frankfurt	1993

Author	Title	Year of publication
Getubig, I., Oshima, H.T.	Towards Full Employment Strategy For Accelerated Economic Growth, Asian Pacific Development Center, Kuala Lumpur	1991
Glanter, Marc	Competing, Equalities: Law and Backward Classes in India, Delhi, Oxford Press	1984
Göser, Barutzki, Frommer, Knabe	Grundausbildung und Berufsausbildung für afghanische Flüchtlinge und der in den betroffenen Gebieten lebenden Pakistani, N.W.F.P. und Baluchistan, Eschborn, GTZ	1981
Government of India	Report of the national commission on self employed women and women in the informal sector, Shramshakti: durchgeführt im Auftrag der indischen Zentralregierung, New Delhi, India	1988
Government of India	The Constitution of India, Nabhi Publication, New Delhi, India	1992
Government of India	Workshop on Vocational Hi-Tech Training 2000 AD, Publ. Central Instructional Media Institute, Madras	1990
Government of India (GOI)	Ministry of Labour, Vocational Training in India, New Delhi, India	
Government of India	Eighth Five Year Plan, 1992-97, Vol. I, Planning Commission New Delhi, India	1992
Government of Pakistan	Pakistan Manpower Review, Islamabad, No. 1, Pakistan	1989
Greinert, W.-D.	GTZ-Bericht zur Sektortagung und konzeptionelle Schlußfolgerungen, Pakistan 1991, Eschborn	1991
Greinert, W.-D.	Instrumente und Strategien der Systementwicklung/Systemberatung, in: Biermann, H., Greinert, W.-D., Janisch, R. (eds.): Systementwicklung und Systemberatung in der Berufsbildungshilfe (Berichte, Analysen, Konzepte), Nomos, Baden-Baden	1994
Greinert, W.-D., Wiemann, G.	Produktionsschulprinzip und Berufsbildungshilfe, Nomos, Baden-Baden, 2. Auflage	1993
Grotzfeld, H.	Art. Freitag, in: K. Kreiser/W. Diem/H.-G. Majier, Lexikon der islamischen Welt, Stuttgart	1974

Author	Title	Year of publication
GTZ	Leitfaden zur Erstellung von Angeboten an das BMZ, interne Schrift zur Qualitätssicherung, Eschborn	June 1992
GTZ	Angebot zur Projektdurchführung Dez. 1981, Eschborn	1982
GTZ	Angebot mit GTZ-Prüfbericht (Pilotphase), Eschborn	March 1984
GTZ	Zielorientierte Projektplanung (ZOPP) Bericht (Hurwitz), Eschborn	March 1986
GTZ	Angebot zur Projektverlängerung Dez. 1987 und Abkommen Mai 1988, Eschborn	1987/88
GTZ	Angebot zur Projektverlängerung, Eschborn	April 1990
GTZ	Zielorientierte Projektplanung (ZOPP), Eschborn	May 1990
GTZ	Angebot zur Projektverlängerung, Eschborn	April 93
GTZ	Leitfaden zur Qualitätssicherung der Projekte, Eschborn	1992
GTZ	Internes Papier und Ergebnisbericht: Zopp-Workshop for the Planning of the Pak-German Technical Training Programme (TTP) in Refugee Affected Areas of N.W.F.P.-Peshawar, Pakistan, von C. Huizenga, Eschborn	Feb. 1993
GTZ	Orga-Handbuch und Zopp-Planungsdokumente, Eschborn	
GTZ	Monitoring und Evaluierung in Projekten der Technischen Zusammenarbeit, Schriftenreihe der GTZ, Nr. 229, Eschborn	1992
GTZ	Gate, Questions, Answers, Information, Nr. 2, Eschborn	1992
GTZ	Orientierungsrahmen informeller Sektor, Eschborn	1992
GTZ	CEFE-Competence based Economics by Formation of Entrepreneurs, Eschborn	

Author	Title	Year of publication
Gunatilleke, Nimal G.	Human Ressource Development in SRI LANKA – Innapropriate output or Failure to utilize resources, in: Human Ressource Development and Utilization: Issues and Policies. Pakistan Manpower Institut and Friedrich Ebert Stiftung, Islamabad, Pakistan	1989
Guptha, B.S.	Statistical Outline of India 1992-93 – published by Tata Services ltd., Bombay	1992
Hanf, T.	Wenn die Schule zum Entwicklungshindernis wird. Bildungspolitik und Entwicklungspolitik in der Dritten Welt. In: Entwicklungspolitik, edited by Hauf/Oberndörfer, Stuttgart	1986
Hanf, T., Ammann, K.	Erziehung – ein Entwicklungshindernis? In: Zeitschrift für Pädagogik Nr. 23	1977
Hartwig, Karl-Hans, H. Jörg, Thieme (Hrsg.)	Transformationsprozesse in sozialistischen Wirtschaftssystemen, Springer Berlin	1991
Hegel, Georg, W. Friedrich	Bd. II Studienausgabe Fischer-Bücherei	
Horkheimer, Max	Traditionelle und kritische Theorie, Fünf Aufsätze, aus Autorität und Familie. Fischer Frankfurt	1992
Huizenga, C.	Zielorientierte Projektplanung (ZOPP)	Feb. 93
Hutton, Caroline; Cohen, Robin	African peasants and resistance to change: a reconsideration of sociological approaches, in: Oxaal Ivar; Barnett, Tony; Both, David (eds.); – Beyond the sociology of development. Economy and society in Latin America and Africa. London and Boston	1975
IDA	Programm zur Steigerung der Arbeitsproduktivität der Menschen im ländlichen Bereich (1973) sowie in den Städten (1975), Washington D.C.	1973/1975
Illich I.	Schulen helfen nicht. Über das mythenbildende Ritual der Industriegesellschaft, Rowohlt, Hamburg	1982
ILO	Aktionsprogramm zur Förderung der Beschäftigung und der Befriedigung von Grundbedürfnissen, Genf	1976
ILO	The Dilemma of the Informal Sector, Report of the Director-General ILO, Genf	1991

Author	Title	Year of publication
ILO	Tradition and dynamism among Afghan refugees, Report of an ILO mission to Pakistan (Nov. 1982) on income – generating activities for Afghan refugees by International Labour Office Geneva UNHCR (= United Nations High Commissioner for Refugees, Geneva)	1982
Islam, A. Mohibul	Islam und Freizeit – ein Widerspruch, in: al-Fadjr, Nr. 5	1984
Janisch, Reiner	Sektorstudie Berufliche Bildung Papua New Guinea, GTZ, Eschborn	1991
Kerschensteiner, G.	Das Grundaxiom des Bildungsprozesses, München	1953
Kingsley, Davis	The population of India and Pakistan, Russel and Russel, New York, S. 108	1968
Klafki, W.	Aspekte kritisch-konstruktiver Erziehungswissenschaft, Beltz, Weinheim	1976
Klein, H.G. and Nestvogel, R.	Frauen in Pakistan, Rahmenbedingungen, Ansätze und Projektvorschläge zur Entwicklung und beruflichen Qualifizierung von Frauen in der Provinz Punjab. GTZ Eschborn	1984
Klein/Kruse	Projektidentifizierungsmission, Dec. 1980, Eschborn-GTZ	1980
Kohlheyer, G. u.a.	Bericht Projektverlaufskontrolle TTC-Peshawar, GTZ-Eschborn	1987
Laaser, U.	Bildung und Wissenschaft in der Entwicklungspolitik, in: Aus Politik und Zeitgeschichte, Heft 25/74	1974
Laaser, U.	Bildungstransfer und Systemwandel. Theorie und Praxis des industriestaatlichen Bildungstransfers in den Ländern der Dritten Welt, Beltz, Weinheim	1981
Lachmann, G.	Sozio-kulturelle Bedingungen und Wirkungen in der Entwicklungszusammenarbeit, Deutsches Institut für Entwicklungspolitik, Berlin	1988
Lannoy, Richard	The Speaking Tree, A Study of Indian Culture and Society, Oxford University Press, London	1975

Author	Title	Year of publication
Lenhart, V.	Bildung und Beschäftigung in der Dritten Welt, in: Haag, E. (Hrsg.): Der Beitrag zur Berufsausbildung zur wirtschaftlichen Entwicklung in Partnerländern, DSE-Veröffentlichung, Mannheim	1982
Lette, Jarik and Frankefort, Ir. D.	Survey on Workshops in N.W.F.P., GTZ-Eschborn and Pakistan/N.W.F.P.-Peshawar	1990
List, F.	Das nationale System der politischen Ökonomie. Bd. IV der Gesammelten Werke, edited by A. Sommer, Berlin	1930
Lohmar-Kuhnle, Cornelia	Konzepte zur beschäftigungsorientierten Aus- und Fortbildung von Zielgruppen aus dem informellen Sektor, Weltforum Verlag, Köln, Hrs. Bundesministerium für wirtschaftliche Zusammenarbeit (BMZ) Bd. 100	1991
Lutz, Burkhart	Der kurze Traum immerwährender Prosperität. Eine Neuinterpretation der industriell-kapitalistischen Entwicklung im Europa des 20. Jahrhunderts, Frankfurt/New York	1989
Malinowski, Bronislaw	Eine wissenschaftliche Theorie der Kultur, Suhrkamp, Frankfurt	1975
Mamoria, D.B.	Social Problems and Social Disorganisation in India, Kitab Mahal, Allahabad	1961
Manpower and Overseas Pakistanis Division	Pakistan Manpower Review, Government of Pakistan, Islamabad	1989
Marcuse, H.	Kultur und Gesellschaft 2, Suhrkamp, Frankfurt	1967
Marienfeld, G., and Jarik Lette	Vocational Training for the informal Sector, GTZ, Eschborn	
Marx, Karl	Lohnarbeit und Kapital, Dietz Verlag, Berlin, 10. Auflage	1946
Marx, Karl	Ökonomisch-philosophische Manuskripte Reclam, Leipzig	1970
Marx/Gold	Projektverlaufskontrolle, GTZ-Eschborn	Oct. 1989
Meadows, D. u.a.	Die Grenzen des Wachstums. Bericht des Club of Rome zur Lage der Menschheit, Reinbek, Rowohlt	1973

Author	Title	Year of publication
Mertens, D.	Schlüsselqualifikation, in: Mitteilungen aus der Arbeitsmarkt- und Berufsforschung, 7.	1974
Ministry of HRD	Programme of Action, New Delhi, India	1992
Ministry of Human Resource Development (MHRD)	Department of Education, National Policy on Education – 1986 (with Modification Undertaken in 1992), New Delhi, India	1992
MOL, Ministry of Labour, Government of India	Report on Working and living Conditions of workers in the POWERLOOM Industry in India, New Delhi, India	1988
MOL, Ministry of Labour, Government of India	Report on Working and Living Conditions of Workers in the HANDLOOM Industry in India, New Delhi, India	1986-87
Möller, S., Schlegel, W., Schleich, B., Walterborn, M.	Wie kann man durch Berufsbildung den informellen Sektor fördern? DSE-ZGB, Mannheim	1986
Moura Castro, Claudio de	Training for Work in the informal Sector, ILO, Geneva	1989
Myrdal, G.	Asiatisches Drama, Suhrkamp, Frankfurt	1971
Nahabhi Publication	The Constitution of India, New Delhi, India	1992
NCRT	National Council of Educational Survey, Volume I + II, Government of India, New Delhi, India	1992
Nell-Breuning, Oswald von	Kapitalismus und gerechter Lohn, Herder, Freiburg	1960
Nohlen, Dieter (Ed.)	Lexikon Dritte Welt, rororo-Handbuch, Rowohlt, Hamburg	1989
Nölker, Helmut	Technik und Bildung – Überlegungen zur Problematik und Begründung einer allgemeinen Didaktik der Technologie	1982
Nölker, H. and Schoenfeldt, E.	Glossar: Internationale Berufspädagogik, Expert-Verlag, Sindelfingen	1985
Nölker, H., and Schoenfeldt, E.	Berufsbildung: Unterricht, Curriculum, Planung, Expert Verlag, Grafenau	1980
Nölker, Helmut	Arbeit und polytechnische Bildung, Die zwiespältige Deutung der Arbeit, Ein historischer Exkurs, in: E. Schoenfeldt (Hrsg.), Polytechnik und Arbeit, Klinkhardt, Bad Heilbrunn	1979

Author	Title	Year of publication
Nurul, A.T.M. Armin	The role of the informal sector in economic development, some evidence from Dhaka, Bangladesh, in: International Labour Review, Vol. 126, Geneva	1987
Pàges, R.	Das Experiment in der Soziologie, in: Handbuch der empirischen Sozialforschung, Ed. Renè König, Stuttgart	1974
Pakistan Manpower Institute	Human Resource Development und Utilization: Issues and Policies, Islamabad, Pakistan	1989
Payr, G., R. Sülzer	Handbuchreihe Ländliche Entwicklung, Landeswirtschaftliche Beratung, Vol. 2, GTZ, Eschborn	1981
Peterßen, W.H.	Handbuch Unterrichtsplanung, Grundfragen, Modelle, Stufen und Dimensionen, Ehrenwirth, München	1988
Pinger, W.	Berufsausbildung als Schlüssel zur Armutsbekämpfung, Bonn	1986
Prasad, Aniradh	Reservation Policy and Practice in India, A means to an End, Deep Publications, New Delhi	1991
Preuss, W.	Entwicklungspolitische Zusammenarbeit mit Asien, internes Papier des Bundesministers für Wirtschaftliche Zusammenarbeit (BMZ), Bonn	1990
Robin, Cathrine	Mud Construction Training in Bost-Mason Training Centre, GTZ-Vorhaben, Studie im Auftrag der GTZ, Peshawar	1990
Rouillard, H.	Süd-Indien, Richtig reisen, Du Mont Buchverlag, Köln	1982
Rouillard, H.	Nord-Indien, Richtig reisen, Du Mont Buchverlag, Köln	1981
Schischkoff, G.	Philosophisches Wörterbuch, A. Kröner Verlag, Stuttgart	1961
Schoenfeldt, E.	Ziele, Motive und Erwartungen der bundesrepublikanischen Berufsbildungshilfe, in: Rolf Arnold (Hrsg.), Berufliche Bildung und Entwicklung in der Dritten Welt, Nomos, Baden-Baden	1989
Schulz, W.	Umriß einer didaktischen Theorie der Schule, in: Die deutsche Schule 2	1969

Author	Title	Year of publication
Schürmann, M.	Querschnittanalyse Sozio-kulturelle Faktoren, BMZ, Bonn	1990
Schwarz, G.	Mikroindustrialisierung: Handwerk und Angepaßte Technologie, St. Gallen, Verlag Ruegger	1980
Seifert, Helmut	Einführung in die Wissenschafts-Theorie, C.H. Beck, München	1975
Sethuraman, S.V. and Maldonado, C.	Technological Capability in the informal Sector, ILO-Publication, Genf	1992
Shirazi, A.	Religion und Politik im Iran, Gesellschaftspolitische Vorstellungen im shiitischen Islam: Differenzen in der »reinen Lehre«, Syndikat Frankfurt	1981
Sigrist, C.	Regulierte Anarchie, Texte und Dokumente zur Soziologie, Walter, Freiburg	1967
Skowronek, Helmut	Lernen und Lernfähigkeit, Grundfragen der Erziehungswissenschaft, 6. Auflage, München, Juventa-Verlag	1975
Speck, J.	Handbuch wissenschaftstheoretischer Begriffe, Band 2, Vandenhoeck, Göttingen	1980
Spranger, E.	Kultur und Erziehung, Leipzig	1928
Statistisches Bundesamt	Länderbericht Indien 1991, Wiesbaden, Metzler/Poeschel	1991
Statistisches Bundesamt	Länderbericht Pakistan 1990, bei J.B. Metzler-Poeschel, Stuttgart	1990
Stockmann, R.	Die Nachhaltigkeit von Entwicklungsprojekten, Westdeutscher Verlag, Opladen	1992
Strzelewicz, Willy	Der Kampf um die Menschenrechte, Societäts-Verlag, Frankfurt	1971
Sturmann, Uwe	Bildung, Berufsbildung ... und was dann? Verlag Breitenbach, Saarbrücken	1990
Tawney, R.H.	Religion and the Rise of Capitalism, London	1926
Thiel, R.E.	Berufsbildung – nur für Eliten?, in: Entwicklung und Zusammenarbeit, Nr. 2, Bonn	1985
Tibi, Bassam	Der Islam und das Problem der kulturellen Bewältigung sozialen Wandels, Suhrkamp Frankfurt	1985

Author	Title	Year of publication
Tuldodziecki, B., K. Breuer, A. Hauf	Konzepte für das berufliche lehren und lernen, Naturwissenschaft, Technische Verfahren, Neue Technologien im Unterricht, Julius Klinkhardt / Handwerk u. Technik, Hamburg	1984
Tworuschka, M.	Arbeit im Islam – Begriff und Ethik – in: CIBEDO-Texte, Nr. 33, Frankfurt	1985
Ulfig, Alexander	Lexikon der philosophischen Begriffe, Bechtermünz, Eltville	1993
UNICEF	Strategie für Grunddienste, Genf	1976/77
Wallenborn	Legitimationsprobleme und Reflexionsbedarf praktischer Berufsbildungshilfe, in: Berufliche Bildung und Entwicklung in den Ländern der Dritten Welt, Hrsg. Rolf Arnold, Nomos Verlag, Baden-Baden	1989
Weber, M.	Die Protestantische Ethik und der Geist des Kapitalismus, Gesammelte Aufsätze zur Religionssoziologie, Bd. I, Tübingen	1922
The World Bank	Vocational and Technical Education and Training, Washington D.C.	1991
The World Bank	Report No. 7530-IN, Staff appraisal report, INDIA, Vocational training projekt, Washington D.C.	04/1989
Werner, Heinz	Glossare zur Arbeitsmarkt- und Berufsforschung, Institut für Arbeitsmarkt, Berufsforschung der Bundesanstalt für Arbeit, Nürnberg	1979
WHO	Programm für eine medizinische Grundversorgung (1975) und Programm »Gesundheit für alle bis zum Jahre 2000« (1978)	1975/1978
Wissing, J.	Modell einer Facharbeiterschule für Entwicklungsländer, Weinheim	1961
The World Bank	India, Progress and Challenges in Economic Transition, Report No. 11761-IN, Washington D.C.	
World Bank Policy Paper	Vocational and Technical Education and Training, The World Bank, Washington D.C.	1991
World Watch Institute Report	Zur Lage der Welt 1993, Daten für das Überleben unseres Planeten, Fischer Taschenbuchverlag, Frankfurt	1993

Annexes

Annex I:	Questionnaire	298
Annex II:	Criteria for Evaluation and Interviews	307
Annex III:	Project Planning Documents TTP/SES-Peshawar	
	A. Problem tree: PGTTP and AGTTP	310
	B. Project Planning Matrix (PPM)	312
Annex IV:	Project Organisation of the Pakistan-German Technical Training Programme, Peshawar, Pakistan	319

Annex I: Questionnaire

Draft: M. Diehl

SURVEY FOR DETERMINING THE CHARACTERISTICS OF ENTERPRISES, ENTERPRENEURS AND EMPLOYEES IN THE INFORMAL SECTOR

01. Survey Conducted By: 02. Date:

03. Country: 04. Place:

05. Entrepreneur (Name and Sex):

06. Type of Enterprise:

- what kind of products (production, assembling, etc.)
- what services (maintenances, tourism, transport, etc.)
- tiny, small, etc.
- legal status
- others

07. Products/Services:

- name the products and approximate value, etc.
- name the services
- others

08. Capital:

- Buildings, machinery, tools, etc.
- others

09. Financing:

- Loan (Family, Friends, Banks)
- Banks (special development programs)
- own capital
- other sources

10. Buildings/Equipments:

- what kind of buildings, e.g. low cost shades, etc.
- what kind of equipment, e.g. production machinery, tools, etc.
- what kind of service equipment e.g. tools kits, cleaning staff, etc.
- others

11. No. of Employees and Kind of Employees:

- Manager
- Supervisor
- Workers
- Helper
- others

12. Machines/Tools:

- Name and Description of machinery (portable/mobile/non-portable)
- Name and Description of tools
- others

13. **Nature of the Products/Services:**

- Description of the Products (Names, sizes, weight, uses, spares, etc.)
- Description of the services (repair, maintenance, cooking, food processing, etc.)
- others

14. **Prices/Quanty of the Products/ Services:**

- Products (mass products, products on order, etc.)
- Services (repair, maintenance, etc.)
- others

15. **Neighborhood markets/ Competitors/Environment (sozio-economic aspects):**

- e.g. industrial estates, street corner jobs, village, rural areas, . . .

- Customers (e.g. sales network, regular customers, marketing necessary, etc.)

- Social Structure and Type of Customers (e.g. expectations in terms of punctuality, quantity, quality, etc.)

- Social Status of buyers/customers, etc.

- other remarks

16. **Qualifications of the Entrepreneur:**

- Formal education
- Non formal educational/technical training
- Professional experiences
- Others

17. **Profile of the Entrepreneur:**

- Production/Service skills (practical & theoretical skills)
- Entrepreneurial Skills
- Canvass orders/costing/pricing
- Process and execution of Orders: (if difficulties, what kind?)
- Process orders in time (promptly): (if not, what kind of deficiencies, etc.)
- Open mind for innovations
- Open for staff training and skill upgrading
- other remarks

18. **Social Role and competencies of the Entrepreneur inside the company and its own sozio-econonmic/cultural environment:**

- Role in the company
- Role in society/social environment
- Social competence (expected, fulfilled, what is lacking)
- other remarks

19. **Profile/Job requirements of the employees from the employers side (expectations):**

- Practical skills/abilities manual, operating machines, etc.

- Flexibility and abilities to adopt or adjust himself in the companies with the regard to production/services, etc.

- Literacy Abilities (Reading-Writing): (passiv/activ)

- Social Competencies:
  (e.g. team work, individual work, etc.)
  (communication skills, languages, etc.)

- Individual Capabilities or ambitions (ability to maintain and expand)

- Competence to deal with dependents/employees & periphery: (depends on the level of the described staff, etc.)

- other remarks

20. **Description of the Employees of the Enterprise and their social levels in the enterprise (if possible for each category of employee):**

1. Levels
2. Type of employees
3. Skills required and the qualifications
4. Competencies

- Schooling (formal or non formal education)
- Vocational Training (formal/non formal)
- Social Background of the employees
- Job Profile and Description/Relation to the Enterprise (profile of employees for each level, if possible)
- Organized in trade unions or other organizations
- other remarks

21. **Criteria for recruitment and employment of staff:**

- Formal Education/Social origin/Social Bond
- Recruitment process and notifying vacancies
- Contracts or verbal agreements
- Rights of dependent employees
- others

22. Nature of Jobs/Payments:

23. Miscellaneous:

24. Remarks:

Annex II: Criteria for Evaluation and Interviews

I. Type of surveyed enterprise (see questions 1-14)

   (1) Number of enterprises (Bangladore/Madras)

   (2) Type of enterprise/company
       e.g.
       - manufacturing enterprise
       - service enterprise
       - repair enterprise

   (3) Category, i.e. classification of enterprise
       - traditional crafts
       - enterprise in the informal sector
       - micro enterprise
       - small industry

   (4) Entrepreneur's capital (in RS)
       - up to 100.000 RS
       - up to 300.000 RS
       - above this sum

       Type of investments/capital
       - tools
       - machines
       - buildings
       - vehicles, etc.

   (5) Number of employees and managers in the company
       - helpers
       - skilled and semi skilled worker
       - foremen/supervisor
       - manager
       - ...

   (6) Type of financing of the enterprise
       - loans from banks, family, etc.

II. Evaluation of the information on the market and sale of products/services (see question 15)

   (1) in the industrial region
   (2) on the street corner
   (3) in the village (semi-urban) environment
   (4) type of customer:
      - individuals (private)
      - local authority/municipality
      - company i.e. as supplier
      - shop (sales) in the bazaar

III. <u>Evaluation of qualification of entrepreneurs (see questions 16 to 18)</u>

   (1) profile of the surveyed entrepreneurs (see question 16)
   (2) demand a profile of entrepreneurs (see question 17)
   (3) role of the proprietor (see question 18)
      - active
      - passive
      - none

IV. <u>Evaluation of the demand profile of employees (see questions 19 and 20)</u>

   (1) formal education
   (2) vocational qualification
   (3) on the job
   (4) systematic/formal training
   (5) social capabilities
      - teamwork
      - communication (reading, writing, articulation)
      - etc.
   (6) entrepreneurs wishes regarding upgrading of employee qualifications

»The questionnaire addressed questions solely from the viewpoint of the entrepreneur and only answers in this context were obtained.«

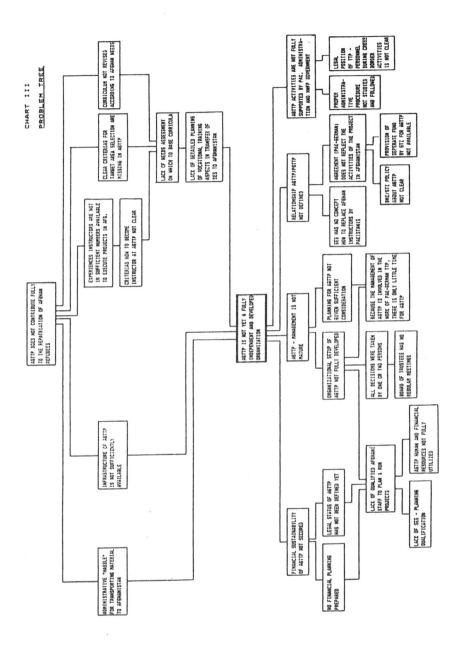

CHART VII
Project Planning Matrix

SUMMARY OF OBJECTIVES	OBJECTIVELY VERIFIABLE INDICATORS	MEANS OF VERIFICATION	ASSUMPTIONS
Super-Goal: Living standard in NWFP improved			
Overall-Goal: (self) Employment opportunities are improved	O1: More skilled workers from NWFP are hired in NWFP O2: Work culture in N.W.F.P is more oriented towards industry	M1 Labor statistics M2 survey among employees	
Project Purpose: VTS in NWFP is increasingly oriented towards sustainable (self) employment of its Afghan and Pakistan pass-outs	P1: SES approach has been institutionalized by June 1996 P2: SES approach is recognized by the authorities of NWFP and the budget to support SES is incorporated in the provincial budget 1996/1997 P3: Agreement to modify all trades in TTC Peshawar towards (self) employment activities based on model AC/R. and R./TV by June 1996 P4: More applicants for SES than seating capacity	M1 Agreed upon organizational chart M2 Budget document 1996/1997 M3 Minutes of meeting DMT-TTC M4 SES admission records	A1 Industrial promotion schemes are effective A2 Other technical training institutions also change their approach towards (self) employment A3 Demand for skilled labor is large enough to absorb pass outs of TTC's A4 political-economic culture in conducive to self employment

SUMMARY OF OBJECTIVES	OBJECTIVELY VERIFIABLE INDICATORS	MEANS OF VERIFICATION	ASSUMPTIONS
Result 1: Pass-outs trained and supported according to SES in centers	* I1.1 From 2000 Pak pass-outs 65% are (self) employed per year * I1.2 From 2000 Afghan pass-outs 65% (self) employed per year * I1.3 320 Pak ladies trained in tailoring and 60% are self employed * I1.4 40 Afghan ladies trained in tailoring and 60% are self employed * I1.5 2320 toolkits are provided to Pak pass-outs by DMT * I1.6 2040 toolkits are provided to Afghan pass-outs out of project resources * I1.7 Pak: pract. tr. to 300 per year superv. worksh. to 90 per year loans provided to 130 per year * I1.8 Afghan: pract. tr. to 300 per year superv. worksh. to 80 per year loans provided to 130 per year	* Admittance and graduation records * Follow-up study * Longterm study (Bremen)	* A1.1 Enough contracts for 800 pract. trainees * A1.2 New donors for 600 trainees basic training * A1.3 June 1994-June 1995: Rs 4 million Pak contribution for 2300 Pak trainees * A1.4 June 1995-June 1996: Rs 5.6 million Pak contribution for 2300 Pak trainees * A1.5 Regular budget is provided by NWFP Govt. after July 1996 (grant + aid)

SUMMARY OF OBJECTIVES	OBJECTIVELY VERIFIABLE INDICATORS	MEANS OF VERIFICATION	ASSUMPTIONS
Result 2: Pass-outs trained and supported according to SES in bazaar	* I2.1 140 Pak pass-outs are trained annually in the bazaar in 70 shops * I2.2 140 Afghan pass-outs are trained annually in the bazaar in 70 shops * I2.3 70% of Pak trainees are (self) employed * I2.4 70% of Afghan trainees are (self) employed * I2.5 280 toolkits are provided to pass outs and lungi money (Rs 1000 per training) is paid to 140 masters	* Contracts with masters and apprentices * Report of supervisors * Voucher of payment	* A2.1 Project approach of apprent. training in informal sector is recognized and adopted by the government
Result 3: Model developed and agreed upon for longterm sustainability of short-term training for (self) employment	* I3.1 Joint task force has been established, is functioning before Oct 1993 and comprises Govt., DMI, project, GTZ and others * I3.2 Proposal for future set up has been developed and submitted as well as agreed upon before Sept 1994	* M3.1 Minutes of meeting of taskforce in project * M3.2 Finalized proposal	* A3.1 Political and administrative support for independent setup * A3.2 Participation of relevant partners

SUMMARY OF OBJECTIVES	OBJECTIVELY VERIFIABLE INDICATORS	MEANS OF VERIFICATION	ASSUMPTIONS
Result 4: Monitoring and evaluation system for formal (2 trades) and non-formal training is developed and functioning	* I4.1 3 per year follow-up studies conducted * Joint plan of operation agreed upon for implementation finalized in July 1993	* M4.1 Reports available	* A4.1 Separate funds available
Result 5: Donors identified, approached and contracts for funds finalized	* I5.1 Rs 8 million out of annual budget are paid by third party donors (results 1,2,3)	* M5.1 Contracts and bankstatements available	* A5.1 Solvent and sympathetic donors available * A5.2 Donors convinced of the approach to be funded

SUMMARY OF OBJECTIVES	OBJECTIVELY VERIFIABLE INDICATORS	MEANS OF VERIFICATION	ASSUMPTIONS
Result 6: Pass-outs trained in AC/refrig. and R/TV according to market needs	* I6.1 20 trained each trade and 50% per year (self) employed according to trade * I6.2 Drop-out decrease 1st group: 15% 2nd group: 10% 3rd group: 5% * I6.3 Field study to identify the needs for refrig./AC + radio/tv is carried out by Oct. 1993 * I6.4 Curricula revised according to the needs before Feb. 1994 * I6.5 Equipment/workshop/ training material for R/TV, AC/refr. installed and functioning before Oct.1994. * I6.6 Instructions for refr/ AC and RTV are trained according to curricula.	* M6.1 Survey and records maintained in TTC * M6.2 TTC record * M6.3 Joint report TTC-DMT-GTZ * M6.4 Training organization setup (workshop, qualifications of instructor, training material, training method) * M6.5 TTC adm. record	* A6.1 Number of admitted trainees according to seating capacity * A6.2 Qualified coordinator will be made by GTZ * A6.3 PTB approves revised curricula based on field studies

SUMMARY OF OBJECTIVES	OBJECTIVELY VERIFIABLE INDICATORS	MEANS OF VERIFICATION	ASSUMPTIONS
Result 7: In house instructor-training scheme of TTC Peshawar is established and functioning	* I7.1 The number of trained instructors and master-trainers for the next three years has to be agreed upon until June 1993	* M7.1 Minutes of meeting * M7.2 Plan of operation	* A7.1 In case that instructor under training will be transferred, DMT provides facilities to allow the continuation of training
Result 8: Employment generation program for two selected trades (long term training) are successfully implemented	* I8.1 Industry and bazaar have interest in 50% on the job training * I8.2 Coordination with agencies helpful in granting revolving loans to 5 trainees in each session per trade for self employment scheme * I8.3 Services are sold/given to refr./AC, R/TV, Small Scale Industry/Bazaris and income is directly reinvested before June 1995 * I8.4 Work-contract with related industries for 25% employment * I8.5 >20 entrepreneurs ask for advice at TTC (refr./AC, R/TV) from Sept 1995	* TTC record & follow-up study	* A8.1 Enough SSI/Bazaris in condition to offer on the job training places * A8.2 Budget and personal resources available for selfemployment scheme * A8.3 DMT allows for two pilot trades to operate according to the setup

CHART VI
DETAILS FOR RESULT 9 OF THE PROJECT-PLANNING MATRIX: AFGHAN-GERMAN NGO IS REGISTERED IN NWFP AND IS IMPLEMENTING SES-CONCEPT

Result 9: Afghan-German NGO is registered in NWFP and is implementing SES-concept	
1.	Assist in registration
2.	AGTTP & PGTTP work out financial/administrative needs for sanctions of GTZ by june 1993
3.	Advice + training: - proposal writing; - accounting & auditing; - reporting; - monitoring & evaluation.
4.	Concept development for SES transfer to Afghanistan
5.	Finance the ongoing projects in Afghanistan (Kunar/Terizai)
6.	GTZ should only contribute to AGTTP on the basis of concrete projects
7.	PGTTP provides software (teaching material)
8.	Provide 1 pick-up car for permanent use of AGTTP

Annex IV:

Project-Organisation of the Pakistan-German-Technical-Training-Programme, Peshawar, Pakistan (Status as of February 1993):

(1) Project Relationship: Directorate Manpower and Training, Ministry of Labour, Provincial Government of NWFP

(2) Overview of the »Main Orga-Structures of PAK-GERMAN-TTP«

(3) Organisation of Project Administration

(4) Organisation of Project Component A (for refugees) with the following Organisation Charts:
- Organisation of Income Generating Scheme in Project Component »A«
- Organisation of Training in Contract Work (Masonry) in Project Component »A«
- Organisation of Training in Contract Work, Component »A« (others than Masonry)
- Organisation of Training in Supervised Workshops in Project Component »A«
- Organisation of Basic and Advanced Training in Project Component »A«

(5) Organisation of Project Component »B«, i.e. integration of the yet existing Technical Training Center (TTC) – Peshawar

(6) Organisation of Project Component »C«, i.e. forming a so-called »Skill Development Center« for target groups in the rural area

(7) Organisation of Project Component »D«, i.e. forming a structure to promote potential small (micro) entrepreneurs and self employment

PROJECT RELATIONSHIP
INSIDE
DIRECTORATE MANPOWER AND TRAINING DEPARTMENT N.W.F.P.

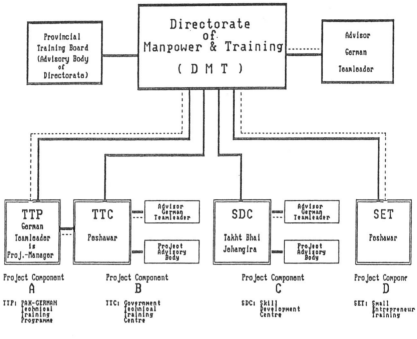

Main Organisation Structure of PAK-GERMAN TTP

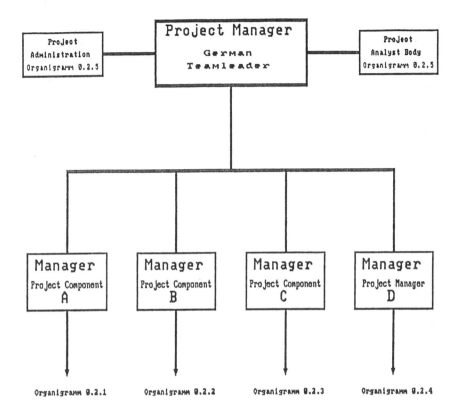

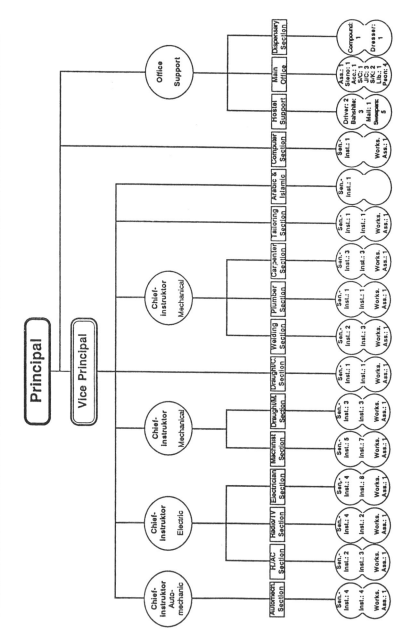

Organisation of Project Administration

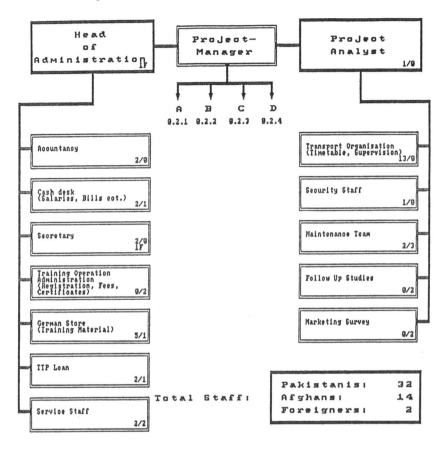

Organisation of Project Component A

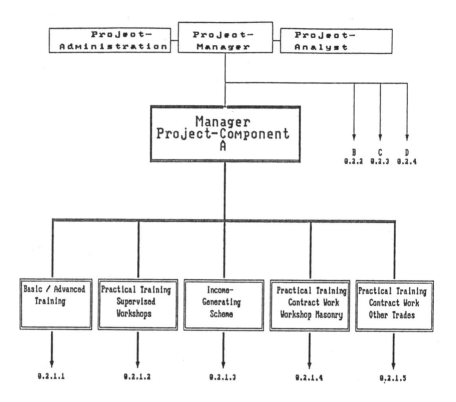

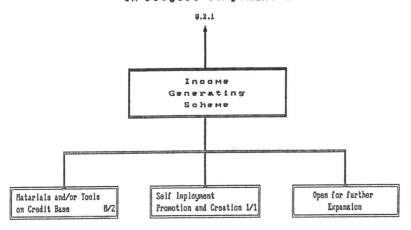

Organisation of Training in Contract Work (Masonry) in Project Component A

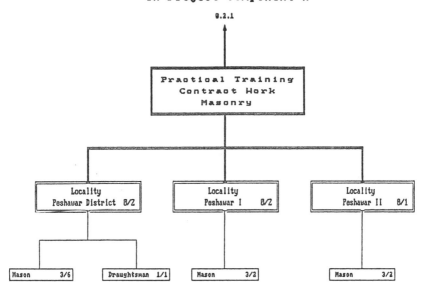

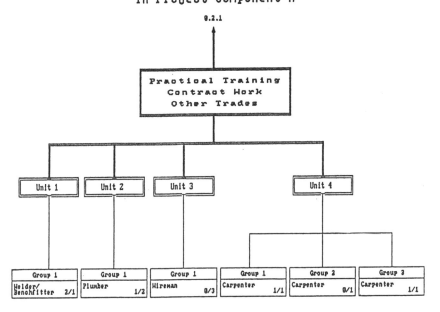

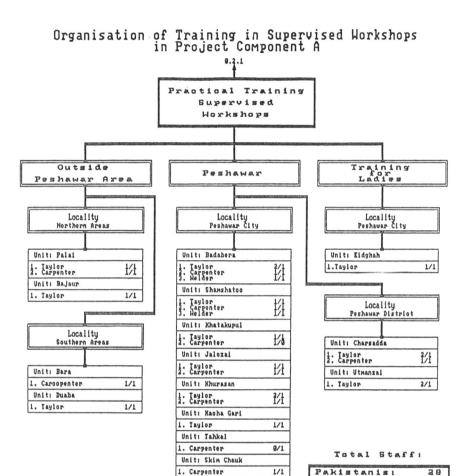

Organisation of Basic/Advanced Training in Project Component A

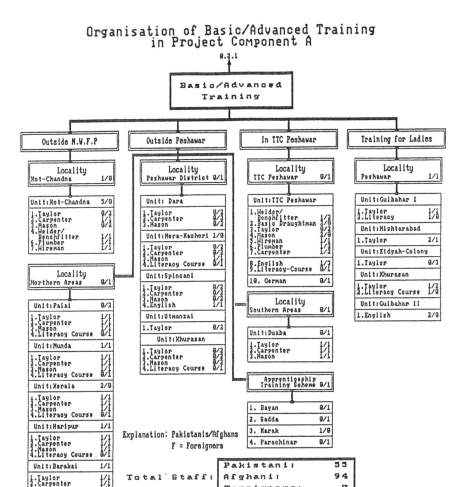

Organisation of Project Component B
Technical Training Center Peshawar

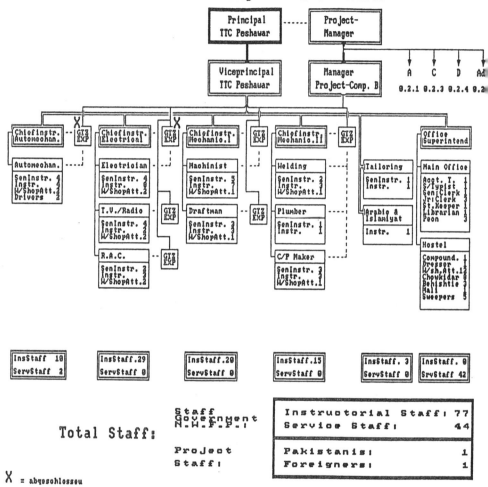

Organisation of Project Component C

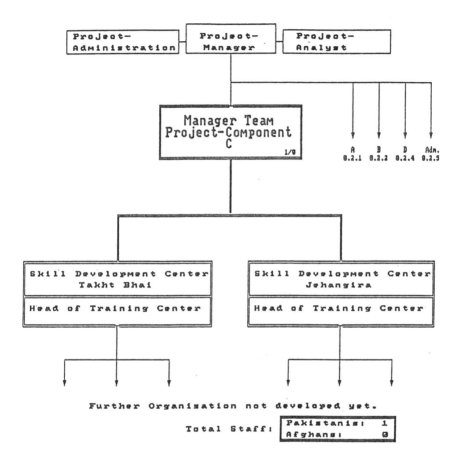

Organisation of Project Component D

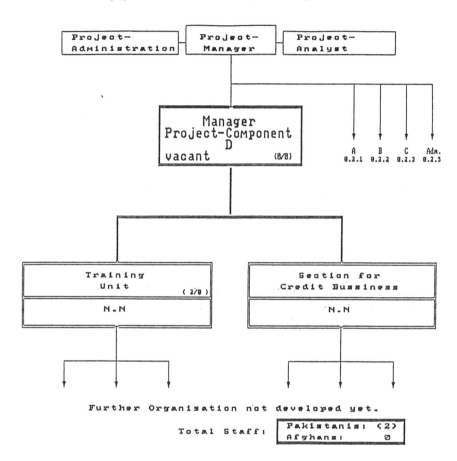